UNDUE PROCESS

THE UNTOLD STORY OF AMERICA'S GERMAN ALIEN INTERNEES

ARNOLD KRAMMER

ROWMAN & LITTLEFIELD PUBLISHERS, INC.
London • Boulder • New York • Oxford

ROWMAN & LITTLEFIELD PUBLISHERS, INC.

Published in the United States of America·
by Rowman & Littlefield Publishers, Inc.
4720 Boston Way, Lanham, Maryland 20706

12 Hid's Copse Road
Cummor Hill, Oxford OX2 9JJ, England

British Library Cataloguing in Publication Information Available.

Library of Congress Cataloging-in-Publication Data

Krammer, Arnold.
    Undue process : the untold story of America's German alien internees / Arnold
Krammer.
        p.   cm.
    Includes bibliographical references and index.
    ISBN 0-8476-8518-7 (cloth: alk. paper)
    1. World War, 1939–1945—German Americans.   2. World War, 1939–1945—Prisoners
and prisons, American.   I.   Title.
    D769.8.A6K73   1997
                                                                    97-008365
                                                                    CIP

ISBN 0-8476-8518-7 (cloth : alk. paper)

Printed in the United States of America

♾ ™ The paper used in this publication meets the minimum requirements of American
National Standard for Information Sciences—Permanence of Paper for Printed Library
Materials, ANSI Z39.4–1984.

Dedicated to

my wife Jan and our sons,

Adam and Douglas,

and

Joyce and Harry Smith

CONTENTS

	Introduction	ix
1.	The Lists	1
2.	Precedents	13
3.	The Net Tightens	23
4.	The Arrests	31
5.	The Process	45
6.	The Camps	83
7.	Life in the Camps	101
8.	Camp Crystal City, Texas	109
9.	Nazis and Troublemakers in the Internee Camps	117
10.	The Exchanges	141
11.	The War Is Over	151
12.	The Issues	171
	List of Internment/Detention Camps During World War II	175
	Notes	177
	Bibliography	197
	Index	205
	About the Author	211

INTRODUCTION

When America went to war in December 1941, the nation prepared for the global conflict to follow. Lives changed direction as thousands enlisted in the military, industry mobilized for national defense and unimaginable profits, patriotism became the watchword for millions, and Kilroy, whoever he was, appeared in the most unlikely places. Songs, movies, and news articles promoted "Americanism" like a sacred mantra, and the Axis enemies were evil incarnate. Racial and language differences among individuals took on a new, and often sinister, meaning.

If the first casualty of war is Truth, the second casualty must surely be the fate of foreigners living in the midst of any nation at war—especially enemy citizens or suspected sympathizers. The emotional stress of war, the unchallenged suspension of legal protection, and arguable threat posed by saboteurs create a dangerous climate for a minority made vulnerable by its isolation and its eagerness to prove its loyalty. Much of the intolerance was sanctioned by law. The Selective Service cracked down on conscientious objectors and pacifists; mob attacks were launched against Jehovah's Witnesses, culminating in bloody scenes in places as widespread as Little Rock, Arkansas, Springfield, Illinois, and Klamath Falls, Oregon. Anti-Semitism, already acceptable in American society and government, reached new heights during the war, such that by mid-1942, a full thirty percent of the classified ads in *The New York Times* and the *Herald Tribune* expressed an open preference for Protestants and Catholics. Black Americans fared far worse as defense industries passed them over entirely, despite their enthusiastic enlistment in the strictly segregated military services. The fate of enemy aliens—Japanese, German, and Italian citizens—living in America was the most precarious of all.

The tragedy of the 120,000 Japanese and Japanese-Americans is well known. A cursory examination of material in the Library of Congress on their forced relocation from the West Coast lists 1,058 published oral histories and books (including a frothy novel by Danielle Steele), in addition to 112 manuscript collections.

What is little known is the story of Germans and German-Americans and other Europeans in America during the war, many thousands of whom were rounded up by federal agents, and paroled or released, and 10,905 others who were arrested, rushed through hearing boards, and interned in prison camps for the duration of the war and beyond. Many were not released until as late as 1947, two years after the war was over. The families of many internees volunteered to join their spouses and parents and were imprisoned as well. The total number of Germans, German-Americans, and German-Latin Americans incarcerated by the Enemy Alien Program in nearly four dozen enemy alien camps across the country is slightly more the 25,000.

The motives for the program are numerous. Primary was the government's understandable prudence, albeit heavy-handed, to lock up potential spies and saboteurs during wartime. Being unable to accurately fathom the ideological allegiance of each enemy citizen, the government cut a wide swath. In terms of the FBI, the need to control the enemy aliens provided J. Edgar Hoover with a reason to argue for marked expansion of the bureau's army of agents and support staff. The threat of internment was also used to divide and intimidate the German community to prevent any hint of disloyalty. Finally, there is a suspicion that since the German community did not support Roosevelt in the election of 1940, the incarceration of a few thousand Germans or German-Americans would not be a political loss.

Little has been written on the subject of internment of Europeans during World War II in America, and our knowledge of the entire episode has been clouded and confused by bad and at times self-serving history, along with the efforts of pressure groups to minimize or deny the scale and scope of internment beyond the Japanese experience. The task of unearthing this story is complicated by the decreasing number of living participants, as well as their varied feelings about recalling these events. Some former internees wish to put it all behind them, while others trumpet the injustice of their particular case to any listener. Many are simply tired of telling the story of German internment to people who don't believe them. A few are ashamed of having been viewed as disloyal, and some fear losing their jobs or business clients if their wartime incarceration becomes public. Most are embittered.

Records are scattered everywhere: in the files of the FBI and the Immigration and Naturalization Service; the records of the U.S. Army, State Department, War Department, and the Justice Department in the National Archives; and in the mountain of Swiss camp inspection reports held in the Auswärtiges Amt in Bonn. Because of bureaucratic inertia and perhaps a government desire to avoid acknowledging a distasteful past mistake, many documents, until very recently, were available only through application under the Freedom of Information Act.

The difficulties involved in telling this story only dramatize the valuable help offered by former internees, researchers, archivists, and librarians. My first thanks go to former internee Arthur D. Jacobs, who has tried, almost single-handedly, to break down the wall of silence around the subject. He and writer Joseph E. Fallon have collected documents, published articles, protested in court, and challenged history books; Jacobs serves as a general clearinghouse of information on the German internees. Another outspoken former internee who, in turn, helped me find others, is Alfred Plaschke; he and his wife Hannelore gave unstintingly of their time, as did Eberhard and Julius Fuhr, Reverend Reinhard Kruse, JoAnn Wartemann Terwege, Gunter and Juergen Koetter, Gerd Erich Schneider, Deborah Ann (Dudel) Lincoln, Joachim Meyer in Bogota, Charlotte Meier in Munich, and Paul Grayber in St. Martin, in the French West Indies. Professor John Heitmann (at the University of Dayton), a child of internees who is currently writing a book about his parents' experience, was especially helpful. Numerous other experts aided me, including Professors Amos E. Simpson (of the University of Southwestern Louisiana), Robert Dippner (University of Nevada at Las Vegas); Karen Lea Riley (Auburn University); Henry C. Schmidt (Texas A&M University); and Stephen Fox (of Humboldt State University), whose new book, *The Invisible Gulag: An Oral and Documentary Bibliography of German American Internment During World War II,* is awaited by interested scholars and history buffs of the period.

Librarians, researchers, and archivists are the often unsung heroes of every large project. Among the best are Max P. Friedman, Stefan Feucht, Johannes Kleinschmidt, Jean Mansavage, Dr. Todd Brereton, Joseph P. Harris at the National Archives Motion Picture Branch, and Marian L. Smith, the outstanding senior INS historian and compiler of the catalogue to the records of the Enemy Alien Program, entitled "INS Records Related to the Detention and Internment of Enemy Aliens During World War II."

A particular debt is owed to Ms. Jude K. Swank, a talented computer expert at Texas A&M University, who typed this entire book, more than once, correcting mistakes and offering suggestions along the way. Thanks also to Mr. Jack Lala for his skilled editing.

Lastly, a salute to Mr. Stephen M. Wrinn, History Editor at Rowman & Littlefield, for his confidence, and to Ms. Deidre Mullervy, for turning a manuscript into a book.

CHAPTER ONE

THE LISTS

Every adult American is familiar with the terrible injustice done to the nation's Japanese population during World War II. The American military along the West Coast, driven by public hysteria and deep-seated racism, forcibly uprooted and unceremoniously transported nearly 120,000 Japanese and Japanese-Americans living in California, Oregon, Washington—78,000 of whom were born in the United States—to "relocation camps" for most of the war. The prejudice against them, the loss of their homes and businesses, the wasted years and anguished questions of loyalty are well known. While the U.S. Supreme Court's recent decision to redress the wrong by awarding each survivor $20,000—fifty years later—is commendable, the experience nonetheless casts a dark shadow over America's image as a beacon of democracy. Yet their story was not entirely unique. American history has almost completely overlooked the arrest and forcible internment of thousands of Germans and others, with their children and families, in federal prison camps—some until well after the war was over: Enemy aliens.

On 7 December 1941, as millions of Americans listened in outrage to news of the Japanese attack on U.S. bases in Hawaii, they would have been comforted to know that the FBI and the U.S. Justice Department had set in motion a program to seize people across the country whose names had been secretly collected years earlier and placed on a list as "dangerous and disloyal."

While the identification of potentially disloyal noncitizens would certainly seem prudent during wartime, the program was created during peacetime, secretly, and gave those so labeled no right to confront their accusers. The collection of thousands of names was the personal passion of J. Edgar Hoover, director of the FBI. Hoover was by nature wary of foreigners and had been steeped in the hysteria and excesses of the Justice Department's Enemy Alien Bureau during the World War I. As a result of this passion, belatedly approved by President Roosevelt, Hoover's general intelligence groups spent years collecting information about suspected subversive activities being conducted in the United States by communist, fascist, and other groups.[1] Indeed, from the moment he was appointed director of the bureau in 1924 by the attorney general, Harlan Fiske Stone—very skeptical about the wisdom of his choice—Hoover believed he had a mandate to snoop. He understood better than anyone else in this century that information was power.

Hoover's concern about internal enemies was shared by many. In January 1934 a New York congressman, Sam Dickstein, created a special committee to investigate Nazi propaganda activities in America.[2] As public concern mounted, all eyes turned toward the FBI. It was imperative that the FBI do something! President Roosevelt agreed. In September 1936 J. Edgar Hoover's FBI began a secret five-year plan to list all individuals who posed a potential security risk to the nation. The order went out to every bureau station and agent in America to put aside all but the most critical cases and start collecting information on any "communist or fascist" subversive individual or organization. Nor was lack of accuracy important. Hoover ordered them to gather all information "regardless of the source from which this information is received."[3] Every government agency was expected to cooperate. Working in partnership with the Army's military intelligence division and the Navy's Office of Naval Intelligence, the FBI in 1939 boasted that it had its eye on "more than ten million persons, including a very large number of individuals of foreign extraction."[4] Hoover assured an awestruck Congress that these lists "have been arranged not only alphabetically but also geographically, so that [if at] any time should we enter into conflict, we would be able to go into any of these communities and identify individuals or groups who might be a source of grave danger to the security of this country." Hoover noted ominously that "their backgrounds and activities are known to the Bureau."[5]

Not that Hoover's enormous power wasn't causing some concern. As early as 1934 Senator Kenneth McKellar of Tennessee tried to get Hoover to disclose information about the FBI's activities. When told that such disclosure would be "unwise," the senator replied, "I think the idea of a Cheka in this country is something that ought not to exist." In 1935, McKellar was more direct and warned: "We are getting to have a tremendous secret service organization. . . . [Such organizations] are frequently used as a means of doing great wrong, and I have my doubts about secret service systems in a republican form of government like ours. I have been astonished at the tremendous growth and the use of large sums of money for the 'secret service' as it is called, of the Department of Justice."[6] By May 1940 Senator George Norris of Nebraska had had enough. He cautioned that unless Hoover was stopped, "there will be a spy behind every stump and a detective in every closet in our land. Unless we do something . . . we will have the organization of the FBI which, instead of protecting our people from civil acts of criminals, will itself in the end direct the Government by tyrannical force, as the history of the world shows has always been the case when secret police and secret detectives have been snooping around the homes of honest men."[7] Others echoed these sentiments, but events in Europe and the presence of an unknown number of foreigners in America seemed to justify the FBI's extreme vigilance at home.

Foreigners in any country have always been viewed with some suspicion, especially during times of international tension. The situation in America was no different. By the spring of 1939 Europe was in turmoil, and the American public grew increasingly anxious about the presence of a possible internal Fifth Column of enemies. Instinctively, America returned to the paranoid years of World War I, when German-Americans were thought to be putting ground glass in America's sausage, poisoning community water supplies, and spreading defeatist or pacifistic thoughts. Rumor had it that the Kaiser's agents were disguised as Bible salesmen; what could be lower? Now, the new war confirmed American's worst fears. The sudden appearance of Fifth Columns in Poland, Norway, Belgium, Holland, and France were significant to Hitler's successes. German citizens and Nazi sympathizers, living quietly among the population, cast off their sheepskins when Hitler signaled, revealing themselves as enemy wolves. As Germany attacked each nation in turn, a hidden force donned armbands and arose to aid incoming troops, help parachutists, draw huge arrows on the ground to point the Luftwaffe toward strategic targets, and sabotage home defenses. Fifth Columnists were disguised as workmen and priests, farmers, tourists, teachers, students, and train engineers. In the case of Norway, the foremost subversive turned out to be no one less than the former Minister of Defense Vidkun Quisling. So important to Hitler's success were internal agents that in 1949 an international council of UNESCO requested the Netherlands' State Institute for War Documentation at Amsterdam to write a history of the subject. The result was the monumental study by Dutch historian Louis DeJong, *The German Fifth Column in the Second World War.*[8] As Americans read about Hitler's successes in the daily news, their eyes began to turn toward the Germans and German-Americans living in their midst.

To be sure, enemy aliens were not legally defenseless in the United States. Indeed, constitutional law was (and is) very protective of people with foreign roots, even those unfortunates with enemy citizenship during wartime. In only a few areas do their legal rights differ significantly from those of native-born or naturalized citizens. Aliens, like Americans, may sign contracts, sue and be sued, own and inherit property, and even serve in the military under certain conditions. The alien's principal shield is the Fourteenth Amendment, which guarantees to any person within its jurisdiction the equal protection of the laws. The amendment does not merely say "any citizen," but "any person." In only two areas does the alien have fewer rights than the citizen. He may not vote or hold public office (although he must pay taxes like everyone else) and may not be eligible to receive certain licenses, such as a license to practice law or medicine. "Pressure groups have sought to bar aliens from becoming architects, reporters, dentists, junk-dealers, surveyors, barbers, steam-boiler operators, taxi-driv-

ers, beauty-shop operators, embalmers, chiropodists, and taxidermists. If
the reader can discover a thread of unity running through these occupa-
tions," commented Ernst Puttkammer, professor of law at the University
of Chicago, "he has found something not visible to the writer." Several
states actually excluded aliens from sharing in their material resources: for
example, Virginia forbade aliens from engaging in oyster fishing, Pennsylvania would not allow them to own a dog of any kind, and Massachusetts
made it illegal for aliens to pick wild flowers! Natural resources belonged
collectively to the citizenry, it was believed, and the noncitizen had no
right to remove anything from the whole.[9] With the exception of these
restrictions, aliens were protected by the broad rights granted to citizens.

This protection existed until the European war broke out in 1939. First
came the Alien Registration Act of 1940, which required all aliens to go to
a U.S. post office to be fingerprinted, photographed, and registered. Another law aimed only at aliens required those who wished to leave the
United States to obtain a permit. In October 1941, even before Pearl Harbor, all aliens with assets over one thousand dollars were required to provide a detailed accounting of those assets to the Treasury Department.
There were, doubtless, numerous state and local restrictions on the movement and employment of aliens and enemy aliens: businesses that wouldn't
hire foreigners or apartment building owners that wouldn't rent to Germans, and so forth. Importantly, however, aliens and enemy aliens still had
access to the judicial system.

Curiously, no one really knew how many German-Americans lived in
the United States. The last trustworthy (read: pre-Nazi) accounting of Germans living abroad, in 1932, led the German public to believe that more
than twenty-five million Americans were exclusively or largely of German
stock. The implication was that they would never go to war against their
homeland.[10] Others knew better. German Ambassador Dieckhoff in 1938
estimated that the number of German-Americans "who still really speak
German, read and write German, think in German, and are fully cognizant
of their German origin," was at most four or five million.[11] Other estimates
of Germans living in America ranged from the millions down to 264,000.[12]

However, only a small percentage of them were interested in joining
such pro-Nazi organizations as the German-American Bund. Ambassador
Dieckhoff illustrated his report by noting that while some 700,000 people
of German origin lived in Chicago and 40,000 of them belonged to some
German association, only 450 had actually joined the Bund.[13] Such a small
organization was more an irritant than a threat. Reports of the membership
in the German-American Bund ranged from the FBI's rather low estimate
of 6,500, to Martin Dies's wildly high figure of 400,000.[14] Congressman
Sam Dickstein, who headed the 1934 probe into Nazi activity in America,
put the number at an even higher 450,000, while Fritz Kuhn, Bund leader,

cited various figures, ranging from 8,299 to 230,000, depending on the group he was addressing.[15] Actual membership hovered around 10,000.[16]

Reports of their activities and publications were always in the news and, despite their small actual membership, public fear widened of the German-American Bund and similar pro-Nazi groups. On 26 February 1938, the Superior Court of Indiana enjoined the Bund from holding meetings in the state, claiming that "Nazi activities are dangerous to the well-being of the commonwealth." In Philadelphia, on 24 March 1938, as the local Bund was celebrating Hitler's seizure of Austria, an anti-Nazi crowd broke into the party; a full-scale riot broke out, and fistfights continued until the riot squad arrived. In addition to their bombastic publications, the Bund had boisterous rallies, meetings, and marches. Yet it must be remembered that however repugnant it was to an overwhelming majority of Americans, the Bund was perfectly legal. The organization was under close scrutiny by the authorities and until the war began had not been accused of any act of sabotage or breach of national security.

To magnify the effect of its numbers, the Bund seemed to court publicity.[17] In May 1939 Bund leader Fritz Kuhn traveled to Germany for a personal audience with Adolf Hitler. That Kuhn was barely tolerated by the Nazis and given only a few moments with Hitler was lost in his triumphant return. The Bund's peak visibility, and perhaps the beginning of its demise, came with its famous George Washington's birthday rally at New York's Madison Square Garden on 20 February 1939. Security was extraordinarily heavy for the event, with some 1,700 police officers on duty. For days prior to the rally, the streets around Madison Square Garden saw protests, marches, and counterprotests, building to some 10,000 howling anti-German protesters by the day of the rally. When it finally took place, the Bund celebration proved to be relatively uneventful, as 22,000 Bundists and sympathizers cheered speeches, chanted, sieg-heiled, and sang nationalistic songs in both English and German. Only one minor incident was reported indoors, and on the streets the New York police made only thirteen arrests, all on minor charges.[18]

The increased Bund visibility and growing public outrage both picked up speed as Europe moved closer to war. In San Diego another George Washington's birthday celebration by the Bund on 25 February was met with jeering, heckling, tomato- and egg-hurling crowds.[19] On 12 March 1939, 342 members of the Brooklyn youth division of the German-American Bund, wearing storm trooper and Hitler Youth uniforms, held a special rally to march, drill, do calisthenics, and dance. They had to be protected from jeering onlookers by more than 250 policemen.[20]

Lest one think that the German-American Bund was the single pro-Nazi organization in America, the civil affairs division of the U.S. Army's Western Defense Command created a long list of organizations whose allegiance to Germany was vocal and potentially dangerous. These groups flooded the post offices of America with many colorfully named newsletters: *The American Ranger* (Beverly Hills, Calif.), *The Patriot* (Beverly Hills, Calif.), *The Herald* (Lake Geneva, Wis.), *The Red Network* (Chicago, Ill.), *America in Danger* (Omaha, Neb.), *Industrial Control Reports* (Washington, D.C.), *Hypocrisy* (Glendale, Calif.), *The Broom* (San Diego, Calif.), *The Individualist* (Lincoln, Neb.), *The Beacon Light* (Atascadero, Calif.), *The Miracle of Happiness* (Los Angeles, Calif.), *The Truth About England and the New Europe* (San Francisco, Calif.), *Today's Challenge* (New York, N.Y.), *Social Justice* (Royal Oaks, Mich.), *The Christian Free Press* (Los Angeles, Calif.), *The South Coast News* (Laguna, Calif.), *The Octopus* (Omaha, Neb.), *Liberation* (Asheville, N.C.), *The Roll Call* (Noblesville, Ind.), *The Revelation* (Indianapolis, Ind.), *Trans-Ocean News Service* (Germany), *The Amerika Herald Lincoln Freie Presse* (Winona, Minn.), *California Demokrat* (San Francisco, Calif.), *The National Patriot* (Los Angeles, Calif.), *Fair Play* (New York, N.Y.), and at least a dozen more. All were pro-Nazi, anticommunist, and wildly anti-Semitic. Many simply reprinted articles forwarded by Nazi periodicals in Germany. The most outrageous of them ceased publication at the beginning of the war or continued only until their readership dried up or their editors were indicted for violation of the Wartime Sedition Laws.[21] The majority of such newsletters, frightening as they were, could be traced to a small number of distasteful organizations. Jack Peyton's "Gentile American Protective League" and "American Patriots" in Beverly Hills accounted for several, Father Charles E. Coughlin's "Christian Frontiers" in Michigan published several others, and William Dudley Pelley's "Silver Shirts" produced others. The Bund was especially active, as were such individuals as German propagandist George Sylvester Vierick, Los Angeles publisher Mrs. Edith Shol, the known German agent Mrs. Leslie Fry, and, surprisingly, a congressman, Stephen A. Day of Illinois. While there are no data to measure the impact of these scurrilous publications on their readers, their visibility was enough to anger the American public. It also made hundreds of thousands of German-Americans and loyal German residents very uncomfortable.

After war broke out, Bund functions attracted fewer members and drew more adverse publicity and bigger protests, and German-Americans grew frightened. They did not fear the Bund, but worried about the tolerance of the American public. The relatively small number of Nazi extremists cast a pall over the loyal immigrant residents and naturalized citizens who were not members or sympathizers of the Bund. German-Americans scrambled to distance themselves as quickly as possible, but an ominous question was developing among the American public. Could the population at large distinguish clearly between the Bund and the loyal German-American community? The answer, notes one scholar, "is a qualified no."[22] While some people did make the distinction, the majority did not; the distinction between such greatly different groups had largely blurred. This occurred partly because of the continual association in the headlines of Nazis with Germans. In addition, Congressional hearings on Nazi activity habitually called both Bundists and non-Nazi German-Americans as witnesses in their proceedings. The public tended to lump them all together. The German-American community found itself confronted by guilt by association; as historian Susan Canedy stated in *America's Nazis*, "The group as a whole was punished for crimes committed by the few due to the solidarity which the group portrayed."[23]

Moreover, the World War I hysteria against German-Americans was apparently still close to the collective surface. While the public and the government may have expressed remorse over the events two decades earlier, prejudice against foreigners—and Germans in particular—had established roots. Finally, there were the movies.

Film depictions of American's German stock generally leaned toward the extremes, with Nazi espionage agents and Bundists in films of foreign intrigue. Movies about average, nonpolitical Germans, thrifty and hardworking, did not sell tickets; evil, monocled Nazi agents and cunning admirers of Adolf Hitler did. Far from providing a balanced portrayal of Germans in America, films unnecessarily fanned the flames of prejudice and xenophobia. First came the newsreels, which emphasized the daily patriotic and heroic events that took place in Germany in the most visual way. Marching troops, overflights, rallies, and street crimes in Nazi Germany were perfect fodder for newsreels, which were produced regularly and shown before the featured movie fare.

In 1935 Time, Inc., introduced a new film vehicle that combined newsreels and movies called *The March of Time*. One, in particular, was a box office and critical success: *Inside Nazi Germany—1938*. The popular film began with a look at the dramatic military expansion and racial madness taking place in Germany. The film moved rapidly to the Bund at home, citing Fritz Kuhn's activities and warning of the danger of Nazi propaganda in America. The docudrama made no distinction between "good Germans" and "bad Germans." Moreover, evildoers could not expect their American citizenship to protect them. Said one character in the film: "We have no quarrel with what we term 'the older order of German people.' But we do object, and we do protest, against the insidious, treacherous activities of Nazi agents masquerading as American citizens." The audience was left with no way to tell them apart.

The first overt feature propaganda film against Hitler's Germany was the 1939 blockbuster *Confessions of a Nazi Spy*. Tough-guy FBI man Edward G. Robinson unearths a nest of Nazi spies in America and tracks their

sabotage and intrigue to the Bund and its German–American dupes and
sympathizers. The German–American Bund proves to be the center of a
Nazi spy ring, gathering intelligence on the American military and attempting to spread class resentment. Predictably the Nazis are stereotyped as
sneering, goose-stepping fanatics out to rid America of its Constitution and
Bill of Rights.[24] In the opening week at the Strand Theater in New York
the film grossed $45,000, more than any show previously released that year.
The National Board of Review of Motion Pictures named it one of the
four best films of the year.[25]

Confessions developed a history of its own. First, Fritz Kuhn sued Warner
Brothers Studio for libel for $5 million; the suit dragged on for nearly two
years and was dropped when Kuhn went to prison for embezzling Bund
funds. Then Germany banned the film, followed by thirteen other countries frightened of angering Hitler. Most importantly, Confessions and similar
films prompted the U.S. Senate to convene a series of hearings 9–26 September 1941 to assess the role of propaganda in American motion pictures.
An underlying question, reflecting a high level of anti-Semitism, was
whether Jewish movie moguls (like the Warner brothers, who released
Confessions) were trying to push America toward war in retaliation for Nazi
atrocities.[26] Anti-Semitism aside, the hearings reflected the government's
honest concern about how movies influenced public attitudes and foreign
policy, especially while the country remained neutral. The hearings were
also an effort to curb America's heightened anti-Germanism and calm the
many thousands of loyal German-Americans who realized the effect that
movies like Confessions had in blurring the distinction between German-
Americans and Nazis. Their safety rested on reminding the general public
that a huge gulf existed between the two groups.

In 1940 Charlie Chaplin appeared in The Great Dictator, a film that paro-
died Hitler and his mannerisms. While a classic showcase for Chaplin's
comedic genius, The Great Dictator's portrayal of Germans further confused
the American viewing public who equated their pronounced "Germanness" with Nazism. As events in Europe continued to unfold—first with
the invasion of Poland in 1939, then, in 1940, the fall of Denmark, Norway, Holland, Belgium, and France—Hollywood kept up a large and steady
flow of prewar propaganda movies, most quite successful at the box office.
The villains were often similar and tailored for the American audience:
evil Nazis, usually overacted, merciless conquerors of defenseless European
countries, turning their malevolent attention on the last bastion of democracy. Predictably, they were halted at the final moment by the heroics and
vigilance of an alert American public. With the appearance of such low-
brow fare as Bowery Blitzkrieg (1941), which pitted ruthless Nazis against
the Bowery Boys of New York's Lower East Side, and Flying Wild (1941),
an equally overdramatic story of Nazi agents in America sent to steal the

blueprints of America's newest fighter plane, Hollywood was on a roll. Only one film, *Nazi Agent* (1942), approached the very real problem facing German-Americans: the distinction between "good" and "bad" Germans. In this film, twin brothers of opposite loyalties, one a patriotic German-American and the other a Nazi spy, struggle over the future of America.[27] The first twin kills his Nazi brother and takes his place in the spy ring, foiling the enemy's plots and barely escaping detection. The *New York Times* screen critic gave the movie a four-star review, called it "tautly intriguing" and "hair-raising," and cautioned movie-goers to "keep your hands gloved or pocketed when you see it, else your fingernails will go."[28] Despite the many implausibilities, the situation captured the concerns of millions. After Pearl Harbor, Hollywood studios could no longer be accused of edging the nation closer to war or of influencing foreign policy. Nazi spy films now appeared in every form: some frightening, others heroic, together with a surprising number of comedies, such as one by the Three Stooges. Some fell into no clear-cut category, such as a Humphery Bogart film called *All Through the Night* (1942) that pitted America's underworld criminals against the best spies Nazi Germany had to offer.[29] How does one categorize *Wild Horse Rustlers* (1943), which portrayed Nazi spies, in modern suits and snapbrims, in the American West? Their heinous mission was to rustle Army-bound horses, and only the frontier heroism of American cowboys saved the day.[30]

In short, many American prewar and wartime films were ideology-driven and, after the war began, understandably anti-German. While they alone could hardly have caused the public to view all Germans as dangerous enemy agents and prepare the way for the round-up of ten thousand enemy aliens, films were enormously influential when combined with earlier-noted factors like the publicity-plagued Bund and America's World War I experience.

One indication that the public was growing suspicious of the Germans in its midst came in 1939 when Congress took up the issue of detaining certain people considered security risks. Representative Sam Hobbs of Alabama introduced a bill that in many ways legitimated the detention process to follow. America already had the power to deport dangerous enemy aliens and criminals, but what should be done with them while waiting for final expulsion? If they were unsavory enough to deport, should they be allowed to remain at large? Congressman Hobbs's bill called for their detention in camps under the jurisdiction of the Department of Labor. The immediate problem seemed minor, since only about 460 aliens and criminals were being readied for deportation, and it was estimated that the legislation, if passed, would affect about fifty people per year. Still, the debate was heated. Some legislators called it "un-American" and labeled such detention camps "concentration camps." Others predicted that the passage of such a law would damage America's relations with other countries and jeopardize the safety of Americans living abroad. Still others thundered that detention was too good for aliens who had turned against their adopted country. They were considered potential traitors by some: a possible Fifth Column living within a country whose isolation from the harsh realities of an approaching European war seemed to be coming to an end. The *Congressional Record* account of the debate is peppered with Biblical quotes, charges of "communistic forces," references to the Thirteenth Amendment to the Constitution regarding slavery and involuntary servitude, and such precedents as *Zakonaite v. Wolf* (226 U.S. 272), and *Wong Wing v. U.S.* (163 U.S. 228). Someone referred to the bill's sponsor as "Heil Hitler Hobbs." Eventually, the Hobbs Bill was enacted on 5 May 1939 by a vote of 289 to 61.[31] The idea of locking up suspicious foreigners was suddenly legal.

On 9 September 1939, with war in Europe a reality, President Roosevelt created the Emergency Detention Program, instructing the Justice Department "to arrest and detain those persons deemed dangerous in the event of war, invasion, or insurrection in and of a foreign enemy."[32] J. Edgar Hoover shifted into high gear, ordering FBI field offices to review their voluminous files and prepare detailed reports on "persons of German, Italian, and Communist sympathies." Hoover commanded his agents to identify their most dangerous cases and prepare a list of pro-Nazi and procommunist individuals "who would constitute a menace to the public peace and safety of the United States Government."

Even with Roosevelt's detention program officially in place, Hoover was skating on thin ice. For the past three years his collection of names of potential security risks had been based only on the verbal authorization of President Roosevelt. A determined legal challenge could jeopardize the use of those names or, worse, sully the reputation of the FBI itself. Equally worrisome was the growing rivalry of the crusading Texas congressman, Martin Dies, chairman of the Special Committee on Un-American Activities, who loudly complained that the FBI was not seriously confronting the Nazi and Soviet threats in America. His committee could do a better job, he assured the public, and he demanded that all information be funneled to him.[33] Hoover had to act. Through a series of deft political moves combined with surveillance of the Dies committee members and dark hints of worse to come, Hoover managed to circumvent Congressman Dies and persuade the president to require that "all state and federal law enforcement officials turn over to the FBI any information obtained by them relating to espionage, counter-espionage, sabotage, and subversive activities."[34] Hoover now held absolute control over all relevant information, and further information now flowed only to the bureau.

All this information was boiled down to produce the secret Custodial Detention Index (CDI), which listed everyone "to be apprehended and interned immediately upon the outbreak of hostilities," as well as those "who should be watched carefully."[35] This was strictly illegal, of course, and did not fall within the FBI mandate, since it was peacetime. Moreover, the list was being drawn from the flimsiest of sources, including complaints filed by angry ex-wives and business partners. Any exposure of the list would have raised a constitutional outcry and bureau agents were instructed on what type of subterfuge to use as a cover for all investigations.

When an accusation was made against someone—and according to the bureau's figures, it fielded some 78,000 accusations in 1939 alone[36]—agents routinely interviewed the suspect's employers, family, friends, and neighbors, searched apartments, and listened to an army of paid informants. Many were on par with that of the lady who turned in her German-born laundry deliveryman because he always whistled: "He could only be whistling because he was happy about Hitler's successes."

Once a name made it onto the CDI, there was almost no way out of the quicksand. When the person moved from one area to another, a copy of his card followed him. If the suspect went to jail for some unrelated reason, surveillance began again when he was released. Upon induction into the military, his name was forwarded to the military intelligence division or the Office of Naval Intelligence. "Cancellation" of a card came only if the suspect died, and even then Hoover demanded a thorough investigation of the facts surrounding the death before cancellation could occur. It was bureaucratic flypaper. The most irrational denunciation from a persistent, and often anonymous, informer could easily put someone's name on the list.

At the same time, the Special Defense Unit of the Justice Department, led by Lawrence M. C. Smith, began creating its own list of those residents it felt posed the most serious security risks to the United States, including the individuals it planned to arrest first in the event of hostilities. The prime sources for such information were Bund membership rosters, subscription lists to German-language newspapers, or names of people who attended German cultural festivities. The Justice Department's master list was known as the "ABC" list.[37]

As the British had a year earlier, the Justice Department placed everyone on the list into one of three categories. But unlike the British, the categories were based on a person's commitment to Germany rather than the documentable danger he posed. For instance, Category "A" consisted of aliens who were leaders in nonpolitical cultural organizations; Category "B" was made up of people who merely belonged to such organizations; and Category "C" contained people who donated money to radical pro-Nazi organizations or somehow indicated their support. Clearly, the government was already preparing for hostilities against Nazi Germany.

The innocent had nothing to fear, according to the Justice Department Special Defense Unit and the FBI, but the guilty certainly did. In mid-

September 1939, Attorney General Cullen Murphy, a Hoover sycophant, called a press conference to place all potential spies and foreign agents in America on notice. The FBI's patience was at an end. "There will be no repetition of the confusion and laxity and indifference of twenty years ago," Murphy warned, apparently unaware of the brutality experienced by German-Americans during World War I. "At the same time," the attorney general cautioned, "it must not turn into a witch hunt. We must do no wrong to any man."[38] Aware that he probably terrified more foreigners than he calmed, Attorney General Murphy clarified his meaning in a hasty talk before the National Police Academy. He reemphasized that the country was prepared to run down spies, "but we will not act on the basis of hysteria. We are just as anxious to protect the rights of our citizens as to see to it that those who attack the United States do not go unwhipped of justice. . . . Twenty years ago inhumane and cruel things were done in the name of justice. . . . We do not want such things done today for the work has now been localized in the FBI."[39]

Lest one judge the Justice Department's stern warning too hastily, it should be remembered that plenty of potentially dangerous people were in this country. Openly or secretly, dozens of organizations across America pledged their loyalties to unfriendly foreign powers; various embassies were bubbling with subversive and clandestine activities, and there were kooks galore. Dangerous people of every imaginable stripe were loose in America—Germans, Japanese, Italians, communists, anticommunists— enemy propagandists and saboteurs, spies, and espionage agents.[40] Any reasonable population during wartime would want such security risks watched and locked up, if necessary. But how does one separate out the disloyal elements from the rest of the population, and what should be done with them?

Chapter Two

PRECEDENTS

United States

America had faced these questions before. When the United States went to war in April 1917, it was almost as a religious crusade. Imperial Germany had invaded neutral Belgium and attacked France in 1914 before turning on Russia in the East. The British fleet had blockaded Germany in turn, and Europe settled in for a war without end, driven by the rapidly improving technology of killing. Propaganda stories of German atrocities, real and imagined, were fed by the British to an increasingly angry and frightened American public. In April 1915 the German military introduced the horror of poison gas against French Colonial and British Canadian troops in the front lines; in May 1915 a German submarine sank the British luxury liner *Lusitania*, killing more than a hundred Americans. Germans and German-Americans living in the United States began to feel pressures in the communities where they lived. In his preparedness campaign of 1915 and 1916, President Woodrow Wilson attacked the "hyphen mentality" of aliens in America and demanded 100 percent Americanism in this time of crisis. The "American melting pot" myth intensified. Before long, the public was shocked by numerous cases of suspicious fires at important factories in New England in 1916, followed in 1917 by the fateful Zimmermann Telegram from Berlin, which offered Mexico an alliance with Germany against the United States, in return for Texas, Arizona, and New Mexico. German *Kultur* became synonymous with barbarism.

America was growing alarmed. There were eight million first- and second-generation Germans in America out of a total population of ninety-three million, and more than 2.5 million had been born in Germany. When President Wilson stood before Congress on 2 April 1917, to demand a declaration of war, he anticipated the public's reaction. He reassured the nation of the loyalty of German-Americans. While he acknowledged that a few would be disloyal—"a lawless and malignant few"—they would be "dealt with a firm hand of stern repression."[1]

According to the acknowledged expert on this period, the German historian Jörg Nagler, Germans and German-Americans were in trouble even before the declaration of war. Assistant Attorney General Charles Warren, a rabid nativist, recommended that the enemy alien population be "controlled" before they could commit crimes.[2] To support this questionable course of action, Warren discovered the Alien Enemy Statute of 1798, which, during the war of 1812, had been resurrected and interpreted to give the president the powers to control the lives and property of the enemy alien population. Basing his actions on that precedent, President Wilson issued twelve regulations on 6 April 1917, which defined the restrictions imposed on all German-born males over fourteen years of age. They were not allowed to own guns, radios, or explosives. Nor could they live within a half-mile of munitions factories, aircraft stations, forts, arsenals, or naval vessels. Irrational xenophobia and wild-eyed nativism was becoming normal. Even before America entered the European fray, German names were becoming suspect, "hamburgers" were "Liberty Steaks," and the Lutheran Church no longer prayed in German. Enemy aliens were also put on notice that anyone posing a possible threat to American security or the war effort could be removed; within days of the publication of Wilson's twelve regulations, arrests began. As if these restrictions were not sufficient, on 16 November 1917, the president issued eight more regulations. Now, 250,000 male enemy aliens had to register at U.S. post offices, and it became unlawful for them to be found without their registration cards. They had to report any change of residence or employment; Washington, D.C., was off-limits to any enemy alien. A year later, on 18 April 1918, President Wilson extended all twenty regulations to cover the 220,000 German women enemy aliens in the United States, signifying America's descent into total war. Interestingly, the task of organizing this phase of Wilson's regulations fell to an ambitious young lawyer in the Justice Department's Bureau of Enemy Aliens, J. Edgar Hoover—giving him his first experience in alien control and, for that matter, extraconstitutional action authorized by the president.

Germans and German-Americans in America were in real trouble. On one flank were the government's increasingly repressive regulations, the U.S. Post Office's new ability to censor mail, the Justice Department's Bureau of Investigation and its army of paid and volunteer informants, and the state and local police, who eventually arrested 6,300 enemy aliens under presidential warrant.

On the other flank were the mobs: employers who fired their foreign workers with suspicious accents, self-styled "patriotic groups" that demanded that Germans kiss the American flag, recite the list of American presidents, or memorize Lincoln's Gettysburg Address. Eight million "hyphenated Americans" were randomly humiliated, harassed, and discriminated against. Mob violence was not uncommon and at least one German, a Robert Prager, was accused of being a spy and lynched by a frenzied mob in Collinsville, Illinois, on 5 April 1918.

Ultimately, 2,048 Germans (out of a total of 254,138 registered male enemy aliens over fourteen years of age) were incarcerated for the remainder of the war, and several thousand others were arrested, interrogated, investigated—sometimes for months—for evidence of disloyalty and finally released. Enemy aliens living east of the Mississippi were shipped to Fort Oglethorpe, Georgia; those west of the Mississippi were shipped to remote Fort Douglas, Utah. Not until March and April 1920—almost a year after the Versailles Treaty was signed—were the last 200 internees released and the camps closed. Families had been broken, businesses lost, and foreigners in America felt a new foreboding that they were not as safe or welcome as they had come to believe. Despite the contribution of German-Americans to the nation's arts, education, architecture, and military, they suddenly realized that they would not be safe during future crises. Cultural assimilation and naturalization did not always protect those who had become 100 percent Americans. The experience created a legal precedent for a later government to restrict the movement of any minority, especially Germans, in any future war. The evacuation of 120,000 Japanese-Americans during World War II could not have occurred without the precedents established against Germans in World War I.

Canada

Canada went through a similar experience. At the outbreak of World War I, about half a million, or 6 percent, of Canada's eight million residents were German or Austro-Hungarian. Unfortunately, the German government considered all Germans to be citizens of the Imperial Reich, with its military obligation, regardless of emigration to a different country. Thus, Canadians saw foreign residents as possible agents of the Kaiser. As in the United States, the Canadian population turned against its German immigrants with shocking hostility; they were harassed, tormented, and routinely forced to demonstrate their loyalty to Canada. Thousands were arrested and interrogated, and 8,500 enemy aliens were shipped to internment camps for the duration of the war. After the war, the Canadian experience too set the stage for the next war: legal precedents were now in place; a justice system insensitive to wartime prejudice had been organized; and the public accepted the reality of political prison camps. The minorities who lived in Canada learned not to take for granted their future safety.

While the Japanese along the west coast of Canada were relocated, as in America, the similarities with the World War II experiences in America end there. Several reasons account for the differences, according to the eminent Canadian historian of World War II, Robert Keyserlingt.[3] For example, after 1939, Berlin no longer considered German citizens who became citizens of new countries to be citizens of the Third Reich, perhaps to punish them for leaving. In their adopted homeland, former German citizens were not seen as committed foreign agents.

The majority of German-Canadians no longer lived in large cities where they could have been seen as threats to defense plants, military bases, or elected officials. Most were overwhelmingly rural—farmers who had moved out west to Canada's small towns. While the number of Canadian residents of German origin had risen to 600,000 in 1939, the third-largest ethnic group in the country, they had long been accepted as loyal Canadians. Moreover, since Canada had largely halted immigration at the beginning of the Great Depression, the 90,000 German immigrants who arrived after World War I had generally arrived before Hitler took power and were long removed from Nazism. Also, many were Jews and anti-Nazis escaping the Third Reich. Fewer Germans than ever had direct ties to Germany.

There were other reasons that Canada treated German enemy aliens and German-Canadians less harshly during World War II than it had during World War I. One major difference was the Canadian prime minister, Mackenzie King. King liked Germans. He began his political career by representing a heavily German constituency located around the city of Kitchener, Ontario; he genuinely admired the Germans, their language and literature, and in 1937 like many other politicians of the decade paid a personal visit to Hitler and came away entranced.

King followed Britain's lead during the 1930s, remaining somewhat isolationist and proappeasement. Like Britain and the United States, Canada believed that a second world war was only a remote possibility. In the early months of the war that began in September 1939, Canadian casualties were mercifully light. In contrast to the huge losses suffered in 1915–1918, Canadian casualties during World War II remained minimal until the 1943 Allied invasion of Sicily. Consequently, the public was not particularly hostile toward former Germans in their midst.

Overall, Canada shared Britain's view of the essential goodness of Germans although this philosophy was debated through to the end of the war. The overwhelming majority were hard-working, private, and patriotic Canadians who had done nothing wrong. It was politically important to separate those "good former Germans" from the "Hitlerite Germans" who represented the "Nazi Tyranny." To tar them all with the same brush was to lose the support of the many "good" Germans and naturalized Canadians.

Lastly, the Royal Canadian Mounted Police (RCMP) were unprepared to root out subversive activity—even had there been indications that such did exist. In 1939, the total strength of the RCMP consisted of only 2,541 mainly uniformed officers; moreover, they were not trained for intelligence work, but as policemen. The head of the tiny two-man intelligence office in 1939 was a young man, Rivett-Carnac, who had just finished seven years of Arctic patrol. Consequently, the RCMP had little information on or interest in the three well-known pro-Nazi and Nazi organizations. (Canadian authorities always believed that the greatest threat was from the political left). There were also very few policemen available to investigate suspected Nazi agents. In any case, the Nazi organizations were not particularly large or deemed dangerous. These organizations consisted of the Canadian Society for German Culture or Bund, the German Workers' Front or DAF, and finally, the NSDAP, an outright Nazi Party. Each was thought to have a membership of under three hundred, although later indications reveal that the membership of the Workers' Front might in fact have surged as high as 2,500.[4] The only pro-Nazi German-language newspaper was the *German Gazette for Canada* (*Deutsche Zeitung für Kanada*), which was subsidized by the German government.

Despite a generally favorable view of Germans, public hysteria arose and came in two waves: September 1939 and again in mid-1940. The first panic came with Hitler's invasion of Poland. Four days later, on 4 September 1939, six days before Canada went to war, 303 Germans and German-Canadians were arrested and sent off to an internment camp without trials. As in the United States, most of the round-ups were made on the basis of little more than a neighbor's accusation or a complaint from a business competitor. After the crisis passed, however, Canadian courts examined the evidence in each case, released the majority, and held on to only the most dangerous individuals.

The next war crisis in May 1940 was earthshaking, as Canada watched Hitler invade Scandinavia, Belgium, Holland, and France. Now began real problems for German-Canadians. Did they speak German at home? What organizations did they belong to? Were they acting strangely or out of place? Just where did their loyalties lie? Public hysteria turned against German-Canadians, as it was in the United States at the same moment. Rumors flew about German spies, saboteurs, and Fifth Columnists. The Canadian government succumbed to public pressure, just as it had in 1939. The regulations restricting the rights of enemy aliens were expanded to include Canadians from Germany naturalized as far back as September 1922. Government restrictions now also included Italian fascists, native Canadian fascist groups, and the ever-feared communists. The RCMP called on its provincial headquarters to collect lists of potential Fifth Columnists. Then came the arrests and round-ups, which rose to 1,200 by the end of 1940.

As in 1939, with the public's apprehension subsiding the Canadian courts began to sift through the cases. Several hundred were released. By mid-1941 the number of internees had dropped to 780, and by the end of 1942, to 411. When the war ended, the Canadian government held only twenty-two enemy aliens. Forty other Canadian-Germans were denaturalized—stripped of their citizenship—and twelve German women and children were exchanged for the same number of Canadians who had been captured at sea. Ninety-eight others were willingly or unwillingly repatriated to Germany. The rest of the enemy aliens had weathered the war, and while several periods of public hysteria had resulted in many hundreds of arrests and episodes of ethnic hostility, German enemy aliens in Canada, in general, were not as harshly treated as they were in the United States. Or in Britain.

Britain

The situation in Britain was different from that of either Canada or the United States. England is less than sixty-five miles from the French coast, and the threat of German invasion was real and immediate. Germany and Britain had been at war since 3 September 1939, when Berlin ignored London's ultimatum to halt its invasion of Poland. The news of Germany's swift victory over Denmark and Norway stunned the British public. When it became known that in Norway the Nazis were aided by the Norwegian army's own Major Vidkun Quisling (providing the English language with a new wartime label for traitors), rumors flew of a germinating Fifth Column of enemy agents in England. The stream of incoming refugees became a source for concern. How many Quislings were among them? A week later Hitler launched his Blitzkrieg against Belgium, Holland, and France. Refugees came flooding across the Channel, as did wild stories about treachery in Holland and France, as Fifth Columns of secret Nazis spies, visiting "tourists," and even German maidservants rose up to greet German parachutists. England was swelling with incoming refugees, not just from France and the Low Countries, but from Poland and Czechoslovakia, in addition to the tens of thousands of anti-Nazis and Jews from Germany and Austria. All crossed the sea to find sanctuary in Britain.

There was plenty to be frightened about. Much evidence does indicate that as early as August 1938 the Germans had mapped out most of Britain's airfields and acquired maps and photos of the major docks, warehouses, oil tanks, harbors, and important highway junctions of London and Hull.[5] Even more ominously, the German consul general in Liverpool was caught buying information from a worker in a munitions factory. Not long afterward, the anxious British public read that three workmen in the great arsenal works at Woolwich were sentenced for giving information to the Germans. Rumors and potboiler novels speculated about the Nazi exploitation of visiting German tourists, youth groups, conferences, and exchange students; one writer claimed that "more than a thousand German girls had been lodged with English families as maid-servant spies."[6] While Germany certainly intended to invade Britain and planned a large amphibious attack under the code name Operation Sea Lion, Hitler's private discussions reveal that he did not intend to rely on any substantial aid from citizens or aliens living there. On 21 July 1940, Hitler told his generals: "We cannot count upon any supplies whatsoever being available for us in England."[7] Unaware of this, British government scrutiny turned toward the thousands of incoming refugees and resident aliens living in soon-to-be beleaguered England.

At first, both the British government and the public were repelled by the prospect of mass internment. As early as 1 April 1939, a subcommittee of the Committee of Imperial Defence initially decided that in the event of hostilities, no automatic internment of enemy alien men would occur. The War Office pressed for stronger measures, and later that month the committee reluctantly approved the reserving of accommodations for 18,000 possible internees. Attention focused mainly on German and Austrian nationals living in Britain, although the home secretary, Sir John Anderson, an opponent of mass internment, pointed out that a greater danger probably existed from Irish extremists, British fascists, communists, and naturalized British citizens. When Hitler attacked Poland in September, Sir John changed his mind. He announced an immediate review of all Germans and Austrians and established 112 alien tribunals to evaluate each case. Each tribunal was presided over by a king's counselor, clerk, and liaison officer appointed by the Imperial Refugee Committee. The proceedings were private, with a detective-inspector acting as secretary. Each enemy alien could bring an English friend (but not a legal representative) with him to vouch for his sentiments and good faith toward Great Britain. The presiding judge determined if the alien was a true enemy (Category "A") or a "friendly enemy" (Category "B"). Those who could convince the tribunal that their German citizenship had been revoked for political opposition or who had spent time in a Nazi concentration camp were declared to be "Refugees from Nazi Oppression" rather than "Enemy Aliens," and placed in Category "C."

At the time, nearly 75,000 Germans and Austrians lived in Britain—men, women, and children—a total of 62,244 German and 11,989 Austrian nationals. Tribunals investigated each case, however briefly, with the following results:

569 —Class "A" or "high security risks" (to be interned)
6,782 —Class "B" or "doubtful cases" (restrictions)
66,002 —Class "C" or "no security risks" (remained at liberty)

Category "C" would soon present a problem: 55,457 of the 66,002 Germans and Austrians were Jews and anti-Nazis who had escaped from Europe. Nonetheless, as soon as Britain went to war with Germany on 3 September 1939, despite the earlier rulings, they all became "Enemy Aliens." By January 1940 the authorities had interned 528 enemy aliens judged by British counter-intelligence, MI5, to be especially dangerous, while placing an additional 8,356 under restrictions. The vast majority, some 60,000, remained at liberty. In May 1940, as Hitler's armies poured into France, the situation for the remaining 60,000 suddenly became worse. On 11 May, after the formation of Churchill's coalition government, a protected zone was declared along Britain's eastern and southern coast, and all German and Austrian men sixteen to sixty years old living within that zone were rounded up and interned. At the end of the month, all German and Austrian men in Category "B" were interned as well.

The arrests were not unlike those to follow a year and a half later in the United States: two policemen usually pounded on the alien's door in the early morning hours and made the arrest. After that, the police methods varied from station to station. Sometimes the aliens were dealt with gently, encouraged to pack, and informed about their destination. In other areas, the arresting officers were brusque, explanations were few, and the aliens were forbidden to bring anything along. Many spent weeks in confinement before being allowed to receive clothing or luggage from relatives.

The public still wasn't satisfied. Almost every day the *Daily Mail* complained that the measures didn't go far enough. Hostility against German and Austrian nationals, now enemy aliens, spread like wildfire. On 25 May, the rector of Oxford University declared, "All aliens are a potential menace and should be interned. That is the general opinion of the university." A few voices in the government tried to dampen the growing anti-alien hysteria. Some cautioned that the alarmist news stories might have been Nazi-inspired; another warned his constituents, "The outcry for internment is coming from all the old appeasers, the friends of Franco, the members of the Economic League, from all those trying to direct attention from themselves."[8] The cries of an angry public drowned out their efforts to calm the country's mood.

Now came the women. What began as silly banter in Parliament regarding equality between the sexes and the danger of women's wiles hardened into a new government program to round up all German and Austrian women, exempting only those in Category "C." Not that all the women in Categories "A" and "B" were blameless. "Although there were probably very few, if any, planted agents amongst them," notes a British former internee, "there is no doubt that a number of them were proud of being Germans, sympathized with the Nazis, and in the event of an invasion would have become a security risk. It was sensible to intern them; they should in fact have been put into category 'A' and interned immediately."[9]

What about Category "C"? The decision came on 10 June 1940, when the unimaginable had happened. The Germans had reached the French side of the English Channel and seemed unstoppable; invasion appeared imminent. Mussolini had just declared war, and Churchill, reluctantly (perhaps recalling his own imprisonment during the Boer War), ordered Sir John to intern all Italian men. With the press and some members of Parliament leading the charge and the military establishment now on board, the government saw little option other than to intern all German and Austrian men in Category "C." Once the decision was made, the War Office, determined to clear Britain of all distractions, firmly rejected many suggestions to raise a Foreign Legion or a Jewish Brigade to fight under British command. The alternative put into effect was to intern both Jews and Nazis in the same camps. The decision reeked of anti–Semitism. Placing citizenship over logic and beset by countless other wartime issues, London ordered all men from Germany or Austria between the ages of sixteen and sixty to be shipped to internment camps. By 13 June 1940, a total of 10,869 enemy aliens were interned—all those in Category "A," all men and women in Category "B," and a few men in Category "C" who had been caught in the protected zones. Ultimately, 22,000 people were imprisoned—Jews, Nazis, and anti-Nazis alike—often giving rise to bizarre situations. One case, reported in the *Daily Mail* on 7 February 1942, was particularly unusual. It seems that a small group of Orthodox Jewish students had come over from a yeshiva in Frankfurt together with their Talmud teacher before the outbreak of the war. They lived with a local rabbi, who had inadvertently failed to register his guests with the police as required of arriving enemy aliens. Both rabbis were summoned before the magistrate and each sentenced to pay a dramatically high fine of £50. In passing sentence, the magistrate commented: "I think it is a horrible state of affairs when men of this description can harbour the enemy in the centre of the biggest city in the world." This group might well have ended the war in Britain's Swanwick Camp, which housed both Jews and rabid Nazis.

At the cabinet meeting of 10 June 1940, the lord president of the council, Neville Chamberlain, reported that Canada had agreed to take four thousand civilian internees; Australia and New Zealand agreed to do the same. Ultimately, none went New Zealand. Only mainland Canada and Australia received internees. Between 30 June and 10 July 1940, four ships sailed for Canada (*Duchess of York, Arandora Star, Ettrick, Sobieski*), and one to Australia (*Dunera*), transporting a total of 11,003 people—hardened Nazis, anti-fascists, Jewish refugees, and Italians. One ship, the *Arandora Star*, was torpedoed off the coast of Ireland with a loss of 661 people.[10]

Hastily, Britain, Canada, and Australia built a network of internment camps to accommodate more than 22,000 internees, although more than half were quickly released on parole or given their liberty. It was far different from World War I when Britain interned 99 percent of its resident enemy aliens in 1914; this time it established a screening process that resulted in internment for only 2.5 percent of them, freedom under restrictions (parole) for 10.8 percent, and unrestricted freedom for 86.7 percent.[11] While Britain and the United States both acted quickly to round up their enemy aliens, the United Kingdom seems to have acted with greater control.[12]

CHAPTER THREE

THE NET TIGHTENS

By mid-1940 Europe had been at war for nearly a year. Americans had watched the Wehrmacht sweep through Belgium, Denmark, Norway, Holland, and into France. American merchant shipping was suffering serious losses, and German U-boats prowled unmolested off the East Coast. In a well-publicized speech to the FBI's National Academy, Director Hoover said "that there is a Fifth Column which has already started to march is an acknowledged reality. That it menaces America is an established fact. That it must be met is the common resolve of every red-blooded citizen. A Fifth Column of destruction, following in the wake of confusion, weakening the sinews and paralyzing it with fear can only be met by the nationwide offensive of all law enforcement!"[1] The public clamored for action: a Gallup Poll of 10 June 1940 posed the question, "Should all people who are not United States citizens be required to register with the Government?" In response, an overwhelming 95 percent of the respondents said "Yes."[2] Clearly, the public was anxious about the presence of spies and enemy agents and wanted them controlled. They were not to be disappointed. On 20 December 1940 the state attorney's staff in Chicago announced that it had seized German-American Bund records that revealed alarming news. The Bund's membership, on paper, numbered in the tens of thousands; still worse, between 1,500 and 2,000 Bundists were currently serving in the United States Army and Navy. Termites had infiltrated America's military defenses!

To stem the increasing American concern, Attorney General Robert Jackson, who displayed little concern about the legality of the FBI's methods, allowed Hoover to convince him to establish the Neutrality Laws Unit (later renamed the Special War Policies Unit), which made a flurry of public arrests. The officials of the Nazi Transoceanic News Service were taken to Ellis Island for deportation, and several hundred Italian and German seamen were arrested in various American ports. In Manhattan, nearly a hundred Italian restaurant waiters, most admittedly having long overstayed their visas after the 1939 New York World's Fair, were rounded up by an army of immigration authorities, Canadian border patrolmen, and New York City police detectives. To impress the public with the Justice Department's ability to protect its citizens, these alien sweeps and arrests were conducted in the middle of the busy lunch hour.

Even the blue-blooded Princess Stephanie Hohenlohe-Waldenburg-

Schillingfürst was swept up by the Justice Department. Princess "Steph" was an international hostess, whose friends included Hungarian and British aristocrats, English and American millionaires, artists and actresses, politicians and beauties. Her difficulties arose when her parties and friendships began to include the leaders of the Third Reich, and she had audiences with Hitler. While her associations were more the pretensions of Viennese high society than political intrigue, her son, Prince Franz Hohenlohe, nevertheless states that his mother had been working since 1938 "to prevent the outbreak of the conflict, and that her reputation as a *femme fatale* merely dabbling in politics was totally undeserved."[3]

Whatever the purpose of Steph's meetings with Nazi leaders, snippets of gossip began to appear in British and American newspapers describing the elegant forty-five-year-old redhead as a secret agent "playing an important part in a system of underhand intrigue and espionage." Waving aside the advice of her friends, the princess left an increasingly hostile England for the United States. From her apartment in New York's famed Plaza Hotel, where newspaper photographs pictured her waving from her bathtub, she set about trying to alert the American public about the approaching war in Europe. Eventually, she became entangled with the German consul in San Francisco, Captain Fritz Wiedemann, with the joint purpose, according to her son, of "acting against his government's policy."[4] In January 1941, Steph realized that her few months' stay had stretched into a year, and her tourist visa had expired. Her son explained that "she wanted to renew it but because of the press attacks upon her and the pressure of her enemies, there was little likelihood that this could be done." The Justice Department ordered her deported. She delayed her departure until April 1941 through hearings, petitions, and appeals. When the authorities finally came for her, Steph developed paralysis of her legs and was taken by stretcher and ambulance to the San Francisco Immigration Station on Silver Avenue. She remained in government hands for several weeks, until a deal was arranged with a special assistant to the attorney general, Major Lemuel B. Schofield (an eventual suitor). She was released on probation, and moved to a suite in Philadelphia's Barclay Hotel. Soon she was again entertaining the rich and famous. Her freedom was short, however; the day after Pearl Harbor, Steph was rearrested by the FBI and shipped off to an internment camp.

Another flurry of public arrests swept up some 380 German and Italian seamen and merchant marine sailors who had been stranded in the United States since the war broke out in 1939. They seemed largely harmless. Most were well known to the authorities, and some were even taking English-language courses while they waited to be exchanged or rehired by their employer, Standard Oil of New Jersey.[5] Still, their predawn arrests were dramatic proof to an anxious American public that the Justice Department was on the job. The waiters arrested earlier in New York and others were taken by government ferries to the already overcrowded Ellis Island reception center, where they remained for months.

Only the 380 seamen went elsewhere. The sailors were placed aboard a heavily guarded military train and taken west. The Italians were left at remote Fort Missoula, in Missoula, Montana, and some of the Germans went farther to a holding facility at Fort Stanton, New Mexico.[6] An additional number were transported to bleak Fort Abraham Lincoln, North Dakota.

Fort Stanton was the first enemy alien internment camp in the United States during the war. An abandoned Civilian Conservation Corp (CCC) camp located on the Fort Stanton Military Reservation in mid–New Mexico, it was renovated between December 1940 and March 1941 to accommodate approximately 400 crew members of the S.S. *Columbus*. This German luxury liner, one of the largest and most opulent steamships in the world, was scuttled by her captain, Wilhelm Daehne, on 19 December 1939, to prevent its capture by the British. The passengers and crew of the *Columbus* were rescued by the U.S. cruiser *Tuscaloosa*, and Captain Daehne and his men became "guests" of the American government. First they were taken to Ellis Island, where they joined the one thousand aliens already being held there. From there they were shipped to Angel Island, near Alcatraz, in San Francisco Bay. During the year they spent on Angel Island, they were frequently permitted to come ashore to San Francisco. Newspaper articles, however, began to reflect the city's nervousness with the so-called dangerous seamen and indicated that they were no longer welcome in San Francisco.[7] The Justice Department then shipped them to distant Fort Stanton.[8] They remained there until the United States entered the war in December 1941, at which time the German "guests" became "enemy aliens."

Other German seamen were taken on to Fort Lincoln, a sprawling, antiquated CCC headquarters post on the desolate windswept plains five miles south of Bismarck, North Dakota. The communities of Missoula, Fort Stanton, and Bismarck were abuzz for weeks with rumors about the objectionable arrivals. Bismarck was particularly concerned, not so much about the danger of the new arrivals but about the possibility that the government would send a company of black troops to guard the interned sailors.[9]

On 27 August 1940, Congress passed the Alien Registration Act (Public Law Number 670), part of the larger Smith Act, which required all noncitizens to register at their local post offices. Those aliens who could not speak English had to furnish their own interpreters. The aliens were then fingerprinted. The authorities attempted to make the fingerprinting more acceptable by pointing out that "nearly all civil service employees, even J. Edgar Hoover, Department of Justice chief, have their prints on file in Washington."[10] The registration process took about fifteen minutes, and at the end

of each day, all registration forms were placed in mail bags and sent directly
to the Department of Justice.

Enemy aliens were at first "uncertain and frightened, but toward the
end, enthusiastic," remembers Solicitor General (soon to be attorney general) Francis Biddle. "The post-office clerks who handled the enrollment
were trained to emphasize politeness and patience." To save time and minimize disruption at work, FBI and other available Justice Department agents
were sent out to register aliens at factories, hospitals, institutions, farms—
even penitentiaries. Seamen were registered by representatives of the Immigration Service who boarded their ships as they docked.[11] All the
information was funneled to the temporary registration headquarters, a
huge, barn-like former roller skating rink in Washington, D.C.

> It was built for roller skating, with high windows, and a glossy
> hardwood floor. Today, instead of the hum of skates, the *Casino* is
> filled with the clatter of hundreds of typewriters, the thud of heavy
> wooden cases in which tens of thousands of records are moved from
> desk to desk, the soft whir of automatic microfilm cameras. . . . Here
> some seven hundred clerks, statisticians, business machine operators,
> experts, and administrators are sorting, studying, reporting the stream
> of data poured into the division's hopper from every community in
> the nation during the four-month period which ended at midnight
> on December 26.[12]

The program went quite smoothly. Only in southern states, Georgia in
particular, with a high degree of nativism and a negligible number of foreign-born residents, were repressive registration measures enacted, generally by executive order from the governor's office. Overall, however, the
first registration of aliens in America since 1917 proved successful.

When the process was completed, the public was hardly calmed to learn
that the country contained more than 4,900,000 aliens—1,000,000 more
than the preregistration estimates—and that among these were 315,000
Germans citizens, 695,000 Italians, and 91,000 Japanese.[13] One out of every
twenty-six people in the country had been fingerprinted and catalogued.
In New York alone, a national high of 500,000 aliens had registered, or
one out of every sixteen residents of the city. That ratio was changing
dramatically, however, as the prospect of war sent foreigners rushing to
become naturalized American citizens.[14]

Then the public read about the FBI's sensational arrest of two German
aliens in Philadelphia, tool-makers in plants with defense contracts, who
were found to own cameras. They were characterized by the FBI as important cogs in a big espionage ring.[15]

The internment of aliens neared reality. The next step was to separate
out the greatest security risks. James Rowe Jr., assistant to Attorney General

Biddle, described the Justice Department's efforts isolate the worst cases: "If the evidence showed he was very dangerous, he was an 'A'. If the evidence was good, he was an 'A-1'. If it was poor, it was an 'A-4'. . . . The program worked quite well."[16]

Questions arose about aliens' legal status. In discussions held in July and August 1940, the War Department and the Department of Justice, regularly at one another's throats, analyzed the legal rights of aliens who were potential enemies, concluding significantly, "Alien enemies should be treated as prisoners of war rather than as criminals."[17] The task that remained was to select the proper sites to house internees.

In March 1941 the Adjutant General's Office in Washington sent out a request for available areas. In response each military district in the United States surveyed its potential sites and reported in. The Fifth Corps area, for example, designated Fort Benjamin Harrison, Indiana, for the detention of enemy aliens and crews of foreign merchant vessels, with Forts Knox and Thomas in Kentucky, Fort Hayes in Ohio, and thirty-six abandoned camps standing by.[18] The Second Corps area, in turn, announced the completion of Camp Upton Enclosure at Camp Upton, Long Island, consisting of 120 winterized tents, an infirmary, a mess hall, a recreational building, and latrines. The camp was enclosed by two barbed-wire fences ten feet high and twelve feet apart. A tower at each corner held a machine gun, and the entire camp was illuminated. District officials reported, "This Enclosure is now available to receive, record, house, mess, clothe, and otherwise care for internees."[19] The Sixth Corps area offered Camp McCoy, Wisconsin, and requested permission from the War Department to augment McCoy's existing security—double fences, subsurface barriers to prevent tunneling, and four guard towers equipped with searchlights—by installing a high-voltage fence.[20] (The request was firmly rejected). The Seventh Corps area suggested Fort Meade and Sturgis, South Dakota, and old Fort Lincoln, near Bismarck, North Dakota. The Seventh Corps area headquarters also patriotically threw in the State Fair Grounds in Sedalia, Missouri, and Hutchinson, Kansas, as well as fifty-five scattered CCC camps, and the Helmer's Furniture Company Warehouse in Omaha, Nebraska.[21] Other corps areas responded as well.

In July 1941, six months before America entered the war, representatives of the Justice Department and the War Department met to hammer out a basic program for handling the potentially large number of enemy aliens. The result was a no-nonsense, eight-page outline of steps and jurisdictions involved.

Once arrested, each enemy alien's case would be evaluated by the Attorney General's Office, with the eventual result of (a) conditional or unconditional release, (b) parole, with or without bond, or (c) internment for the duration of the war. To prepare for the third possibility, the program called for the construction of major detention camps to be located in the south-east, the middle south, and the southwest parts of the country. Opening with a reminder of the excesses of World War I, the outline listed the many restrictions that would immediately apply to enemy aliens in the event of war, from barring entry to restricted zones in such areas as the Hawaiian Islands, Alaska, and the Canal Zone, to forbidding possession of numerous items, such as firearms, ammunition, cameras, shortwave radio receivers, signaling devices, codes and ciphers, and the like. The agreement's major flaw was that it relied entirely on FBI reports; aliens were to be arrested "on the basis of information submitted to the United States Attorney by a Federal Bureau of Investigation agent. . . ."[22] Everything depended on those files—the Custodial Detention Index.

In 1944, looking back on this Justice—War Department agreement, FBI Director Hoover championed it as the nation's guarantee against "difficulties arising from overinternment . . . interference with labor through reckless internment activities, and the internment of persons solely because of careless statements prior to the outbreak of war."[23] But he failed to mention that soon after the war began, the War Department and the Justice Department had a serious falling out over many of the points they had agreed to and that the agreement served as nothing more than a procedural guide. As of July 1941, the basic framework for the Enemy Alien Internment Program was complete, and many thousands of German and Italian citizens living in America grew frantic.

In an effort to calm "American-Aliens," as he called them, Attorney General Francis Biddle, an intelligent and principled humanitarian, assured readers of the widely read government magazine *State Government* that the Justice Department was dedicated to its name—to the task of justice.[24] To help accomplish this, Biddle enlisted the help of the Philadelphia lawyer Earl G. Harrison. Biddle appointed Harrison commissioner of the Immigration and Naturalization Service. Harrison echoed the call for calm and pointed out that compared to World War I, only a tenth of the number of German aliens lived in the United States. Moreover, four out of every five German noncitizens had family ties in America, and more than half were over forty-five years of age and thus considered no military threat. America currently has "the smallest proportion of aliens to the total population in our history—approximately 3.5 percent! . . . The 'American Alien,' for much the greater part, is neither a refugee, nor, at any time, an enemy alien. He is, in reality, an immigrant—a product of American history."[25]

The public generally agreed. In May 1939 Americans celebrated a much-touted new holiday, "I Am an American" Day, to congratulate naturalized U.S. citizens. The holiday became a minor July Fourth festival, wrapped in patriotism and family outings. In May 1941, more than 750,000 New Yorkers packed the Central Park Mall to hear speeches by Secretary of the Interior Harold Ickes and Mayor Fiorello La Guardia. In Chicago, 100,000 people trooped to Soldier Field to hear Vice President Henry Wallace, Speaker of the House Sam Rayburn, and other national figures deliver a stirring radio broadcast to the country.[26] German, Italian, and Japanese citizens in America were somewhat calmed.

A number of organizations sprang up to counter the general American view that German-Americans were automatically sympathetic to Nazism. The Loyal Americans of German Descent, the German-American Congress for Democracy, the German-American Democratic Society of Greater New York City, the Wisconsin Federation of German-American Societies, the German-American Anti-Nazi League, and others worked to rally German elements in American society to illustrate their loyalty.[27]

The big question concerning Biddle's "American-Aliens" boiled down to: "Who is loyal to America and who is not?" A former German diplomat provided one explanation in February 1942 in a *Harper's Magazine* article entitled "Your German-American Neighbor and the Fifth Column."[28] German immigrants to America, like immigrants anywhere, said Wolfgang zu Putlitz, were understandably torn between sympathy for the land of their birth and loyalty to their adopted country. While the great majority of Germans in America were devoted to their adopted homeland, the diplomat admitted the existence of many whose hearts remained with Germany.

The largest group of Germany's supporters, he said, were nationalists—"simple-minded believers in the myth of German racial superiority. They are no worse than Kipling in this respect," he added pointedly, "and certainly not more beastly than certain proponents of Ku Kluxism in the 1920s." Another group of supporters were those overawed by the Nazi government's economic achievements. They were generally more sympathetic to Hitler if they lived safely in the United States and had not experienced firsthand the tyranny and corruption that went with these economic achievements. A final group simply could not imagine joining Russians and Englishmen, Germany's old World War I enemies, to fight against the Fatherland, especially before America joined the war in December 1941.

America's real enemies were not these conflicted but loyal German-Americans, but rather fell into three general groups: First, zu Putlitz said, "a very small number of bankers and businessmen who have a material stake in the Nazi success, either because they still own German properties or because they are being paid handsome commissions to handle Nazi business. Secondly, individual fools and hotheads, or criminal types, happy to pick up a bit of Nazi easy money." Lastly were "those immigrant citizens who for one reason or another have had a hard time in this country, and for whom adherence to the Nazi idea is a cheap fashion of 'revenge' against the country in which they failed to make good."

According to zu Putlitz, America had nothing to fear from such groups of strutting Nazis as Fritz Kuhn's Bund. "Can it be imagined," he asked rhetorically, "that a real fifth column would be led by men as boastful and hungry for publicity as the paltry and amateurish leaders of the Bund?" "No!" he declared—ignoring the very methods of Hitler's success. The reason for the Bund's supposed impotence was that the organization required members to hold American citizenship. "American citizens of German origin, considered collectively, are useless as Nazi instruments of immediate action for the reason that the Nazis have no unbreakable hold over them."

These words of reassurance notwithstanding, plans on the internment camps went forward. With an agreement in place, a huge list of suspects compiled, Congressional and public support, and reports about military sites coming in, the only remaining issue concerned the actual camps—who would run them. The issue of control was settled quickly. The army would maintain and transport arrested aliens until they reached the camp proper, at which time they would be handed over to the Immigration and Naturalization Service (INS) of the Justice Department.

On 10 October 1941, two months before America entered the war, a confidential directive, one of many between the Office of the U.S. Attorney General and INS directors around the country, was sent to the director of Ellis Island in New York harbor. The INS official was instructed to prepare for the arrival of foreign internees and informed that "It has been estimated that there will be six hundred arrests monthly in the State of New York, and two hundred in the State of New Jersey."[29]

Chapter Four

The Arrests

The Japanese, Germans, and German-Americans, it is now clear, were under government scrutiny long before the attack on Pearl Harbor. In an astonishing revelation that came in 1981, thirty-five years after the end of World War II, a lengthy article in *The Los Angeles Times* revealed that agents of the Office of Naval Intelligence (ONI) and the FBI actually broke into the Japanese consulate in Los Angeles in the spring of 1941, long before Pearl Harbor. Lieutenant Commander Kenneth Ringle, reportedly the model for heroic protagonist Victor Henry in Herman Wouk's novel, *Winds of War,* disclosed for the first time that in the break-in agents had "removed and photographed everything in the consulate's safe, then replaced each item as it had been. . . . We had the police outside watching. We had the FBI. We even had our own safecracker . . . [whom] we checked out of prison for the job."[1] The break-in was worth the risk, however. The secret files in the consulate's vault revealed the names and whereabouts of more than 450 Japanese agents in Southern California. When the FBI and the ONI fanned out to arrest spies after Pearl Harbor day, they were working from the enemy's own lists; equally important, the authorities knew when they had completed the roundup. Moreover, the consulate break-in yielded something even more valuable: evidence that officials of Imperial Japan looked upon most American Japanese, both resident aliens (Issei, who by law could not be naturalized) and American-born (Nisei), not as potential allies but as untrustworthy cultural traitors. The later backlash and relocation of 120,000 American Japanese was not necessary on security grounds, since both J. Edgar Hoover and President Roosevelt had received a copy of Lieutenant Commander Kenneth Ringle's lengthy break-in report.

An equally startling revelation regarding the treatment of German aliens was recently found in the FBI files. An 8 December 1941 memorandum from J. Edgar Hoover to Major Lemuel Schofield of the INS not only confirmed that the government had indeed developed a massive list of people targeted for arrest in the event of war, but more importantly, that the majority of those to be arrested immediately were American citizens rather than Germans enemy aliens. According to Hoover's memo, the number of individuals considered for immediate custodial detention were:

German aliens	636
American citizens sympathetic to Germany	1,393

Persons of German descent whose citizenship is unknown   1,694
Italian aliens   77
American citizens sympathetic to Italy   49
Persons of Italian descent whose citizenship is unknown   211
                                            TOTAL   4,060 [2]

Clearly, the Enemy Alien Program singled out greater numbers of German-Americans (1,393), either native-born or naturalized citizens, than German resident aliens (636). Hoover considered German-American citizens more dangerous, with their presumably excellent English and their ability to assimilate into the mainstream; German citizens who lived in the United States would be more visible, less trusted by the American public, and easier to catch. For whatever reason, the program was extra-legal and begun under false pretenses.

Attorney General Biddle was in the middle of a speech in Detroit when the Japanese attacked Pearl Harbor on 7 December 1941. "Stunned and troubled," he made his way back to his Washington office where his assistants had already prepared the necessary orders for the internment of enemy aliens. Curiously, a substantial number were arrested just *before* the Japanese attack on Pearl Harbor, and four days before Germany or Italy declared war on the United States on 11 December. The procedures had long been established. Now, President Roosevelt immediately issued Presidential Proclamation 2525, modeled on the Enemy Alien Act of 1798; together with Roosevelt's Proclamations 2526 and 2527, the orders gave the government full authority to detain enemy aliens and confiscate enemy alien property at will. However, though Germany and Italy had not yet declared war on the United States, government officials were already discussing the fate of their citizens in the United States. On the afternoon of 8 December, Biddle took a draft proclamation authorizing their arrest to the White House for the president's signature; after a brief discussion about the number of German and Italian aliens in America and the possibility of interning them all, Roosevelt told Biddle, "I don't care so much about Italians. They're a lot of opera singers. But the Germans are different; they may be dangerous." [3] Biddle left with his authorization and telegraphed J. Edgar Hoover to begin the roundup of enemy aliens deemed dangerous to the security of the United States. Hoover and the FBI, however, were way ahead of him.

With the war a reality for America, the FBI went into action. All bureau field offices were put on full alert. Offices operated around the clock, and annual leaves and vacations were canceled. Protective guards were stationed around the Japanese embassy and its consulates in major cities (and for good measure, the German and Italian missions as well). After the Axis countries declared war on America on 11 December, telephone connections with enemy countries were severed lest spies in America communicate the nation's emergency security measures and level of morale. Then the FBI, often together with an ONI officer or a member of the local police, went out to round up those the CDI lists deemed the most dangerous American citizens and enemy aliens.

Along with the Japanese, hundreds of Germans and Italians were arrested during the next several days—before either Axis nation declared war on the United States on 11 December. In Houston, Texas, the FBI began its roundup hours after the Japanese attack was announced, initiating a twenty-hour blitz that bagged seventeen accused Nazis, nine Japanese, and two Italians. They were taken to San Antonio's Southern Pacific Railroad Station under heavy guard and placed in a special immigration car.[4]

The FBI is not normally legally allowed to make arrests on its own authority, only on warrants issued by the Justice Department. "But on that Sunday night," recalled Attorney General Francis Biddle, "Hoover was authorized by the President to pick up several hundred without warrants, and this procedure was followed for a short time until the more dangerous had been apprehended."[5] Over the next several days, the FBI arrested 857 Germans and 147 Italians in thirty-five states, including, for a few days, the entire German and Italian communities in Hawaii. The commissioner of the INS, Earl G. Harrison, put the total number at "more than one thousand . . . before day's end on December 8, 1941."[6] Several thousand more were detained for questioning, and still others were told to hold themselves in readiness. The Justice Department's other agencies, for their part, rounded up for questioning an astounding 60,000 enemy aliens, mostly Germans. "We thought we were off to a pretty good run," Assistant Attorney General James Rowe Jr. crowed some years later.[7]

At the end of this first sweep and after the suspicious characters had been separated from the others, the FBI ended up with only 400 German "possibles." J. Edgar Hoover must have wondered if his massive several-year effort to collect the names of potential spies had been worth the time. In fact, in a memorandum to his assistants, Clyde Tolson, E. A. Tamm, and D. Milton Ladd, dated 9 December 1941, an apparently embarrassed J. Edgar Hoover noted, "I told Mr. Shea that this morning the Attorney General decided not to issue a press statement because we had only taken into custody a little over 400 Germans, that if this figure were given out public opinion would be very unfavorable."[8] By the following day, 10 December, the INS had detained an additional 457 Germans. An INS memo noted that "Mr. Hoover says this is practically all whom it contemplated to arrest at the present time, though there may be a few more."[9] This proved to be an understatement—by the thousands. By 11 December, the FBI was able to announce that the number of German aliens currently under arrest had risen to 1,002.[10] By 8 January 1942, the number of German enemy aliens arrested in the United States had risen to 1,243, and by 16 February 1942, the Justice Department had interned 1,393 Germans, 2,192 Japanese, and 264 Italians. Internment differed markedly from the mass exclusion program against the Japanese which began the following month on the West Coast and the individual exclusion program that occurred largely against German aliens on both coasts. Enemy aliens were arrested on suspicion of disloyalty—not a crime. Circumstances had placed their names on Hoover's list. But by the end of the war, 10,905 Germans (along with 3,278 Italians) would have been rounded up and unceremoniously shipped to distant, spartan camps for the duration of the war (and beyond).

Some of those arrested during the first days after Pearl Harbor were actual spies. Such people were criminals, and if caught they were tried for espionage and jailed if found guilty. Most were Japanese. Acting on the evidence secured during the spring 1941 break-in at the Japanese consulate, the authorities had a list of more than 450 genuine Japanese spies. In one dramatic arrest, the ONI and the FBI had to drive at breakneck speed to catch a Japanese naval officer, Itaru Tachibana, and a valet named Toraichi Kono, with a truckload of documents that revealed Japan's entire espionage effort on the West Coast of the United States. Some Japanese spies were not even Japanese. William A. Schuler was arrested at his home in Palos Verdes, California, for sending radio messages to the Japanese (he was sentenced to six years at a federal penitentiary); the Reverend Kurt E. B. Molzahn, a German national, was caught stealing military information, as it turned out, for the Japanese (Molzahn got ten years); Dr. Otto Willumeit, head of the Chicago German-American Bund, and Gerhard Wilhelm Kunze, another Bund leader, were nabbed transmitting U.S. defense secrets to Germany and Japan (five and fifteen years respectively); and Dr. Wolfgang Ebell was arrested for operating an "underground railroad" to assist Japanese and German spies fleeing to Mexico (five years). Samuel Eliot Morison, the premier historian of American naval operations in World War II, was convinced that disloyal elements along the East Coast aided the enemy. "The U-boats were undoubtedly helped by enemy agents and clandestine radio transmissions from the United States."[11]

Several years later, in 1943, a book by Alan Hynd entitled *Passport to Treason* uncloaked, in authoritative detail, the existence of a large, malevolent network of German spies and saboteurs throughout America and the FBI's heroic efforts to protect the public. The book is larded with praise for Hoover's insight in collecting in advance the names of dangerous people and is sprinkled with stories of invisible ink, crafty spies, and buxom couriers, and it assured America that many on Hoover's list were genuinely dangerous. Hoover's "G-men" were on the job. Interestingly, considering the FBI's penchant for occasionally pursuing an investigation with no legal foundation, only a flash of their badges, author Hynd notes that the G-men were so respectful of the law that they adhered to it even when doing so meant the loss of valuable evidence. "They are not permitted to enter private premises without a search warrant, and to have sworn out a warrant would have been to tip their hand."[12]

Ten days after the attack on Pearl Harbor, Hoover decided to enlarge the pool of suspects. On 17 December 1941, he sent an encoded dispatch to all FBI offices in which they were "instructed to furnish to the Bureau . . . the names concerning persons of *American citizenship, either by birth or naturalization,* who you believe should be considered for custodial detention. . . ." (emphasis added)[13] The Constitution, in effect, had been set aside—a position that was upheld after the war by the Supreme Court in *Johnson v. Eisentrager* (339 U.S. 763). Enemy aliens were not within their rights to demand equal protection under the law.[14]

While the list of dangerous enemy aliens swelled, and the prospect of mass incarceration became a real possibility, the government turned its attention to the question of enemy diplomats.

Hoover considered diplomats of enemy countries (and their staffs and families) to be a far greater security threat than regular aliens. Diplomatic staffs regularly concealed trained espionage agents who had access to codes and sophisticated spy and communications equipment. The FBI swarmed over Washington's Embassy Row the moment the news came in from Pearl Harbor. Despite the outraged protests, most of the Axis nations had realized the crisis was coming and had their suitcases packed when the FBI arrived. Only the Japanese resisted, stalling the agents while continuing to haul armloads of secret documents out to a bonfire on the front lawn of the embassy. The staff of the Japanese Consulate in Los Angeles never knew that the ONI and the FBI had already been there.

Diplomats are protected by a mantle of legal immunity, and Washington maintained this protection to insure the safety of American diplomats in enemy hands. Thus, it was clear that these contingents of Axis diplomats could not be thrown in jail or taken to a common detention center. Instead, the State Department decided to transport the entire enemy diplomatic colony of Germans, Japanese, Italians, Hungarians, and others, numbering in the hundreds, together with mountains of luggage and personal belongings (in the case of one diplomat numbering 292 pieces of luggage including a Maytag washing machine, an Estey spinet piano, an electric refrigerator, five bicycles, golf clubs, an RCA cabinet model radio, and a Royal typewriter), to such luxurious hotels as the Greenbrier in White Sulphur Springs, West Virginia, the Grove Park Inn, in Asheville, North Carolina, the Gibson in Cincinnati, and the majestic old Jung Hotel in New Orleans. There they remained in splendid isolation for several months, complaining loudly about their treatment.[15] After a few weeks they were joined by hundreds of Axis diplomats and their families from diplomatic posts throughout Latin America. The majority of diplomats had been repatriated to Europe by April 1942.

American diplomats in Germany were not as lucky. They were rounded up and held as prisoners at Jeschke's Grand Hotel in Bad Nauheim, harassed by the German authorities and, sadly, totally ignored by the U.S. State Department. After numerous false starts and anxious hungry days filled with internal squabbling and unbecoming pettiness, the 150 American diplomats and their staffs were finally released on 22 May 1942. On 30 May, the S.S. *Drottningholm* sailed into New York harbor with 875 passengers—military attachés, journalists, and diplomats, including Admiral William D. Leahy—crowded along the rails and singing "America the Beautiful."[16]

Ordinary Germans and Japanese in America were not protected by such immunity, however, and for many still living the nights of 8–15 December 1941 remain a nightmare. Those arrested, often in the middle of the night, tell of being shuttled by police vans or INS buses to one of more than fifty temporary detention areas—local police stations or county jails, INS centers, National Guard armories, or CCC camps. Some ended up at one of six Homes of the Good Shepherd, leased by the INS, in Buffalo, Philadelphia, Cleveland, Milwaukee, Chicago, and Omaha. Others were ferried to the decrepit reception halls of Ellis Island, ironically, the place that had welcomed so many millions of immigrants to America in better times. Now they huddled and waited, many with their families, in perplexed and often fearful anticipation. Most describe being arrested before they could pack any belongings and had to survive the next several months with what little they had brought.

Most were peaceful people with no greater disloyalty to the United States than a chance remark or the complaint of a disgruntled neighbor. A scant few worked in any war-related industry. In fact, according to the government's lists of February 1944, they worked in a total of 1,139 different professions and jobs. They ranged from bakers, sausage-makers, and carpenters, to weavers, glassblowers, and a Ph.D. in literature. One was an officer in the Merchant Marine. At the start of the war, their ages ranged from sixteen to seventy-one with an average age of thirty-nine.[17]

The sticking point is that the aliens in America had been investigated and listed, secretly, *during peacetime*, by an organization (the FBI) now considered by historians to have been notoriously irresponsible and biased at the time.[18] Average Germans living in the United States found that an incautious pro-Nazi remark (if reported) or complaint by an unscrupulous business competitor or spiteful neighbor, had been enough to have their name placed on the FBI's Custodial Detention Index. There is no way to quantify the danger the enemy aliens may have represented, but according to an authoritative study, "the great majority of people in America of German descent or German birth were not as impressed with National Socialism as most of the Nazis in Germany chose to think."[19] Whatever danger those arrested may have posed, the roundups were much the same. Curiously, Hoover saw nothing wrong with Nazism as it was established in Germany, maintaining cordial relations with Nazi officials—even swapping autographed photos. He broke ties, reluctantly, at the insistence of his advisors, only three days before Pearl Harbor.

The experiences of Alfred Plaschke, then ten years old, born and raised in America, were not uncommon. His father, Rudy Plaschke, was German-born and co-owner of a small garage in New York. He never became an American citizen. "My father was certainly pro-German, a nationalist," his son recalls, "but that wasn't a crime. The problem was that my father's partner, Walter Ehrhard, was a real Nazi. Sometimes customers at the United Motor Service garage 'sieg-heiled' him when they came into the office. But, unlike my father, Ehrhard was an American citizen, so the Justice Department decided to lock up my father instead." In October 1940 they moved their garage business and families from New York to Valesco, Texas, a small town near Houston. It did not take long for the authorities to follow them. A little more than a year later, Rudy Plaschke was arrested. Alfred Plaschke remembers vividly when they appeared. "They burst into our apartment at 4:30 in the morning on December 8, 1941, ransacked the place, and simply took him away. We later learned that he had been taken to Houston, where he was held for several days. My mother, nearly hysterical, finally located him on January 1st at the Shepherd Drive jail in Houston. He was charged with operating a radio transmitter— what nonsense! My folks did have a radio, an old Midwest, but it was a receiver, not a transmitter. We suspected that Papa had been turned in by his business partner."

On 4 January 1942, the FBI swooped in again to arrest Rudy's wife, Bertha Plaschke. No reason was given at the time, but a later announcement on the front page of the local newspaper, *The Freeport (Texas) Facts,* noted dramatically that "at the time of her husband's arrest, it is said that Mrs. Phelaske [sic] cursed both officers and the American government and made threatening remarks to the officials who took her husband to Houston." (Says Al, "My mother never uttered a swear word in her entire life!") The news account ended with the terse statement that "No date for trial and formal investigation of either Mr. or Mrs. Phelaske [sic] has been announced."[20]

With his parents under arrest, young Plaschke and his younger brother suddenly found themselves alone.

So my brother and I joined our folks at the Shepherd Drive jail; there was nothing else we could do. My brother and I played all spring in the fenced-in yard between the jail and the fire station, and in June, all of us were all taken to Seagoville prison, a pretty little place, really, near Dallas. Nearly a year after my parents were arrested, in early spring, 1943, our family was loaded on Greyhound buses and driven across Texas to Crystal City.

The night after the Plaschkes were arrested, the feds picked up Erich Alfred Schneider. He and his wife Frieda had emigrated to the United States in 1928 from Dresden and moved to Houston where Erich worked as a painter and decorator. His son remembers a quiet, mannerly gentleman who was involved with the local German community, but certainly not a Nazi. The FBI saw him differently, however. Firstly, he never took steps to obtain American citizenship. In addition, he entertained visiting German sailors, made speeches favoring Germany in meetings of his painter's union, and was observed giving the Nazi salute to German ships tying up at the Houston Ship Channel. One December evening between 7:00 and 8:00, three FBI agents forced their way into the Schneider house. Within twenty minutes, the father, mother, thirteen-year-old Gerd Erich, and his fifteen-year-old sister Margot were escorted out of their house with only the clothes on their backs. That was the last time they ever saw their house, car, or possessions at 626 Hahlo Street, Houston.

The family was taken to the fire station on Kirby Drive, where they remained for the next two weeks. There they met the Plaschkes, with whom they remained friends for the next fifty years. Men and boys over the age of twelve were taken to Fort Sam Houston in San Antonio, and the women and children were taken to another site. After three weeks, the men were moved to Stringtown, Oklahoma. Because of his youth, Gerd Erich was returned to his mother. The women and children were then bussed to the Women's Federal Prison in Seagoville, Texas, where, three weeks later, they were reunited with the men from Stringtown. After a year at Seagoville, the Schneiders, Plaschkes, and dozens of others were moved to the family detention camp at Crystal City, Texas. They still didn't understand why they were arrested or how to get released.[21]

The causes for the arrest of others were more justified. For example, Martin George Franz, alias "Dutch," arrived from Germany in the United States in 1926, but never acquired American citizenship. In the late 1930s, he regularly visited crew members on German ships when they docked at nearby ports, occasionally attended meetings of the pro-Nazi Silver Shirts and the Stahlhelm (Steel Helmets), and his name was found on a list of "Agents" carried by yet another German suspect. Others appeared even more suspicious. Werner Ernest Seifert was born in Wilhelmshaven in 1907 and entered the United States in 1937. He associated with members of the Liederkranz Club and the Stahlhelm. He, too, entertained German sailors, made speeches favoring Germany in meetings of his painter's union, and was observed giving the Nazi salute to arriving German ships. Others' Nazi sympathies appeared stronger. Werner Ernest Seifert was born in Wilhelmshaven in 1907 and entered the United States in 1937. He associated with members of the Liederkranz Club and the Stahlhelm. He also entertained visiting German sailors, was observed giving the Nazi salute, praised Hitler and National Socialism, and stated that he would fight for Germany in a war against the United States. Seifert whispered to his friends that he was in the German Secret Service, and like others, his name was found in the notebook of a name already on the FBI Custodial Detention List, suspected Nazi organizer George Karl Gerhard Stubbe. Stubbe, in turn, was guilty of associating with Christian Iden, a German geologist caught mapping the Gulf Coast, who celebrated Hitler's birthday every 20 April and who tried to sell a new gun invention to visiting German sailors. At the top of this rather small heap in the Southwest, according to the FBI, was a German immigrant named Hermann Koetter of Houston, Texas. He was clearly a staunch German nationalist, and somewhat eccentric, but probably never a danger to the national security. Nonetheless, the FBI rated him "A-1" on the Custodial Detention List, and his friends and acquaintances, in turn, found themselves in trouble. Harry Oscar Veis was arrested because he possessed a suspicious list of moving-picture titles "that might be a code key"; Heinz Woeltje was arrested for soliciting funds to be sent to Germany; Walter Erich Adler was a skilled tool machinist with a hobby of photography and a past membership in the Stahlhelm. Wives were considered equally dangerous, and were generally rounded up as well. Arrests were filmed by the army.[22]

Interestingly, the FBI files also reveal that at the beginning, in mid-1936, J. Edgar Hoover was concerned that he didn't have enough information on each suspect. He chided his special agent in charge, R. J. Abbaticchio, for failing to supply all facts about the enemy aliens being arrested. "It is noted," Hoover warned Agent Abbaticchio, "that the reports reflecting apprehensions of enemy aliens by your office do not set forth all the information obtained from a review of your files. The Bureau desires that immediate steps be taken by you to remedy this situation and that the Bureau be advised when this has been done." Four days later, on 6 January 1942, Agent Abbaticchio assured the director that he had been forwarding his information, including exhibits and results of searches, to the United States Attorney, as required by policy, since the Justice Department needed the information to conduct its hearing boards. "I trust that the Bureau will sanction my handling of the situation in this manner under the circumstances which existed in this district. . . ."[23] Hoover then seemed satisfied with the level of data being collected on each person arrested and the route by which that information reached the hearing boards most efficiently.

Now came Hermann Koetter. His actual arrest was routine. He was picked up on 7 December 1941, directly after the attack on Pearl Harbor. FBI files today show that Koetter was on Hoover's CDI list of security risks. Hermann was 100 percent German—a colorful character whose ties to his native Germany were deep-seated and visible. In his younger days, during World War I, he had been a sailor in the German navy, was captured and spent time as a prisoner of the Chinese in Tsing-Tao, and married a girl from Tsing-Tao's German colony. Eventually, Hermann and Gertrud made their way to São Paolo, Brazil, where their already substantial "Germanness" was further reinforced by the large, notoriously nationalistic German community in Brazil. Their sons, Juergen and Gunter, were born in Brazil and with their mother sent to Germany for a proper upbringing. Hermann continued to work as a sailor. In 1924 Hermann entered the United States illegally by jumping ship in New Orleans; he sent for his family in Germany and settled down in the small town of Lamarque, Texas. Along the way Hermann learned a dozen skills, which the FBI now feared he might use on Germany's behalf.

He never troubled to cover up his Germanness. The Koetter family maintained a German household, cooked German foods, read German newspapers, and was involved in German cultural and singing societies. In the 1930s, foreigners stood out—especially in the South. Even Hermann Koetter's sons today concede that the trappings were there, although they doubt if their parents were devoted to Hitler. His name must have made Hoover's CDI list early in its creation, and the Koetters were among the first arrested on 7 December. At the time of his arrest and internment, Koetter was a successful painting contractor in Houston, with two sons in college. Once the Koetters were arrested, everything moved with efficiency. Both were taken to the Yale Street Police Station in Houston, fingerprinted, photographed, and placed in cells. A large group of men, including Hermann, were shipped to a recently completed enemy alien transit camp at Fort Sam Houston, Texas, and after that to Stringtown, Oklahoma. The women, meanwhile, were shipped to Seagoville, Texas, where they remained for six months. The men arrived to join their wives in Seagoville in June 1942. From Seagoville, most internees were taken by military buses to the large family camp at Crystal City (Uvalde), Texas, where they spent the remainder of the war. Sons Juergen and Gunter were never arrested.

What made the Koetters's case especially unusual is that while they were languishing in a west Texas internment camp for aliens of questionable loyalty, their sons joined the armed forces. Astonishingly, Gunter rose to become a general's aide, and Juergen was recruited to join the team of scientists who worked on a supersecret radar project whose importance was second only to the development of the atomic bomb. Each passed every level of security clearances. It is ironic that while Koetter's case was not aided by his sons, neither did it hurt their careers. Gunter and Juergen were never removed from their jobs. In fact, they continued at their posts until the end of the war, among the nation's most trusted and loyal soldiers.

On 8 December, the day after Pearl Harbor, FBI agents closed in on

Princess Stephanie Hohenlohe, at liberty in Philadelphia since April when she was first arrested (and released) for overstaying her visitor's visa. According to her son's account, Steph and her seventy-six-year-old mother were standing outside a Philadelphia cinema, when they were attacked by a group of men they thought were gangsters. Steph's elderly mother began to scream as they were pushed into a waiting car. "One of the men holding her back said, 'Stop shouting for the police. We are the police!' "[24] According to *The New York Times*, the FBI had been keeping her under close scrutiny for several weeks. "Last Saturday she left her undisclosed hideaway, got into her automobile with many pieces of baggage. Federal agents trailed her in three cars, finally picking her up somewhere between Philadelphia and Washington."[25]

Whatever the true story, Steph and sixty-five other aliens were arrested and transported to the immigration station in Gloucester City, New Jersey. Apparently overwhelmed by her current dilemma, she tried, unsuccessfully, to commit suicide by swallowing sleeping pills. She was saved by the director of the immigration station. From Camp Gloucester, the princess was transferred to Seagoville, Texas, where she remained for the duration of the war.

On 16 February 1942, it was her son's turn to be arrested. Prince Franz Hohenlohe was picked up while visiting friends in Katonah, New York, taken to Ellis Island, and held for a hearing in July. Five weeks later he was transferred to Camp McAlester, Oklahoma. At the end of November 1942 he was refused a new hearing, and in May 1943 he was sent to Camp Kenedy, Texas. It was not until February 1944, exactly two years after his arrest, that he was released on parole. Franz finished the war in the U.S. Army and was later part of the American occupation force in Japan.[26]

On the same night, 16 February, FBI agents arrested Jacob Reseneder, a German national who had emigrated in 1926. FBI files indicate that Reseneder spent much of the 1930s embroiled in Nazi Bund activities. His daughter Othilia (Tillie), then ten years old, vividly recalls the moment in December 1941 when "brusque agents rousted us out of our beds in the middle of the night and ransacked our apartment." He was taken to Ellis Island, where Tillie, her sister, and mother joined him. The whole family was soon shipped to the family camp at Crystal City, Texas, where they were held for almost four years. They were freed in December 1945, seven months after the war ended in Europe, and eventually deported.[27]

The Graber family from Elizabeth, New Jersey, remembered the nightmare of their arrest. One evening when Heinrich Graber, a skilled research technician, came home from work, his wife mentioned that two well-dressed men were parked in a Chevy across the street. They'd been there for the past several days. He thought little of her observation. That evening at six o'clock, two FBI men banged on the door and arrested him. Mrs.

Graber, eight months pregnant, fainted and tumbled down the stairs. Two weeks later she gave birth to a baby boy—injured in a way that left him permanently handicapped due to the fall. The agents ushered Heinrich to the local police station for questioning—no recourse offered, nor explanation given. The next day, and for the following two weeks, the family huddled in the unheated, rat-infested arrival hall on Ellis Island. Without explanation, they were put on a train for Dallas, Texas. After three days and nights of traveling, they found themselves in an empty corner of the Dallas train station, cold and hungry.

Paul Graber (today spelled Grayber) remembers the terror when, after sitting with his parents for hours in the same huge station, suddenly the doors were thrown open and in strode two men in cowboy boots, ten-gallon hats, and heavy overcoats.

"You the Garbers? Grabbers? Whatever?"
Dad said we were.
One of them shook his head and said,
"Damn! You don't look like criminals to us."

The deputies bought them hot coffee, chocolate, and hot dogs and drove the Grabers to the internment camp at Seagoville. From there they were later bussed to the family camp at Crystal City.[28]

The Theberath family was arrested at their home in Milwaukee at 2:30 A.M. by the FBI on the night of 8 December 1941. The family of five was inexplicably split up. Peter and Marie Theberath, the parents, were shipped to Fort Oglethorpe, Georgia, and their children Gertrud, fourteen, and Friedrich, thirteen, were turned over to the Milwaukee County Children's Home; for some weeks, no one knew what had happened to the other son John, seventeen. Six months later, Peter, still in a state of shock, wrote to a relative in Germany from Fort Oglethorpe that:

> Marie and I were awakened and taken into custody [8 December 1941]. I was in prison for 4 months. Marie was released on Feb. 11th, but *everything* was gone, *no children, no home.* In one word everything *robbed*, the children placed in separate homes, the mother helplessly thrown into *the street* [writer's emphasis].
>
> We arrived here on April 9th and no news yet from our family. The last time I saw John and Marie was in the prison on April 5th and I have not seen Gertrude and Friedrich since December 8th. These are ridiculous conditions. . . . All hope that the war will end soon.[29]

The letter never made it past the U.S. National Censorship Office in Washington, D.C. Undaunted, Peter wrote numerous letters to the Swiss Legation in Washington, D.C., whose Department of German Interests watched over the fate of German internees. Eventually, the exasperated assistant commissioner of the Immigration and Naturalization Service, W. F. Kelly, told Edward J. Ennis, head of the Alien Enemy Control Unit, to "get to the bottom of the case and really provide a solution which would be best for both parents and the children." This case, as well as some others, eventually even reached the desk of General Edwin Watson, secretary to President Roosevelt.[30] The overwhelming number of cases in which families were split up, however, never created any official interest at all.

Chapter Five

The Process

An enormous new program had come into being. Attorney General Biddle appointed Edward J. Ennis, a respected attorney with the Immigration and Naturalization Service (INS), to head the Alien Enemy Control Unit. Together, Ennis and INS chief Earl G. Harrison worked with Biddle to establish the internment process. They began by separating the problem of alien control into two main areas of need. The first was that of protecting national security by the arrest of "dangerous alien enemies," and the second was that of controlling the "travel and other conduct of the entire alien enemy population." Equally important, the Roosevelt administration hoped that all this could be accomplished without losing the support of the "large German, Italian, and Japanese population which is loyal to the U.S., or of the Four Freedoms for which we are fighting. . . ."[1] It was to be no easy task. Ennis's first job was to sift through the many cases of people arrested from the FBI lists and release all but the most dangerous. To evaluate the cases, he created a network of small tribunals called Civilian Alien Enemy Hearing Boards. Under the original plan, each hearing board was to be composed of three representatives, one each from the local office of the United States Attorney, the Immigration and Naturalization Service (INS), and the FBI. Their recommendation on each case was to be forwarded to the Attorney General's Office in Washington for final disposition. It soon became clear that there weren't enough federal representatives for the many hearing boards required (ultimately ninety-three such boards in eighty-six judicial districts), and panels of prominent local citizens in each particular community were assigned to carry out the evaluation process of alien cases. In districts with large numbers of detained aliens, several hearing boards were established, five in the southern district of New York alone.

On 2 February 1942, the Justice Department established the first set of rules for all Alien Enemy Hearing Boards. "Any enemy alien who has been for any length of time an *officer* in any of the following German organizations or who has for any length of time participated in the significant activities of these organizations may for that reason alone be properly interned. . . ." Those German organizations were: the German-American Bund (*Amerikanischer Volksbund*); Association of German Nationals (*Reichsdeutsche Vereinigung*); Friends of the New Germany (*Freunde des Neuen Deutschlands*); the central organization of the German American National Alliance (*Deutsche-Amerikanische Einheitsfront*); German-American Vocational League (*Deutsche-Amerikanische Berufs-gemeinschaft*); Kyffhaesuser League (*Kyffhaesuser Bund*), Kyffhaesuser Fellowship (*Kyffhaesuser Kamerad-schaft*), Kyffhaesuser War Relief (*Kyffhaesuser Kriegshilfswerk*).[2]

Within a short time the system was reduced to a simple equation: the hearing boards submitted their evaluation of each case to Ennis's Alien Enemy Control Unit, where final authority rested. Ennis's unit usually but not always concurred with the board. On occasion the Justice Department was tougher than its hearing boards, sometimes overruling, without explanation, a board's unanimous decision to release the alien.

In one representative case, the process went like this. On 2 June 1942, Edmund Adolph Dropman was arrested at his home in Honolulu, Hawaii, and brought before a four-member board. He was allowed to bring witnesses and despite the restriction against it, an attorney as well. After several lengthy (and tedious) question–and–answer sessions to establish the correct spelling of his name, his birthplace in Germany, and his failure to become an American citizen, Dropman was excused while the board heard the government's charges against him. Special Agent Wayne Gregg of the Counter Intelligence Corps enumerated them. Dropman didn't value citizenship enough to become naturalized; his two closest friends were already in custodial detention; his brother was a high German government official in occupied Danzig; his mother, living in the state of Washington, had a photo of that brother, in full Nazi regalia, on the wall; his substantial income was of possibly illegal origin; he had been arrested for wife-beating; he often kept company with "women of ill-repute"; and "many informants stated that the subject, while drunk, had bragged that he and Hitler were the two smartest men in the world," and "America is foolish not to side with the Germans in the conflict against Britain and Russia."

His two witnesses, fellow businessman in the furniture trade for nearly a decade, spoke to clear Dropman's name.

Q: "Did you ever hear him praise Hitler?"
A: "No."
Q: "Did you ever hear him speak German?"
A: "The only German I ever heard him say was 'prosit,' when we drank beer together."

Dropman's lawyer blamed the entire matter on the defendant's wife, whom he characterized as a vindictive shrew. She was the instigator of this whole problem.

The board then heard from Officer William Kaina of the Honolulu Police Department, who advised that he knew from other sources that the subject was definitely pro-Nazi; that the subject had no respect for the law; was an unscrupulous businessman; and that he was "a man of very low morals, intemperate habits, and a man that could not be trusted in any respect." Several more informants spoke to the board, attesting to Drop-man's domestic brutality, drunkenness, and pro-Nazi statements. A repre-sentative of the Mercantile Bank discussed Dropman's financial improprieties, and several informants even stepped forward to name the prostitutes he frequented ("Bunny" and "June"). The hearing lasted three days, several hours per day. The transcript of questions and answers covered forty-five pages. On 5 June 1942, the board met and ordered that Edmund Adolph Dropman be interned.[3] He appears to have received a fair hearing.

A hearing board could make one of three recommendations: (1) uncon-ditional release, (2) parole, or (3) incarceration in an enemy alien camp. The board hearings were adversarial, and the public and press were strictly prohibited. The person arrested was not permitted to have a lawyer present (although some did, as in Dropman's case), but could bring along a friend or relative to attest to his character and loyalty. Many aliens, however, have disputed this. "Absolutely untrue," mutters Koetter. "Very good friends of mine were denied access to make such presentations for me—at least ten of my friends told me that the FBI specifically told them this was not permitted." Because some immigrants did not speak English, the proceed-ings often had to be conducted through a translator. Apparently, the irony and unconstitutionality of forbidding those arrested to be represented by counsel were lost on Attorney General Biddle, who remarked that "This exclusion greatly expedited action, saved time, and put the procedure on a prompt and common-sense basis."[4]

Whatever the make-up of the community hearing boards, their mem-bers served throughout the war without salary. They often had to make difficult (and arguably illegal) decisions based on little more than infor-mants' hearsay, heavily accented testimonies that were difficult to under-stand or evidence made through translators, and simple gut instinct. Sessions frequently lasted late into the night, and if board members had doubts about an arrested person's loyalty, they generally ruled in favor of the government. Prompted by the aggressive standards of the FBI, the Jus-tice Department, in fact, removed hearing officers thought to be too le-nient.[5] At times, an arrested alien had to wait weeks or often months until the hearing board reviewed his case. Officially, the lengthy wait was attrib-uted to the initial overload at the beginning of the war, but most arrested persons believed that it was malicious or purposeful design to keep them in the custody of the War Department for as long as possible. Despite wide-spread criticism by hundreds of arrestees of the slipshod and interrogative methods employed by the hearing boards, one State Department official, Eugene V. Rostow, declared at the war's end that "the examinations were smoothly conducted, and they did nothing to lower prevailing standards of justice."[6]

Most former internees find that questionable. One of them, Martin George Dudel of Seattle, Washington, simply calls that "hogwash." Dudel

emigrated to America in 1899 and worked his way across the country as a
$10-a-week actor and part-time news correspondent, eventually settling in
Seattle. He applied for American citizenship in 1908 but did not continue
the process after getting his first papers. For the next thirty years, Dudel
was a German citizen living in America, embracing his German heritage
through organizations like the *Portland Theater-Verein* (*Portland Theater Organization*), various *Saengerfest* (*Choral Festival*) groups, and the German
Dramatic Club of Seattle. For a period of time, he edited a small, nationalistic German-language newspaper called *Nachrichten* (*News*), and later an un-
abashedly pro-Nazi weekly called the *Washington State Staatszeitung*
(*Washington State State-Newspaper*). Dudel championed "Germanness" and
called for American isolation and an understanding of Germany's destiny.
His politics were clear, but his influence and potential danger seemed minimal. In fact, the paper went bankrupt for lack of subscribers in 1939, due
largely to its increasingly unpopular political views. When the FBI came to
arrest him on 8 December 1941, they found a sixty-one-year-old man,
living in the past, surrounded by theatrical costumes, a variety of hobby
crystal sets and wireless radios, and volumes of German-language newspaper clippings collected over the years. Everything was dutifully catalogued
and confiscated for the duration. Dudel spent the next ten days at the
Seattle Immigration Station before he joined a trainload of other internees
bound for Fort Lincoln (or the "Fort Lincoln Concentration Camp," as he
bitterly referred to it from then on).

On 23 January 1942, Dudel was notified by the INS of the District of
North Dakota that his case would be heard by the local alien enemy board
on 28 January. This was his moment. Drawing on his newspaperman's
skills and orator's sense of drama, he cited the words of Abraham Lincoln,
Woodrow Wilson, Ghandi, and President Roosevelt. He closed his appeal
to the hearing board by saying:

> The government has given you the right to sit in judgment over
> me. You sit to decide whether or not I am to be given a clean bill of
> health and returned to my loved ones and many friends, who have
> never lost faith in me, or whether I am to be retained in confinement
> for the duration of this war. Whatever your decision may be, I shall
> abide by it unflinchingly. . . . I bear no ill will towards you or the
> government you represent, for I am a Christian man; I have no hatred
> in my heart and peace and understanding will be the goal I strive for
> to the end of my earthly days. If we still bear the love for the Mother
> who gave us life, do not hold this against us. One cannot tear Mother
> Love from one's heart. I would not ask it of you as an American.[7]

According to a letter from the board still among his papers (retained by
his daughter), the members of the alien enemy board upheld the appeal

and placed Dudel on parole. He promised in writing to report biweekly to the office of the FBI in Seattle, to observe curfew from 8 P.M. to 6 A.M., to remain within five miles of his residence, and to stay clear of restricted areas. On 9 April, five months after his arrest, Martin Dudel was released from Fort Lincoln and returned to his home in Seattle. In an ironic twist, Dudel's home state of Washington fell inside the coastal exclusion zone, an area where enemy aliens adjudged potentially dangerous to the war effort could not reside. His story will continue later in the chapter.

The government issued its final rules for the treatment of enemy alien detainees on 28 April 1942. In ten tightly typed pages, the Justice Department itemized how the detainees were to be treated in custody, and outlined, albeit in very general terms, the government's basic obligation. From beginning to end, it is a pledge of humane treatment. The Rules for Detainees (Instruction No. 58) open with the assurance:

> Detainees must at all times be protected against acts of violence, insults, and public curiosity. Physical coercion must not be resorted to and, except in self-defense, to prevent escape or for purposes of proper search, no employee of this Service under any pretext shall invade the person of any detainee. No measures calculated to humiliate or degrade shall be undertaken.[8]

From this promise, based on the Geneva Convention of 1929, the rules went on to assure the basic requirements of sanitation, exercise, food, clothing, bedding and towels, work, recreation, religious services, visitors, and so on. The rules closed with the statement, "The spirit of the Geneva Convention, as well as the letter of these instructions, must be carefully followed at all times."[9] Washington hoped that if the United States followed these rules, Americans held in enemy hands would in turn be safe from retaliation or brainwashing. Judging by the injustices suffered by American civilian, diplomatic, and military prisoners in both Japanese and German care throughout the war, Washington's humanitarianism was not reciprocated.

By mid-1942, the number of aliens apprehended exceeded 8,000: 4,611 Japanese, 2,869 Germans, and 1,364 Italians. Of this number, James Rowe Jr. estimated that "internments have run about 50 percent of the cases heard; 33 per cent have been placed on parole, and 17 per cent have been released."[10] One year later, the trend was reversed as most of those arrested early in the war were reexamined and released, and those apprehended later in the war were arrested on better evidence and were generally interned.[11]

Even adherence to the Geneva Convention was resented by some Americans, who felt that the aliens were already being treated too well. The chairman of the Oregon board, one Dr. Everson, declared that, "The alien is not entitled to a hearing; it is not a trial. It is a courtesy that is granted to the enemy alien by the Government. The Government is under no obligation to conduct a hearing in any of these cases." The only goal of the hearing is "to determine their present loyalty to the United States, or possible subsequent acts of disloyalty."[12]

More than a million enemy aliens watched in horror as the FBI searched for dangerous and disloyal individuals. The public read that "four persons had recently been sentenced to ten years in the penitentiary in Oklahoma under the state criminal syndicalism statute, for having in their possession, when their premises were raided, books written by Marx, Lenin, and Stalin."[13] Americans were growing hostile toward anarchists, radicals, and "un-Americans." To protect themselves, law-abiding German and Italian citizens—the overwhelming majority—gathered items that might allow espionage and sabotage and surrendered them to their local police precinct stations; within weeks, the New York City Police Department took in nearly 3,000 cameras, 250 shortwave radios, and dozens of pistols and shotguns. Accusations and searches often revealed additional contraband. The *New York Times* carried a large photograph of a pile of guns and radios; the caption read: "Property Collected by Police from Aliens Here."[14]

If public intolerance for enemy aliens was fast increasing, the next few months of 1942 brought only worse news and heightened tension. "West Coast Japanese and Nisei at first had little to fear, and in many cases they were shown sympathy for their awkward position."[15] But within months, as Japanese military forces continued their astonishing victories across the South Pacific, the public mood in America changed. On 15 February 1942, a lone Japanese submarine inched close enough to the California coast to shell an oil refinery near Santa Barbara. Also on that day, Singapore fell to the Japanese, followed by the Dutch East Indies on 8 March. Then came the disastrous defeat of an Allied fleet at the Battle of the Java Sea on 15 March. Rumors flew that the Japanese communities on the West Coast were poised to aid the enemy. Newspaper headlines grew larger and more lurid, and petty injustices (such as being dropped from the ROTC program) were becoming daily occurrences. West Coast congressional delegations led by Senator Hiram Johnson harangued the army to remove all Japanese from the coastal states. Lieutenant General John L. De Witt, the sixty-one-year-old commander of all U.S. Army units west of the Mississippi, the Western Defense Command, was the answer to their fears. If there ever was the wrong man for the moment, it was General De Witt. His father had been a general, a much-decorated war hero, but the younger De Witt spent World War I as a supply officer, far from combat. In January 1942 he was an excitable, myopic man who seemed to realize that his moment had arrived. From his office in the Presidio in San Francisco, De Witt shrieked alarms about the impending Japanese invasion. His searchlights probed the skies over San Francisco to seek out Japanese planes, and the population was terrified. De Witt claimed the nightly interceptions of hundreds of unidentified radio signals and shore-to-ship signal lights came from the enemy. Although a thorough investigation proved every case unfounded, the public's sympathy for its Japanese neighbors was eroding quickly. Facts were never considered and intelligence information not consulted, and De Witt ignored a stream of advisors who implored calm. In January 1942 he personally gave James Rowe, Jr., the assistant attorney general, his views on sabotage: "I have little confidence that the enemy aliens are law abiding or loyal in any sense of the word. Some of them yes; many, no."[16] His views played into the hands of California's xenophobes and racists, who demanded the forcible relocation of 120,000 Japanese residents: 42,000 Issei, those born in Japan but prevented by American law from becoming U.S. citizens, and 78,000 Nisei, American-born and citizens by birth.

At the beginning, De Witt thought that such a massive relocation would be unmanageable. So did J. Edgar Hoover, who felt that the FBI should concentrate on handling those individuals who had been identified as potentially dangerous. But then came the report from Frank Knox, Roosevelt's secretary of the navy. Returning from an official investigation of the Japanese attack on Honolulu in early 1942, Knox reported to the president that Japan's success at Pearl Harbor was due entirely to the size and effectiveness of Japan's Fifth Column in Hawaii. The navy had not been unprepared, after all. The resulting Roberts Report (named after Supreme Court Justice Owen Roberts) concluded that the Japanese Fifth Columnists aided the attackers with acts ranging from military espionage, to harvests planted in the shape of huge arrows visible from the air and pointing to targets. This information was later proved wrong. In fact, long before Pearl Harbor, local Japanese in Hawaii had aided the FBI in pointing out potential spies among them. Nonetheless, the public's glare slowly began to focus on hundreds of thousands of peaceful Japanese-Americans, and, four days later, after Germany's 11 December 1941 declaration of war on the United States, on German enemy aliens as well. Companies, concerned about government red tape and investigations, randomly discharged any worker who couldn't prove citizenship. German and Japanese employees were fired out of hand. The situation became sufficiently serious to call for a presidential proclamation on 11 July 1942, pointing out the injustice of firing people solely because they were noncitizens. Moreover, President Roosevelt stated that no law forbade the employment, even in war industries, of aliens, including enemy aliens. Nevertheless, groups like the American Legion fanned the flames of anti-Japanese and anti-German hysteria, and newspaper headlines demanded action.

In January 1942, to comply with the regulation that enemy aliens must give one week's advance notice before leaving on an overnight trip, the

world-famous Wagnerian soprano of the Metropolitan Opera, Lotte Leh-
mann, an Austrian citizen, made front-page news (and got plenty of free
publicity), when in an effort to embarrass the government she dramatically
registered her upcoming concert appearance in Raleigh, North Carolina.
In this case, the drama worked, and the government reduced its requirements for travel notification. After that point, applicants for travel permits
needed to appear in person only once, and all renewals could be handled
through the mail.[17] Any change of address was another matter, and enemy
aliens were required to report seven days in advance ("on a printed postcard—Form AR-11—which is available at all post offices")—or else. Despite these restrictions, thousands of German enemy aliens in America tried
to live normal lives, always conscious that the net might tighten further or
that they might inadvertently fail to follow the rules.

Anti-Nazi refugees, certainly not dangerous, also had to toe the mark. J.
Edgar Hoover was suspicious of all foreigners, even those with a history of
resistance to the Nazis. He believed that anti-Nazis might be communists or
Nazi plants, after all. The sensationalist Hearst newspaper, the *San Francisco
Chronicle*, declared that "Some of the most savage enemies of America and
liberty have come disguised as refugees from Hitler."[18] FBI files today bulge
with investigations of such literary luminaries as Thomas Mann, Heinrich
Mann, Bertold Brecht, Lion Feuchtwanger, Hannah Arendt, Erich Remar-
que, Ernst Bloch—even Albert Einstein was not exempt from surveillance.
The FBI spied on hundreds of other anti-Nazis who had settled in Mexico,
among them Anna Seghers, Egon Erwin Kisch, Ludwig Renn, Gustav Re-
gler, and Bodo Uhse.[19] Even youngsters who arrived in America were subject to restrictions. Gerhard Weinberg, a thirteen-year-old Jewish boy
whose parents fled from Nazi Germany to the United States in 1940, found
himself classified as an enemy alien. At fourteen and eager to perfect his
English, Gerhard became a member of his Albany, New York, high school's
debate team. Despite his youth and obvious anti-Nazi roots, he was periodically humiliated because he had to register with the authorities to compete.
It was an embarrassing beginning for one who became one of America's
premier historians and a noted author on World War II.

This unreasonable suspicion of Jewish immigrants and exiles to America
was also caused by a nasty and dramatic rise of anti-Semitism during the
1930s and the war years. Jews in New York were terrorized by roaming
bands of thugs, and a wave of anti-Semitic vandalism against Jewish-owned
businesses swept the country. A special billy club was invented by the
founder of America First, Inc., disbanded after Pearl Harbor, which was
called "The Kike-Killer." The U.S. Patent Office dutifully awarded the
billy club patent number 2026077.[20]

As the war wore on, anti-Semitism continued to grow and apparently found fertile ground in a large percentage of the population. Eventually, this virulent anti-Semitism reached into Congress itself, as when Mississippi's John Rankin, a notorious racist, delivered a speech against Walter Winchell in February 1944, calling him "that little kike." He was loudly applauded by other members of Congress.[21] That same year when people were polled about which groups should be allowed to immigrate to the United States after the war, 68 percent of those surveyed voted to admit Britons; 57 percent, Russians; 56 percent, Chinese; and, in last place, 46 percent said Jews should be allowed to immigrate.[22]

The government continued to urge calm. "So long as the aliens in this country conduct themselves in accordance with the law," Attorney General Biddle assured them in his statement of policy on 19 December 1941, "they need fear no interference by the Department of Justice or by any other agency of the federal government." This was not just a matter of democracy, Biddle admitted. Putting altruism aside, Biddle continued frankly: "This assurance [of protection for aliens] is given not only in justice and decency to the loyal non-citizens in this country but also in the hope that it may spare American citizens in enemy countries unjust retaliation."[23] More accurately, enemy aliens were being held as bargaining chips to be used in any future exchange for Americans in enemy hands.

At the same time, enemy aliens still had much to reassure them. Aliens of Axis countries living in the United States realized that despite the temporary restrictions on their lives, the continued publication of newspapers in their languages demonstrated the stability of democracy and provided them with a forum to air their grievances. More than 1,000 non-English newspapers and periodicals, printed in thirty-eight languages, were published in America. German newspapers topped the list at 178, most of which were distinguished old-line papers, like the *Florida-Echo* of Miami, Schenectady *Herald-Journal*, Ohio *Gross- Daytoner-Zeitung, Katholisches Wochenblatt* of Omaha, the New York *Staatszeitung* with a daily circulation of 50,000, and the militant anti-Nazi New York weekly, *Neue Volkszeitung*. A November 1940 survey by *Fortune* classified only a dozen as outright pro-Nazi.[24] Among them were such periodicals as the *Portland* (Oregon) *Nachrichten*, *Waco* (Texas) *Post, Milwaukee Deutsche Zeitung*, and Fritz Kuhn's *Deutscher Weckruf und Beobachter* ("German Awakener and Observer"). Some of the pro-Nazi publications closed their doors soon after the war began, notably the *Deutscher Weckruf und Beobachter*, the *Portland Nachrichten*, and the Philadelphia *Herald*; others just became more cautious about what they said. However, aliens could see that the majority of newspapers continued publication, even including the viciously anti-Semitic *Buffalo Aurora* and the *Christliche Woche*.

Italian-language newspapers in America also continued publication during the war although, like the other pro-Axis papers, circulation dwindled for lack of readers and advertisers. Of the 129 Italian publications in America in 1942, 80 were deemed profascist—notably the Boston *Gazzetta del Massachusetts*, the Philadelphia *L'Osservatore*, and the New York *Il Grido della Stirpe* ("The Cry of the Race"). While they, too, were careful about the tone of their contents during the war, they continued publication alongside anti-fascist newspapers like *La Voce del Popolo* of Detroit, the moderate *Il Progresso Italo-Americano* and *Corriere d'America*, and the small socialist weeklies of New York, *Il Martello* and *La Parola*. Even the openly pro-Nazi and anti-Semitic Hungarian papers like Cleveland's *A Jo Pasztor* ("The Good Shepherd") and the equally offensive Bridgeport *Egyetertes* were available, as were the two large Hungarian anti-Nazi dailies, the *Amerikai Magyar Nepszava* in New York and *Szabadsag* in Cleveland.[25]

Concern in the alien communities deepened to fear in mid-January 1942 when all noncitizens were ordered to go again to their local post offices to apply for certificates of identification. They had one week to complete the application process. They were required to bring three recent passport-type photographs and fill out a lengthy questionnaire. To deter fraud, the postman who delivered the official certificate was required to compare the photo with the recipient. The certificate was to be kept on one's person at all times. A copy of all information was sent to the local FBI field officer. The attorney general tried to soften the blow by claiming that the certificates were designed to protect aliens as much as for national security reasons. Earl Harrison, commissioner of the INS, joined other Washington officials in assuring aliens that the new registration program was not a reflection on the loyalty and goodwill of the great majority of Germans, Italians, and Japanese living here. They were reminded that the identification cards described them as "alien of enemy nationality" and not "alien enemy."[26] On 29 January, a newly formed patriotic group called "Americans of German Descent" and other groups of loyal enemy aliens held a large war-bond rally in New York. The group was headed by the great-great-grandniece of General von Steuben, the German hero of America's Revolutionary War. The evening culminated in a rousing speech by one-time presidential hopeful Wendell Willkie, who spoke against the "rising tide of thoughtless prejudice and to eliminate intolerance [*sic*]." "They must be protected in their rights and their liberty for they are of the very marrow of the bone of America."[27]

Meanwhile, the newspapers had earlier that month announced that the immigration service's three detention camps at Fort Lincoln, North Dakota, Fort Missoula, Montana, and Fort Stanton, New Mexico, would be converted from open holding areas to virtual prisons. All three camps were to be patrolled twenty-four hours daily by guards on horseback and in automobiles, armed with submachine guns. There would be new fences with guard towers, floodlights, and trained guard dogs.[28]

Growing alarmed at the increased restrictions, the American Committee for Protection of the Foreign Born, representing 150 organizations, sponsored a "Conference for Mobilization of Foreign Born for Victory in 1942" to assure the nation of their loyalty.[29]

Shortly after the new registration requirements went into effect, in an attempt to dispel misunderstanding and halt rumors among aliens, the Justice Department issued two informative pamphlets that were made available at every post office. The first, published in February 1942, was an eight-page booklet entitled "Regulations Controlling Travel and Other Conduct of Aliens of Other Nations." The second was a more comprehensive forty-five-page pamphlet with simple answers to some two hundred questions, such as, "Is an alien of enemy nationality who makes his livelihood by the use of photographic equipment required to surrender such equipment?" (Answer: "Yes. However, he may apply for a special permit . . ."), or "Are aliens of enemy nationalities permitted to sue or defend any suit brought against them?" (Answer: "Generally, yes"), or "Are aliens of enemy nationalities permitted to travel by plane?" (Answer: "No alien of enemy nationality is permitted to make any flight of any nature in an airplane or other aircraft.") However, the brochure brought a bit of good news to Japanese aliens, who alone had been historically denied the opportunity to become naturalized American citizens: "Can an alien of the Japanese nationality become a naturalized citizen of the United States?" (Answer: "An alien of the Japanese race is not eligible for naturalization unless such alien is serving or has served honorably in the armed forces of the United States during the Second World War.")[30]

Hardly calmed by this, many watched as a flurry of presidential proclamations regulated their conduct, established curfew hours in specific places, and designated, in detail, more than one hundred places on the West Coast alone that enemy aliens were not permitted to enter. Hydroelectric plants were off-limits, as were dams, radio stations and relay towers, docks and harbor wharves, and vast areas of Los Angeles County, San Francisco County, and Alameda County, among others. On 4 February 1942, Attorney General Biddle announced that the entire coastline of California, extending from 30 miles to 150 miles inland was a restricted area for all enemy aliens, and would be regulated by strict curfew laws.[31]

And what of the thousands of enemy aliens living in these places? The answer came toward the end of February 1942 when President Roosevelt signed Executive Order 9066, and the situation took a new turn. The president granted the War Department sweeping powers to designate prohibited military areas in the United States and to exclude anyone—citizen or enemy alien alike—from these restricted zones. The word "evacuation" began to appear in government and military directives.

General De Witt's recommendation to the Secretary of War, dated 14

February 1942, was worthy of a Nazi racial theorist. "In the war in which we are now engaged," he said, "racial affinities are not severed by migration. The Japanese race is an enemy race and while many second and third generation Japanese born on American soil, possessed of United States citizenship [sic], have become 'Americanized,' the racial strains are undiluted. . . . It therefore follows that along the vital Pacific coast over 112,000 [sic] potential enemies, of Japanese extraction, are at large today." The fairness of the relocation program may be gauged by General De Witt's astounding statement to the *Washington Post* on 15 April 1943, that: "A Jap's a Jap. It makes no difference whether he is an American citizen or not . . ."[32] General De Witt, based on an illogical argument trumpeted by the distinguished and normally liberal newspaper columnist, Walter Lipmann, concluded, "*The very fact that no sabotage has taken place to date is a disturbing and confirming indication that such action will be taken*" [emphasis added].[33] Innocence was proof of guilt.

The story of the injustice is well known; 120,000 Japanese were taken to relocation centers—euphemistically called "planned communities," in the words of the noted wartime sociologist Emory Bogardus.[34] Actually, they were grim camps in the desolate Owens Valley, where the populations lived in wretched conditions and under armed guards for the next three years. Forty-three percent were over fifty years of age or under fifteen. None worked as weapons experts or industrial specialists, since anti-Japanese prejudice on the West Coast had long restricted most to employment on small vegetable farms or in domestic service. A number of Japanese-Americans were so ashamed that their loyalty to America was questioned that they committed suicide. As noted earlier, not a single act of sabotage had occurred in the two months since Pearl Harbor. Nonetheless, forty-two thousand Japanese citizens and seventy-eight thousand U.S. citizens were stripped of their rights and property and transported to distant camps without so much as a hearing by the government or an immediate lawsuit on their behalf by any civil-liberties organization.[35] The authorities had no concept of the size of the civil damage that such actions would bring to America. The door was now open to the often brutal treatment of Jehovah's Witnesses, conscientious objectors, pacifists, communists, as well as thousands more enemy aliens. And the Supreme Court supported every violation. *Time Magazine* said, "All they forfeit is their freedom."[36] *Harper's* went so far as to conclude that "in the long run the Japanese will probably profit from this painful and distressing experience."[37] On the other hand, one of President Roosevelt's friends, a Chicago businessman named Curtis B. Munson, warned the president that "we are drifting into a treatment of the Japanese corresponding to Hitler's treatment of the Jews."[38]

Now came a new bombshell. On 1 April 1942, now that the West Coast seemed secure, the FBI announced that it was tightening control over the

256,000 enemy aliens in New York City. It is worth noting that even then when people were asked which group of aliens was most dangerous, "the Germans clearly outdistanced the Japanese." While the East Coast generally feared the Germans most, and the West Coast the Japanese, when people were asked which groups of enemy aliens in America were secretly loyal to a foreign government, 82 percent said the Germans were, 29 percent pointed to the Italians, and only 24 percent said the Japanese were.[39]

The goal of these new restrictions in New York was "to choke off possible fifth-column activity in the city." Patrolmen and detectives were issued lists of aliens who were registered with the government. "In each case," the newspaper warned, "they will check home and business address, daily activity and routine." Furthermore:

> They will note which aliens live in war industry areas or work in war plants. They will determine how long these aliens have been employed at their jobs, whether any have recently gone to new jobs and what the new jobs are . . .
>
> Dossiers will be made of all aliens of enemy nations. The records will check also on the number of persons in each family, and on the whereabouts of each member of the family.

The article in *The New York Times* continued with the warning that "The police check-up and dossier system is only the beginning of a more intensive watch of aliens. Similar action is to be started by police departments in other cities, towns, and villages throughout the United States so that government operatives may be able to put their fingers on any alien in any community at almost any time." Lastly, "New York detectives will not stop with the check of registered aliens. They will follow any leads that turn up as they collect information for their dossiers; they will penetrate any institutions run or dominated by groups from enemy nations. This will include charitable institutions."[40]

The very next day, on 2 April 1942, *The New York Times* published a photograph of a tent city, surrounded by barbed wire, and guarded by a rifle-wielding MP. The caption described the sprawling scene: "Ft. Devens, Mass., site of New England's only concentration camp for enemy aliens is expected to go into active service later this month."[41]

America's enemy aliens were under scrutiny, and not only by the ubiquitous FBI, Office of Naval Intelligence, Justice Department, local police departments, and fledgling vigilante groups. A relatively new group interested in the German enemy aliens was the Office of Strategic Services, the OSS, best known for its intelligence work abroad. On 22 December 1941, President Roosevelt approved a plan to establish the Foreign Nationalities Branch (FNB) within the Office of Coordinator of Information, an agency whose functions were largely taken over by the Office of Strategic Services in June 1942. The FNB was created to organize contact with recent foreign refugee groups as well as with groups of foreign extraction living in the United States. It was hoped that these groups had brought with them valuable information or that groups already in the country might offer significant intelligence information. From 1942 to 1945, the FNB produced thousands of reports, bulletins, specials, news notes, public meeting reports, as well as two editions of the *Handbook for Foreign Nationality Groups in the U.S.* The FNB distributed its classified publications to employees of the Department of Justice, the director of the OSS and other OSS offices, and President Roosevelt. Again, the government could peer into every German-American community, cultural group, and ethnic newspaper, providing itself with a barometer of activity levels for authorities and producing an unplanned goldmine for future researchers. The foreign nationalities branch of the OSS reported on the "German-American Press," "German Emigration in the U.S.," "The Bund," "The Political Attitudes of Germans in New York City," as well as in San Francisco, Illinois, Pittsburgh, Detroit, and Wisconsin—the FNB even investigated topics like the motives of "German Societies Which Pledge U.S. War Aid" and "Pro-German Propaganda by Indirection in the German Language Press."[42]

The authorities put enemy aliens across the country on notice. They could be scrutinized and searched at will; their lives, and those of their families and coworkers were open to investigation. Investigation to many aliens was synonymous with harassment, for they realized that government agents poking around at work could possibly cost them their jobs or reputations. On the West Coast the situation was about to get worse for German and Italian enemy aliens.

General De Witt, in his plan to evacuate the Japanese from America's West Coast, also strongly recommended that the 58,000 Italian and 22,000 German aliens living in the same area be collectively relocated.[43] If this evacuation was to be expanded to include the East Coast as well, the number of German and Italian aliens and their families would total nearly eleven million. This was a different matter, and the plan was met with immediate and determined opposition from nearly every quarter. "In the case of the Japanese," one army report concluded, "their oriental habits of life, their and our inability to assimilate biologically, and, what is more important, our inability to distinguish the subverters and saboteurs from the rest of the mass made necessary their class evacuation on a horizontal basis. In the case of the Germans and Italians, such mass evacuation is neither necessary nor desirable."[44] The Tolan Committee reached a similar conclusion. Directly after the president's Executive Order 9066 on 19 February, Congressman John Tolan convened the House of Representative Select Committee to evaluate the development of the relocation and internment program thus far. Among their findings (which were generally favorable), the Tolan

Committee recommended the relocation of the Japanese, but rejected any serious consideration of the mass roundup of German and Italian aliens. Questions of legality aside, it would have disastrous economic and social repercussions. Mass evacuation of German and Italian aliens "is out of the question if we intend to win this war. . . . Their incarceration for the duration of the war is unthinkable. . . ."[45]

President Roosevelt agreed and on the following day issued Executive Order 9106. Numerous government restrictions on German and Italian aliens were to be lifted, and they were encouraged to become American citizens as quickly as possible. Following the British lead, the order recommended that civilian hearing boards examine each internee. Those deemed dangerous were to be imprisoned in internment camps; the rest should be released. No restrictions were lifted for Japanese aliens or Japanese-Americans; the government was establishing two separate evacuation policies.

In any case, further internments would be a logistical nightmare. Where would the government put another 75,000–80,000 internees? State political leaders were already uncooperative. On 25 February 1942, a congressional committee polled the governors of those states that might serve as evacuation areas for enemy aliens removed from the West Coast region. The poll found that enemy aliens, particularly the Japanese, would not be welcome. Arizona was especially vocal. "We do not propose to be made a dumping ground for enemy aliens from any other State," thundered Governor Sidney Osborn. "We not only vigorously protest but will not permit the evacuation of Japanese, German, or Italian aliens to any point in Arizona." Idaho's Governor Charles Clark stated that it would "be a serious mistake to send enemy aliens to Idaho . . ." Kansas Governor Payne Ratner noted, "The infiltration of enemy aliens into our loyal Kansas communities would distinctly menace the security of our war industries . . ." Arkansas Governor Homer Adkins reflected the feelings of his constituents in stating, "We are always anxious to cooperate in any way we can, but our people, being more than 95 percent native born, are in no manner familiar with [Japanese] customs and ways and have never had any of them within our borders, and I doubt the wisdom of placing any in Arkansas." Finally, Governor Harlan Bushfield of South Dakota summed up the general political feeling toward any arrival of enemy aliens, by stating bluntly, "The people of South Dakota do not want evacuated enemy aliens within our borders."[46] Public sentiment was not with the plight of the enemy alien. The prospect of including Germans and Italians as well as Japanese only complicated the situation.

It quickly became apparent that it wouldn't happen. First, there was no place to put them, but there were many other reasons as well. Germans and Italian aliens were spared from mass relocation, according to the distinguished historian Stephen C. Fox, for five basic reasons. Germans and Italians were widely identified with "American values" such as home, family, hard work, cleanliness, order, patriotism, and so forth. It was easier to justify the internment of the Japanese; their culture was mysterious and sinister to most occidental Americans. Moreover, the Germans and Italians were primarily widely assimilated, unlike the Japanese. The public recalled the humiliating abuses that German-Americans had suffered in World War I and were cautious about making a similar mistake again. The Germans were also heavily represented in vital defense industries. If yet another reason was necessary, it would have been strictly political: members of Roosevelt's administration cringed to imagine the effect such mass evacuations might have on the future of the Democratic Party.[47]

Mostly, however, the issue was numbers. According to the 1992 Congressional Commission on Wartime Relocation and Internment of Civilians, "In 1940, 1,237,000 people of German birth lived in the United States, the largest foreign-born ethnic group except for the Italians. Further, if one considered the children of families in which both parents were German-born, the number of Germans in the country reached 5 million. . . . A population of that size had political muscle; the industrial northeast, the midwest and the northern plains states all had substantial German American voting blocs."[48] For military authorities, any mass evacuation of Germans and Italians in the United States would have been a disaster. When the War Department polled military commanders along the East Coast about possible evacuation programs to include German and Italian aliens, the scope of the problem and its potential ramifications became clear. For example, the Second Corps commander recommended a prohibited zone ten miles wide along the seacoast from the Delaware-Maryland state line northward to the eastern tip of Long Island. At the time, no one could even guess the number of German and Italian aliens living within that area. New York State alone contained more German aliens than the number of Japanese, both aliens and citizens, on the whole Pacific Coast. Attorney General Francis Biddle felt that any German or Italian evacuation on the East Coast posed "gravest consequences" for the nation's economic structure and war morale. Moreover, if the army was allowed to intern Germans and Italians indiscriminately, politicians, well-known writers, and business leaders could wind up in reception centers with the Japanese.

Many Germans and Italians had lived in America for decades; some had sons who were killed at Pearl Harbor or who were fighting bravely in the Philippines. There were thousands of anti-fascists and Jewish refugees from Nazi Germany. (It was estimated that there were 10,000 alien anti-Nazis on the West Coast alone, many of whom had been hounded or tortured by the Gestapo and who had more reason than most to hate America's Nazi enemy.) Thoughtful Americans wondered if a blanket policy might even jail an obscure fisherman in San Francisco who had never bothered to take out citizenship papers named Giuseppe DiMaggio, the father of the celebrated baseball great, Joe DiMaggio. What about Albert Einstein, Bruno Frank, or Thomas Mann? All were German citizens during the war and consequently could be subject to arrest.

While restricted military zones were eventually created along the entire continental defense system, commanders were informed that no mass evacuation of German or Italian aliens would take place. Instead, defense commanders were authorized to arrest only the most potentially dangerous individuals in the evacuation zones, alien or citizen, under the broad authority of Roosevelt's Executive Order 9066. These arrests were collectively known as the Individual Exclusion Program.

This program never amounted to much. As late as 1 July 1943, a total of 268 people had been deemed dangerous enough to require them to leave the area. They were not arrested outright. The process was quite passive for those war years: when enough evidence pointed to a particularly dangerous individual, the person received an order in the mail from the army to show cause why they should not be required to leave the military district. Because of the great potential for the violation of individual rights, as there was with Hoover's CDI list, the exclusion orders were used quite sparingly. For example, a total of 32,952 cases investigated within the Eastern Defense Command yielded only sixty-six exclusion orders.[49] Most were German-born, although the investigations produced two itinerant Palestinian rug merchants caught trying to buy military information around the Norfolk Naval Station. Interestingly, of those investigated, few were actual enemy aliens; almost all were naturalized American citizens.

Some of those who received exclusion orders simply refused to comply. Never mind the often ample evidence of potential disloyalty. They contended that the program was an unconstitutional persecution of Germans and dared the government to do something about it. To the frustration of the authorities, they were winning. The exclusion program had turned into a cat-and-mouse game. In one celebrated case in Philadelphia in 1943, Mrs. Olga Schueller, an American citizen since 1920, refused to leave the area as ordered. Although the government had determined that she had very close ties to several subversive German organizations, Mrs. Schueller told news reporters that she was 100 percent American: she owned a small restaurant, had one son in the navy and another working in a local war plant. Far from calming the authorities, the news about her two sons was disturbing. "It is true," said Mrs. Schueller, "that I am president of the ladies' auxiliary to the Bavarian Charity Society. I am also an officer of the German-American Federation, that was at one time known as the Central Bund. What's the matter with that? The members are patriotic American citizens." To the army's outrage, her position was upheld by a federal judge.[50]

In several exclusion cases, mainly on the West Coast, the suspects fought

back. On 25 September 1942, Henry L. Beach, a twenty-five-year-old
Seattle-born mechanic received a summons in the mail. He was to appear
on 2 October at a hearing board in the Multnomah Hotel in Portland,
Oregon. For some reason, his loyalty was being called into question by
General De Witt's Western Defense Command and the Wartime Civil
Control Administration. He had to prove why he shouldn't be required to
leave the Northwest Coast. The citation was accompanied by an eighteen-
page questionnaire that inquired about every phase of his life, beliefs, family, business, and other private matters. When he arrived at the hearing, he
was informed that no charges had yet been made against him, nor would
he be able to meet his accuser. Beach was also assured that he hadn't endan-
gered any defense materials, premises, or utilities. Nevertheless, Beach was
put under oath and, in his words, "subjected to a severe two- and-one-half
hour inquisition, examination and 'fishing expedition' relative to my actions, thoughts, ideas of government, war, religion, politics, and fraternal
and social affiliations." The board members read numerous statements reportedly made by him but refused to disclose the sources or dates of these
statements. At the end of the day, Beach was sent home to await the board's
findings. Much to his relief, he received a letter from the Western Defense
Command on 19 October 1942 informing him that "upon the findings
and recommendations thus far presented the commanding General does
not at this time contemplate the issuance of an individual exclusion order."
     But Beach's ordeal was far from over. On 6 January 1943, he received a
new summons and an identical questionnaire. This time he was to report
on 3 February 1943, to the very same room, in the same Multnomah Hotel
in Portland, for questioning by another hearing board. Bewildered, he appeared as ordered. A new group of board members asked the same type of
questions, covering the same material, all under oath and recorded by a
court reporter. Again, Beach was read accusations from nameless sources.
As before, he was dismissed to go home and await the board's decision.
Instead, he went home, contacted a lawyer, and sued Lieutenant General
John De Witt, and the members of the two hearing boards.
     His complaint before the federal district court charged that the defen-
dants caused him considerable loss of time, annoyance, and expense; that
he was being deprived of his rights and liberties as an American citizen;
that he had been threatened, and was continuing to be threatened, with
exclusion from his home and family; that the hearings were conducted
behind closed doors and not open to the public; that witnesses against him
were not identified; that his lawyer was not allowed to speak or examine
witnesses; that he had not been indicted by a grand jury; and that as far as
he knew, there was no charge of any nature pending against him.[51] Beach
was going to court simply to stop future harassment and get the court's
assurance that De Witt would not issue an exclusion order against him.

The army ducked for cover and pointed up the chain of command. Eventually, the matter reached the desk of John J. McCloy, assistant secretary of war. Responding to McCloy's interest in the Beach case, General De Witt assured Washington that "it is not contemplated that an exclusion order will be issued against this individual." "But," McCloy wrote to the attorney general, "General De Witt feels it is important that it shall not appear that the decision not to exclude was the result of the litigation." Consequently, McCloy decided that "the case should be permitted to proceed to a conclusion favorable to the government or, alternatively, that after consultation with the Western Defense Command, a stipulation be entered into making it clear that the complaint was defective and consequently could not reasonably have had any bearing on the decision not to exclude."[52] The problem was solved: Henry Beach would be found innocent of any suspicious intentions and be allowed to remain in the Northwest Coast; his legal complaint, "flawed" as it was, had no bearing on the issue, and the military's right to exclude potentially disloyal individuals from sensitive coastal zones would not be weakened.

Kenneth Alexander, a resident of Oregon, not only fought exclusion but demanded that General De Witt pay him for his lost wages of $200 a week, and damaged reputation in the community. Alexander was born in Britain but had been an American citizen since 1915. He served in the U.S. Army during World War I. On 27 February 1943, he received an evacuation notice and the opportunity to challenge it by appearing before a hearing board on 11 March. The morning-long session was like the hearings: tedious questioning, statements from nameless sources, and implications of disloyal behavior. He was dismissed to wait for the results. Instead of going home, Kenneth Alexander went to a lawyer. His Civil Complaint, No. 10514 before the U.S. Circuit Court of Appeals for the Ninth District, blamed Lieutenant General John L. De Witt. He sued De Witt for $50,000. Alexander's argument was that he was not a member of the U.S. military and consequently couldn't be ordered by the military to leave any area; martial law had not been declared; he was an American citizen, and the courts were still open to decide his guilt or innocence; the hearing board process was arbitrary and capricious. The complaint never came to trial; Kenneth Alexander was never excluded, and the case languished in the legal pipeline until the war ended.

Another complaint against General De Witt in mid-1943, this time by an enemy alien in California, brought the government's most frank admission of possible error in policy. Max Ackerman brought suit against the general for the usual illegalities and inconvenience. This time the case went to court, providing the Justice Department with the opportunity to state its final position on the topic. "When a military commander acts in good faith within the scope of the duties imposed upon him by the President, he is not personally liable when afterwards it is determined that such action was taken under a mistake of law."[53]

The longest and certainly the most convoluted fight against the government came in the case of Dr. Hans Zimmerman in Honolulu. This was not an exclusion case but an arrest. Within twenty-four hours of the attack on Pearl Harbor, federal agents arrested the "doctor" of naturotherapy on suspicion of potential disloyalty. Little could they know they were beginning a legal tangle that would continue until 1946. Hans Zimmerman was born in Germany in 1905, emigrated to America in 1927, and after a stint in the U.S. Army, became a citizen in 1935. Along the way, he married and divorced his first wife and married his current wife Clara. He also obtained a diploma from Dr. McFadden's School of Naturotherapy and opened a small Naturotherapeutic clinic in Honolulu. At this point Zimmerman's behavior moved from eccentricity to fraud. He seems to have bamboozled most of his friends and associates, claiming a medical degree from the St. Louis College of Physicians and Surgeons, an internship at Grace Evangelical Hospital in Kansas City, and a host of medical memberships and awards. His friends who served as witnesses praised Zimmerman's loyalty and patriotism.

However, a number of confidential informants, identified in the stenographic records only as HO-13, HO-27, and HO-37, told the hearing board a different story.

"Confidential Informant HO-27 advised that information has come to him indicating that the Subject is a rabid pro-Nazi; that he expresses himself freely along Nazi lines. However this informant has no definite information that the Subject is engaged in sabotage or espionage activities."

"Confidential Informant H0-37 advised that he had had a conversation with Subject who made the following remark: 'I hope Germany wins the war and am not afraid to say so, so strong do I believe in them.'"

He was remanded for internment and sent off to a temporary camp on Sand Island, Hawaii. Now the army's problems began. Zimmerman complained at every turn and filed grievances against every authority figure who crossed his path. He fired off letters to judges, friends, the American Civil Liberties Union, and the editorial pages of local newspapers. Zimmerman's own lawyer told him to "get it out of your head that the United States Government has any grudge against you. They would rather have you a free citizen than an incarcerated one." Undaunted, he continued to protest. At his request, his wife filed a Writ of Habeas Corpus on 20 February 1942, which was denied. She tried again, this time in the Ninth Circuit Court of Appeals, and again his writ was denied, reflecting the tenuous nature of the legal rights of civilians in areas under military control during wartime. On 1 March all detainees at Sand Island, including Zimmerman, were shipped to the mainland. His new home was Camp McCoy, near Sparta, Wisconsin.

The government was in a quandary. In a private letter from Brigadier General Thomas Green, military governor of Hawaii, to Colonel Archibald King, of the Judge Advocate General's Office in Washington, D.C., Green admitted, curiously, that "the question of the sufficiency or insufficiency of such evidence has no bearing on our legal right to hold Zimmerman in custody. . . . The Contact Office, G–2, feels very strongly about this case and believes that, although it has not been able to discover any specific facts clearly justifying his internment, it would be extremely dangerous to allow this man to remain at large, and has insisted very strongly that he remain interned. Because of this belief and insistence of the Contact Office, G–2, this office has continued to intern Zimmerman."[54]

Meanwhile, however, while he was en route to Wisconsin, his case went all the way up to John J. McCloy, assistant secretary of war, who determined that Zimmerman was not guilty of any supportable charge. It recommended "unconditional parole." To the astonishment of all, Zimmerman refused to accept the government's release. He intended to continue his fight in court. His case had already become somewhat of a cause célèbre, and was described in an article in a law review.[55]

Zimmerman then applied to the U.S. Supreme Court for *certiorari*, (*Zimmerman v. Walker*, No. 823), asking for a review of the appeals court's decisions. The Supreme Court dismissed his appeal for review since he had already been exempted from internment on 2 March 1943. He was asked not to return to Hawaii for the duration of the war and spent the next two years in San Francisco and Chicago.

The end of the war did not halt Hans Zimmerman, however. Zimmerman now unveiled his major punishment of the people who caused him so much trouble. He was suing for $575,000—an unthinkable amount in those days—$75,000 for losses suffered in his "medical" practice, and $500,000 compensation for humiliation and character defamation suffered through illegal imprisonment.[56] Named in the suit were high army and navy officers and the civil ex-governor of Hawaii, who, Zimmerman's complaint charged, "entered into a confederation to deprive him of his civil and constitutional rights." Also included were the members of the hearing board that first sent him away. Since the war had been over for more than a year, most of his defendants had moved on to different locations and jobs. But Zimmerman assured the readers of the *Chicago Daily Tribune* that he knew where they were and intended to embark on a 15,000 mile journey to deliver subpoenas to each person in turn: General Short in Texas, Generals Green and Morrison, and Captain Mayfield in Washington, D.C., hearing board member Frank Thompson Jr. in Michigan, General Emmons in Alaska, and so on. Military men knew they had nothing to fear from legal redress, since the government had made its position clear in an earlier case (*Max Ackerman v. General De Witt*): especially during wartime, they had to follow orders from their superiors and were not responsible for any flaws later found in those orders or in the laws that they represented.

Civilians had no such protection. Attorney General Tom Clark received a number of pleas from former members of Zimmerman's hearing board. Frank E. Thompson, now head of his own engineering company in Grand Rapids, Michigan, was especially concerned. In a letter to Attorney General Clark, five days after Zimmerman's announcement in the *Chicago Daily Tribune*, Thompson first recalled those "very upsetting days right after Pearl Harbor, when things moved rapidly." Then, after discussing Zimmerman's suit, Thompson reminded the attorney general that: "At the time that the Alien Enemy Hearing Boards were set up and we were sworn in, we were assured that any action against the members of the Boards for damages of this nature would be defended by the Attorney General of the United States, and that furthermore, if action and judgment were rendered against us by any court, that the Congress of the United States would appropriate such money necessary to pay judgment."[57]

Days later, Thompson received a calming letter from the secretary of war himself, assuring him that, in case of legal problems related to his war work in Hawaii, the government was standing by. "[I]n the event that you are served with process in any suit resulting from action taken by you as a member of an Alien Enemy Hearing Board in Hawaii, the Department of Justice, upon your request, will represent you in any litigation. It is suggested that if you are served with process in any such suit, you immediately communicate with the Attorney General, likewise advise The Judge Advocate General of the Army."[58]

Hans Zimmerman finally ran into a brick wall. The military members involved in his internment were protected by the traditional, though selectively endorsed, dictum of following orders. Civilians were protected by the full weight of the Department of Justice. Thus died the longest legal battle by an internee.

Lieutenant General Hugh A. Drum, commanding general of the Eastern Defense Command, pleaded with the War Department to give him more authority to enforce the exclusion orders. This was a military process, Drum argued, enacted during wartime for the security of the coastal areas. The suspects, all civilians, were openly refusing to obey military orders during wartime. To prevent the "emasculation" of the exclusion process, General Drum requested that he "be given authority to convene military commissions for the trial of violators of military orders and regulations." To impress Washington with the gravity of the matter, the general included a cross section of the most dangerous individuals currently under exclusion order—all of whom were clearly security risks.[59]

In this matter he came up against the civil libertarian Attorney General Francis Biddle. On 17 April 1943, Biddle fired a memo to the president questioning the wisdom of so broad an exclusionary program in the first place.

> We [the Justice Department] have not approved the Army procedure, which does not permit the persons excluded—American citizens—to confront witnesses before the Military Tribunal. This is against a fundamental conception of constitutional rights. Prosecution would have little practical effect. Bail would be granted and the individuals would go on living where they chose until the cases were ultimately decided by the Supreme Court. If the Army believes that they are dangerous they have the express power to exclude them under the Executive Order. . . . Exclusion is based on MILITARY danger. This element is entirely lacking from these cases.[60]

In the end General Drum did not receive the added authority he requested, and most excluded individuals spent the war having their cases reviewed and rereviewed; only a tiny fraction of those excluded actually moved inland.

In total, of seventy-six individual exclusion cases targeted by the Eastern Defense Command:

—twenty-seven cases came under immediate review,
—twenty-three cases were amended,
—twelve cases were suspended,
—three cases were dropped when it was learned that one was already interned, and two had sought safety by joining the army,
—two died and,
—six cases remained active and unchanged.[61]

One of those who did move inland was Martin Dudel of Seattle, Washington. Released from Fort Lincoln on parole in April 1942, he gratefully returned home. Less than a year later, on 20 March 1943, things went sour for Dudel once again. He received an individual exclusion order, one of only 173 such cases in the entire Western Defense Command. The order gave him forty-eight hours to present himself to the authorities. In addition to being fingerprinted, photographed, and required to provide a sample of his handwriting, he was instructed to inform the authorities of his new address—away from the coast, the mode of transportation, and the route he would take to get there. The exclusion order also reminded him to present himself to the nearest FBI office at the city of his new residence. Although many "excludees" challenged the order, Dudel did not. Resigned to his situation and aware that too much fuss might be considered a violation of his earlier parole and land him back in Fort Lincoln, Dudel moved to Chicago, where he had many friends and job possibilities. In a sympathetic gesture, his wife's train ticket and travel expenses were provided by the War Relocation Authority, making the move less difficult.

The Dudels remained in Chicago until December 1944, when the requirements for "excludees" were relaxed enough to allow their return to Seattle. That many of the "excludees" were naturalized American citizens (not including Dudel) offered a new option for the government: denaturalization. The final decision on anyone's loyalty rested with the Justice Department. The civil action to cancel American citizenship was based on the premise that the defendants had mental reservations at the time they took the oath to support the laws and Constitution of the United States. Thus, they had obtained their certificates of citizenship fraudulently. This cancellation of citizenship was not to be confused with "losing" citizenship or "expatriation," since citizenship was illegally procured, and the alien had never really obtained citizenship in the first place. On 26 March 1942, three months after Pearl Harbor, Attorney General Biddle announced to the newspapers that he was recommending "prompt action" to "cancel the nationalization certificates of American citizens whose course of conduct, activities and statements show their true allegiance and fidelity to be to a foreign country rather than to the United States." The attorney general further announced that the government already had thirty cases "ready for action" and several hundred other cases all over the country "under study." While Biddle assured the American public that "such action would not be taken without the full authorization of the Justice Department in Washington," he warned troublemakers, "Holding office or active membership in the Bund and similar organizations is regarded as evidence of lack of attachment to the United States." In case anyone failed to see the gravity of denaturalization, Biddle announced that those Germans and Italians whose certificates of naturalization were canceled would be "interned for the duration of the war."

Their "cloak of citizenship is a sham," growled Hoover and pushed his agents to intensify their efforts.[62] By 30 June 1943 the FBI had completed over 2,000 investigations for denaturalization. Of those cases, the Justice Department felt only 492 warranted further action, resulting in 119 successful denaturalizations. Thirty of those 119 were denaturalized because they had purchased "Rückwanderer Marks," a German investment program created to sell marks at a discount price and hopefully bring Germans home.[63] The Justice Department viewed such investments in an enemy economy as a strong indication of potential disloyalty. As of June 1945, a total of 198 naturalization certificates had been canceled, of which ten cancellations were later reversed by higher courts.[64] Considering the relative ease of decertification, the process proved a judicious use of a powerful bureaucratic weapon that might easily have been misapplied during wartime.

If the number of German aliens in America precluded any serious thought of relocation, the number of Italian aliens would provide further deterence. There were over 690,000 Italians, as compared with 314,104 registered German aliens. Many never became American citizens simply because of their difficulty with English; thousands more believed that having American-born children automatically conferred citizenship on parents or grandparents. They were also among the most visibly patriotic people in the country. Of the 14,738 aliens interned during the war by the Justice Department, only 3,503 were Italian (plus the 1,210 Italian seamen held at Fort Missoula, Montana). It was apparent that Italian aliens constituted no serious danger, and any new harassment was causing the Roosevelt administration increased political opposition. To eliminate political backlash, Attorney General Biddle chose Columbus Day, 12 October 1942, a day of significance to Italian-Americans, to announce in a speech at New York's Carnegie Hall that Italian aliens in the United States would no longer be classified as "enemies." He further delighted the Italian community by indicating his hope that Congress would eliminate the use of literacy tests in the nationalization process and free the aliens "to participate in the war effort without handicaps."[65] The Italian community celebrated its return to the fold and embraced the war effort and Roosevelt's administration with enthusiasm. Historians speculate that Biddle's decision might well have bolstered the strength of the Italian anti-fascist underground and softened resistance to the later invasion of Sicily. Of the 3,503 Italians taken into custody during the war, only 112 were considered dangerous enough to be interned for any length of time.[66]

The day after Biddle's Columbus Day speech, General John De Witt, who had demanded the mass expulsion of all enemy aliens from his West Coast Command area, was forced to follow suit and reluctantly removed many of the restrictions on both Italian and German aliens.[67] While the release from restrictions did not necessarily liberate those already in confinement (such as the German or Italian seamen at Bismarck and Fort Missoula), it made future alien control more manageable and calmed the public.[68]

Within weeks, the Justice Department announced five categories of people who were declared exempt from arrest:

1. German or Italian aliens seventy or more years of age.
2. Patients in hospitals, inmates of orphanages, and the totally deaf, dumb, or blind.
3. Relatives—wives, parents, or children of men in the armed forces or of men who died in the line of duty.
4. Those waiting for final citizenship papers—a common problem since the naturalization courts were often a year and a half or more behind schedule.
5. Refugees—driven from their countries for religious, ethnic, or racial

discrimination, or because of their activity against political systems abhorrent to Americans.[69]

There was a sixth exemption category, which has only recently come to light: alien enemies in the armed forces. As early as 1937 the high proportion of aliens in the military led to a policy decision to restrict more from joining.[70] That policy was shelved as the war in Europe loomed and America needed to beef up the army. The Selective Training and Service Act of 1940, the "draft," authorized the military to induct anyone except public officials, employees in essential industries, ministers, divinity students, college students, and persons mentally or physically unfit to serve. Nowhere did the act bar noncitizens or individuals of questionable loyalty. Taking advantage of the new act, a large number of aliens enlisted to escape the poverty of the Great Depression or to speed up their naturalization. A further 4,000 enemy aliens were drafted, a direct violation of the Hague Convention of 1907; legal as long as the alien conscripts are not directed to fight against their own countries. According to one insider, "It apparently was the intent of Congress to induct into the Armed Forces enemy aliens, disaffected Americans and potential subversives, and then leave it up to the Armed Forces to decide what to do with them."[71]

To resolve the question of too many aliens in the armed forces, the immigration authorities tried to quickly naturalize as many soldiers as possible. Thomas Shoemaker, deputy commissioner of immigration, was dispatched to military bases around the globe to administer the oaths of citizenship to foreigners in the American military. Often large groups were sworn in together, as provided for by the Second War Powers Act. Little effort was made to establish their loyalty.

Especially troublesome new citizens, however, were culled out of the ranks and sent to special units that were kept isolated or assigned to remote posts. The War Department ordered that anyone in the ranks "whether citizen or alien, who is definitely suspected of subversive activity or disloyalty, *even though an investigation has failed to uncover specific evidence in justification of this suspicion, the subjects will be assigned to organizations . . . where duties of a harmless character will be given them" [emphasis added].*[72]

In May 1942 the War Department reassigned 1,500 alien suspects (approximately 1,000 Germans, 150 Japanese, and miscellaneous Europeans, including Italians). Fifty more were reassigned monthly. They were organized into quartermaster service companies of approximately 175 men each, and sent out under "loyal" officers to distant bases in the United States. They received uniforms different from those of regular GIs and were humiliated in many ways. Their tasks were to "do the work formerly performed by the CCC company at the same post," and most of the men spent the war years under close scrutiny making camouflage netting, painting barracks, planting trees, and collecting garbage. Foolishly, considering their potential disloyalty, they were often housed close to the thousands of German POWs maintained at many of the same bases, posing a variety of genuine security problems. When their hitch was over, they were given honorable discharges and released. A few dangerous types were discharged early, and their paperwork turned over to the FBI. On one occasion the army unearthed two particularly vocal Nazi sympathizers. One of the men, it turned out, had actually been an officer candidate in the German army. Both men were discharged but later arrested by the FBI in a roundup of dangerous alien enemies. This time they were sent to an internment camp.[73]

Meanwhile, the arrests continued. According to the FBI's yearly summary of activities, the bureau apprehended 9,405 enemy aliens during the fiscal year 1942, of whom 4,764 were Japanese, 3,120 were Germans, and 1,521 were Italian. In one operation the FBI arrested 923 people across the country who had invested money in Berlin's Rückwanderer Marks scheme. Of those 923, 72 were released, 300 placed on parole, but a substantial number, 426—many of whom had been working in war plants— went to internment camps.[74] Several other particular cases made the headlines, such as the arrested alien who worked as a pantryman in the officer's club at a military reservation on Governor's Island, New York.[75] (Who knows what secrets he might have overheard?) Another, rounded up in a dragnet in Dallas, turned out to be an old customer; it seems he had been arrested and released before. This time he was simply fingerprinted, photographed, and thrown back into the pond.[76] More serious, however, was the arrest of sixteen people in Brooklyn, including a family of five, all violently pro-Nazi. One worked in a war plant. All echoed the Bundist call for race riots, strikes, and aid to escaped German prisoners of war.[77] One enemy alien, for reasons known only to himself, couldn't take the pressure any longer. On 24 June 1942, fifty-one-year-old Albert Wilhelm Kuhn, no relation to the notorious Fritz Kuhn, folded his clothes neatly on the Forty-Fifth Street dock of New York's brackish East River and drowned himself. The police found only his enemy alien registration card in his pockets. A brief FBI investigation indicated that he had an unblemished police record. The mystery was never solved.[78]

On 28 June 1942, newspaper headlines shouted the alarming news that eight German saboteurs had been arrested as they landed on the East Coast from a U-boat. Nazi spies had arrived in America! On the same day, in an unconnected news story, two German-born, naturalized U.S. citizens were arrested in Detroit for aiding an escaped German POW; they would be tried for treason. While the cases were unrelated, the Justice Department tried them together. The trials were speedy and sensational.[79] To send a sobering message to Berlin against sending future espionage teams to

America, and to make a clear example of traitors at home, a military court
sentenced six of the ten men to death (the others became state's witnesses).
On 8 August 1942, five of the eight saboteurs and one of the two men
from Detroit were executed in the electric chair one after another; in the
words of one prison official "at ten and one-half minutes per man, the
swiftest multiple electrocution ever carried out."[80] Berlin apparently got
the message and never sent another sabotage team to the United States. But
America also heard a message; in the minds of the American public, enemy
aliens, even naturalized American citizens, were interchangeable with
enemy saboteurs landed on American shores by Nazi U-boats.

All eyes now turned to enemy aliens, and the number of arrests soared.
Sometimes the arrests seemed frivolous, such as that of twenty-eight-year-
old German-American Bundist, Edwin Westphal, who was sentenced to
six months in the workhouse "for causing a near riot . . . on the night of
May 29 when he told a group of soldiers and sailors they were 'crazy to be
working for Uncle Sam at $21 a month.' "[81] Days later, The New York
Times announced that the authorities had picked up a thirty-nine-year-old
German named George Calvin Mains who had passed himself off as an
American citizen in order to get a job as a carpenter on a war contract.
Mains had lived in the United States for many years; his wife and son were
Americans. The mortgage on his home on Long Island was about to be
foreclosed, he said, and he badly needed work. Mains was detained on Ellis
Island as an enemy alien.[82]

Other arrests were more serious. The FBI fairly crowed to announce
that Herman Agne, a thirty-nine-year-old German-born baker had been
arrested. He was described by FBI agents as "one of the most dangerous
German-American Bundists in the country." As Attorney General Biddle
had earlier threatened could be done, Herman Agne's American citizenship
was promptly revoked, and he was sent to the Gloucester, New Jersey,
Detention Station, pending a hearing.[83] Within one month, a special grand
jury was convened in Chicago to investigate seditious activity by enemy
aliens in the Illinois area. The United States attorney said that the grand
jury would be asked to continue sitting through July and August. He went
on to say that "the inquiry already has uncovered at least half a dozen
enemy aliens, most of whom have been interned after hearings before the
enemy alien board."[84]

On 29 June, the day after the capture of the U-boat spies, the Justice
Department conducted a massive sweep of potentially dangerous enemy
aliens in New York City. The population along the East Coast was nervous
and saw saboteurs in every doorway. That evening a group of roaming
vigilante thugs paid a visit to an apartment building where several German
families lived. The landlady lied to the bullies, denying that any Germans
lived there, and the gang moved on to another suspected building. Later

that night seven FBI agents, guns and all, appeared to arrest any German citizens in the building that the thugs had first visited. Alfred Heinrich R. Heitmann, twenty-nine years old, was picked up and shipped to Ellis Island. Alfred was not an average enemy alien: he worked for an American company, Standard Oil. For several years after leaving Bremen, Germany, in 1933, Heitmann worked for Shell Oil and was based largely on the Dutch island of Aruba, off the Venezuela coast. In 1938, Heitmann switched to Standard Oil and became an assistant engineer on oil tankers in and around New York.

In fact, Heitmann believed that his arrest may have stemmed from his employer's wartime problems. Standard Oil had been involved in a number of actions that skirted the law and, to many, smelled of treason. It shared patents with the German chemical company, IG Farben, for instance, and the Department of Justice was pressing hard to separate Standard's American interests from those of America's enemy. The two countries also shared a tangle of patents and cross licenses for synthetic (Buna) rubber. Perhaps most worrisome to the government was Standard Oil's secret program to sell oil to Germany, which would then be used to sink American and British ships. These transfers to blacklisted countries even before 11 December often took place in or around Aruba. It could well have been that assistant engineer Alfred Heitmann was present at such a transfer and British intelligence reported his name to the FBI.[85]

Whatever alerted the FBI and caused his arrest, Heitmann remained on Ellis Island for a month. After a ludicrous hearing at which he was accused by a Chinese laundryman from New York of making pro-Nazi remarks in his presence, he was sent to Camp Meade, Maryland, then Camp Forrest, Tennessee, spent a short time at Fort Lincoln, North Dakota, and finally went to Camp Seagoville, Texas, which was enlarged to include some men. Initially, his biggest problem was his separation from his wife Caroline, who had no idea where her husband was being held or why. They were not reunited until she joined him at Seagoville.

Poor treatment of the internees who were held at military bases was a serious problem. The military was unsure about the legal status of the Germans in their midst. Were they criminals? Prisoners of war? Part of the West Coast relocation program? Was their care outlined by the Geneva Accords of 1929? The answer to all these questions is "no." Their conditions improved or deteriorated as the newspapers reported recent battles won or lost by the Allies against the German army. Camp Meade, Maryland, in particular, was uncertain about its German internees and provided them with the lowest level of care available. Heitmann was so angry at his treatment that, at the first opportunity, he placed his name on the list for repatriation to Germany. Only a pleading letter from his wife caused him to change his mind, and he remained in the United States.

German internees who were paroled and employed by American companies during the war were often treated as badly. The FBI regularly dropped by those companies employing parolees, especially if they were alerted by an anxious coworker, or if the company manufactured an item used in defense work. Wilhelm Wartemann's experiences were most unpleasant. The refrigerator engineer from Fort Worth, Texas, arrested on 8 December 1941, was paroled in March 1942. Four of his children, however, remained wards of public welfare at the All-Church-Home in Fort Worth, and his wife Anna and remaining child, a five-month-old daughter, lived with a friendly sponsor farm family, the Brauers, in Midlothian, Texas. She received $34 per month from the Swiss Legation. When Wartemann was paroled, he drew an unfortunate sponsor: Mr. Hutchinson was an outspoken patriot and anti-Nazi. Hutchinson also happened to a own a furniture/refrigeration store in downtown Forth Worth, and in a deviation from policy, Wartemann's sponsor also became his employer. The situation quickly became untenable. In May 1942, Hutchinson called the authorities with complaints about Wartemann's pro-Nazi attitude and Wartemann was rearrested. For the next year and a half, he was bounced between Fort Lincoln, North Dakota, and Ellis Island, while petitioning the authorities to allow his fractured family to join him at the Crystal City family camp.

One of the more curious episodes to indicate the growing public hysteria triggered by the June landing of Nazi spies concerned forty-nine-year-old Otto Kiessling, an American citizen since 1928. He was drunk and disorderly in a New York tavern, and, in the words of the legal complaint, "made insulting remarks about the American flag and the American Legion and spat upon the American flag and an American Legion button.[86] He was hauled into court and jailed. His bail was set at an astonishing $100,000. At nearly the same time, the University of Missouri announced its new policy to refuse to admit "citizens of the countries at war with the United States."[87]

The FBI also seized several thousand guns in other raids, as well as short-wave radios, cameras, and more alarmingly, 1,652 sticks of dynamite and caps. In its monthly update, the Justice Department stated that as of 28 November 1942, "the attorney general has acted upon 3,067 Germans, ordering release for 423, parole for 1,134, and internment for 1,426. Cases otherwise disposed of, 11, and reconsiderations and re-hearings came to 73."[88] Aliens who were released from internment and were allowed to stay in the United States had to agree, prior to their release, not to discuss their experience. It was a rule that both the Justice Department and the internees took seriously. By the end of 1943, the FBI had arrested another 5,027 enemy aliens, mostly Japanese. A few Germans were arrested, but hardly any Italians, for reasons discussed earlier. Among the 5,027 arrests for 1943, the FBI also bagged twelve Hungarians, eleven Romanians, and one Bulgarian who alone remained interned for the duration of the war. (To these figures must be added the 802 German seamen and 1,271 Italian seamen interned for the duration. They constituted a separate category, whose presence in America was neither residential nor military.)

For the first time, interestingly, the FBI included in its annual reports the number of alien residences it had searched. Previously, searches were considered normal police work and went unrecorded. Since the public was encouraged to report any suspicious activity or statement to the FBI, this raw, unproved data gradually developed into dossiers. Agents could "drop in" on suspects for an interview to "clarify some matters." One former internee recalls that "sometimes they just dropped by to see if there was a picture of a relative in the Wehrmacht. Sources for their questions were never disclosed."[89]

"In my case," says Arthur Jacobs,

> the FBI ransacked our home three times. Each time they searched our home they came up empty handed—no contraband or propaganda. During their ransacking searches they would throw items all over the place out of drawers onto the floor; and invariably they would leave all the cabinet doors ajar. It would take my mother hours to get things back in order. After each search my mother would be in tears and frightened and devastated. As a last resort, my mother turned to our minister. After she pleaded with him for help, the minister remarked, "Mrs. Jacobs, I too am a German; if I say anything in the matter of your husband, I will be arrested as well."[90]

In 1943, the FBI acknowledged 24,662 searches of alien residences, a colorless tally of the terrifying experiences that disrupted the lives and damaged the belongings of the suspects—and usually revealed little. The numbers increased in every category in the reports for 1944 and 1945.

For the many thousands of German and Italian aliens at liberty across America, the FBI was a constant presence. It drew on an army of voluntary and paid informants, often from the American Legion, to penetrate any suspected pro-German organization. No group was safe from investigation, from the Sons of Hermann clubs in Maryland, to the Echo Singing Society in New Braunfels, Texas, to Delta Phi Alpha, the German Language Honor Society (Lambda Chapter) at West Virginia University in Morgantown. FBI agents and informants copied down the license numbers on automobiles parked at German cultural events. The authorities even confiscated the guest book from Seattle's Blanc's Cafe—a record of more than forty years—where a group called the "German Roundtable" had met for decades. Looking through the pages, one sees the names of foreign dignitaries, local politicians, and visitors from Wiesbaden, Mexico City, and Nome, Alaska. The last entry reads: "This book was taken by the FBI September

3, 1943, and returned February 25, 1946."[91] Archival folders today bulge
with tedious investigations of a large number of German (and Italian)
groups.[92]

The major problem—as always—concerned separating the dangerous
aliens from the others. On 5 April 1942, the Justice Department invited all
state attorneys general to a conference in Washington to attempt to define
uniform standards for loyalty and adjudication.[93] Evaluations of loyalty, suspicious behavior, and the like differed widely from hearing board to hearing board. One alien might be released or paroled, while, for the same
suspicious behavior or group membership, another might be interned. Ennis's Alien Enemy Control Unit, responsible for the ultimate disposition of
each alien's case, often acted capriciously and, critics charged, with unnecessary severity.

Lambert Dietrich Jacobs was one of those caught up in the bureaucracy
in November 1944. Jacobs was German-born and had lived in New York
for years but had never become an American citizen. His problem started
out as a minor matter: he had not reported a recent change of address.
Then, an investigation revealed that he had reported to the German consulate in New York after September 1939 to register for military service, as
was required of German citizens by Berlin. The FBI was told that he had
made some remarks about Stalin and Roosevelt at a local tavern, and they
ransacked the Jacobs's apartment for contraband or Nazi propaganda. They
did not find anything. The net tightened when the FBI accused Jacobs of
having attended a Bund function and produced a list indicating that he had
applied to join the Nazi Party. He vehemently denied both charges but to
little avail. The FBI raided his apartment once again but found nothing.

Several weeks later he was called before a hearing board in Brooklyn.
Everything seemed to be going well. Jacobs even brought a Jewish family
friend to speak on his behalf. There was only one disquieting exchange:
Jacobs was asked if he would join England and America to fight Germany.
Where did his loyalties lie? After a thoughtful few minutes Jacobs told the
hearing board he would refuse. The board determined that he was a nationalist rather than a Nazi; it recommended that he not be interned, that "parole would sufficiently protect the country's interests."

To everyone's dismay, including the members of the board, the Alien
Enemy Control Unit in Washington rejected the board's decision and ordered Jacobs interned for the war. His internment seemed so unnecessary
that the chairman of the board wrote personally to the acting assistant attorney general, C. E. Rhetts, to protest the government's action. "Over and
above the apparent injustice to the subject if internment is ordered," attorney Daniel Priest wrote in his three-page letter, "the Board believed that
internment would be a mistake in that it would be necessary . . . also to
intern his semi-invalid wife and two half-grown boys . . . both of whom

are American citizens." The letter concluded that all the boards in Brooklyn have regularly paroled or released aliens of Jacobs's type. "His internment would be inconsistent with positions heretofore taken and approved by your office."[94]

The government's answer came on the night of 3 November 1944, when the FBI burst into the Jacobs's Brooklyn apartment and, before the eyes of his terrified family, arrested Lambert. They hauled him to a holding area on Ellis Island, where he was eventually joined by his wife and two young sons. He requested another hearing, where it was agreed that he had, indeed, done nothing wrong. He was caught in the system, however, and he and his family were shipped to a family camp at Crystal City, Texas—on the other side of the world from their apartment and friends in New York. "His only mistake," says his son Arthur angrily, today a retired Air Force major and professor at Arizona State University, in Tempe,

> was not telling the board what they wanted to hear—that he was willing to fight against Germany. I'm sure the question was only a formality, but his answer was included in the board report to the Justice Department. Had he said he was willing to fight Germany— after all my father "voluntarily" registered for draft—they would have been satisfied and let him go. On the other hand, my father did tell the board that if Germany invaded the U.S. he would help to defend against such an invasion. His statement that he would not fight Germany only convinced the Alien Enemy Control Unit that he must be a secret Nazi party member. Still, despite the difficult years which followed—our repatriation and expatriation to Germany and our awful treatment there—I'm proud that my father was truthful.[95]

Eberhard Fuhr, then fifteen years old, believes his problem was being a smart-aleck kid. His parents, Carl and Anna, emigrated to the United States in 1927 when he was two years old and his brother Julius was five. A third brother, Gerhard, was born in Cincinnati in 1929. His father became a baker in America, and the household maintained its German ways. The family never considered applying for American citizenship. In 1940, the Fuhr family registered according to the Alien Registration Act and complied with all restrictions placed on enemy aliens after the outbreak of war in December 1941. Because of the family's visible pro-German sentiments, Eberhard's parents were arrested early in 1942, suspected of being on the fringes of the German-American Bund. "If anything," remembers Eberhard, "my parents were unreconstructed monarchists who saw Hitler as a caretaker who would one day restore the Hohenzollerns to the throne."

Carl and Anna were shipped to Seagoville, Texas; ten-year-old Gerhard, faced with an orphanage, chose to go with his parents. Eberhard learned about his parents' internment when he returned from summer camp in

North Carolina. "Where's Mom and Pop?" he remembers asking his older brother, Julius, as he walked in the door. "They were interned two weeks ago. We didn't want to get you upset, because you couldn't do anything about it anyway."[96] When Julius went off to college in the fall, on a football scholarship, Eberhard was left at home alone, paying for groceries with money he earned from a paper route. Soon, Julius quit college, and the two boys tried to maintain the household alone. Eberhard, now sixteen, continued high school and maintained his paper route; Julius went to work moving heavy barrels in a brewery.

For the next year, while his parents were interned at Seagoville and later at Camp Crystal City, Texas, Eberhard remembers being "hounded" by the FBI at work and at school. His first encounter with the feds came in November 1942, when he was asked to go downtown to answer questions about his family's loyalties. "All [the authorities] presented was raw FBI data, which is maybe somebody calls in and says, 'You know, this guy's got bombs in his house,' or something, and the FBI puts it down. . . . It becomes fact." He was released and sent home.

Several weeks later it happened again. This time FBI agents hauled Eberhard out of the house one evening after school and took him to the Federal Building downtown. There, in a darkened room, with a bright light focused in his face, they asked him endless questions, not questions about national security but personal questions—about who he was dating and why he was dating her. "It was like a scene out of bad movie," Eberhard recalls.[97] Again, he was sent home.

Suddenly, on 23 March 1943, without warning, the other shoe dropped. Eberhard was sitting in his English class at Woodward High School in Cincinnati when the principal nervously called him out of class, and he was arrested in the hall by a pair of FBI men. He was marched to the street in handcuffs, as his classmates gaped in astonishment. (His photo was removed from the school yearbook.) Eberhard's brother, Julius, was picked up at work at the brewery on the same day. Both were taken to the Hamilton County Workhouse in handcuffs. The next day they were brought to the Federal Building for a hearing.

"While we were sitting in a waiting room, I began reading the local *Cincinnati Enquirer*," Eberhard recalls. "Suddenly I was reading about myself. The headline said: 'Brothers Want to Help Hitler.' I could hardly believe it." According to the paper, an unnamed FBI source (Fuhr today believes it was his estranged uncle who turned them in) said the brothers reportedly revealed that they "didn't feel they owed allegiance to the United States and would refuse to serve if drafted." They also allegedly stated: "The United States hasn't got a chance in this war." (That was enough to get them arrested.) A misleading photo accompanying the article displayed a variety of Hitler pictures and propaganda items that had been accumulated from other seizures, none of which had been found in the Fuhr home. The article ended with the words, "They will be given a hearing before the Civilian Alien Hearing Board, *then transferred to a temporary internment center at Chicago . . .*" [author's emphasis].[98] "We were dumbfounded! The decision had already been made," Eberhard said, punctuating his anger by pointing his finger in the empty air. "The hearing we were waiting for was just a formality. So much for justice."

"My brother was the first to enter the hearing room," says Eberhard,

> I was next. Neither of us was permitted to bring a witness or lawyer, and we couldn't be present at each other's hearings. They questioned me for a couple of hours: 'Did I like Hitler?' 'Why did we have a picture of Hitler at home?' 'Did we attend German-American Day at Cincinnati's Coney Island amusement park?' 'Why did I go to a German language class on Saturday mornings at Hughes High?'—every question was designed to make me look like a wild-eyed Nazi. One question asked of me was: If your German cousin came up the Ohio river in a U-boat and asked you for shelter, what would you tell him? Being a smart-ass fifteen-year old, I told him the Ohio was probably too shallow for a U-boat. Besides, a German cousin wouldn't speak English, and I don't speak enough German.

The next morning the boys were ordered interned, just as the newspaper predicted. "We were not allowed back into our house, even to lock up our belongings or turn off the electricity, water, or gas. The house was soon vandalized and we lost everything." Eberhard and his brother were handcuffed uncomfortably together, facing each other and walking sideways, and driven to a transit internment facility in Chicago. "They treated us like mass murderers." During the auto trip to Chicago, Eberhard recalls that even when answering nature's calls, "one of the two Federal Marshals was required to cuff himself to one of us, and the three of us jammed and contorted ourselves to a urinal or into a toilet stall, with little regard to modesty." They were taken by train to Uvalde, Texas, where they joined their parents at nearby Camp Crystal City. To this day, Eberhard wonders if he had been more cooperative he might not have been sucked into "this paranoid program" that was responsible for his internment for the next four years—from 1943 until 1947, long after the war's end.[99] Since the enemy alien program was not harnessed to the military, the internees—largely only the German internees—were not released at the end of the war.

Most former internees remember similar scenes, including a mortifying loss of bathroom privacy.

> I was nineteen years old when the FBI men came to arrest me. It was 1:30 P.M. on October 21, 1942. It was unusually warm for Iowa, and

I left without a coat; they told me they only wanted to question me and that I'd be home soon. Instead I was taken on a long drive to Omaha to the Good Shepherd Convent, where I remained for three months. After a hearing I was sent to Seagoville, Texas. But I'll always remember how embarrassing it was to be locked in the rest room and have an FBI man standing guard outside the door.[100]

It is clear from the records that the FBI often wriggled to remain within the law, especially when no executive search warrants or presidential warrants were available. A case in point concerned Mrs. Anna Koehlein of Toledo, Ohio (who was turned in to the bureau by a Mrs. Eugene Nowack of the same address); Mrs. Koehlein had apparently failed to surrender a shortwave radio, and, said her boarder, Mrs. Nowack, "she had given her camera to a nephew to avoid the regulations." Furthermore, she had taken a trip to Hoboken, New Jersey, on Christmas 1941, where she remained until 21 January 1942, "without having requested permission of the appropriate United States Attorney to make this trip." The FBI sensed villainy in Mrs. Koehlein's activities, but with so many accusations they required a complicated warrant for multiple searches.[101] The Justice Department, however, found no grounds for the issuance of such a search warrant and denied the bureau's authorization. Hoover became apoplectic and fired off a barrage of angry letters to the attorney general. He predicted that the entire Alien Enemy Control Program would be "severely hampered" unless multiple spot searches were authorized. In this case, the Justice Department held firm. Often it did not.

In other cases, generally involving a single accusation against an individual, the bureau sometimes apprehended suspects and handed them over to the INS for internment without any warrants at all, eventually leading the INS and Ennis's Alien Enemy Control Unit to warn the bureau that arrested aliens would be turned loose after forty-eight hours if no proper warrant was forthcoming. The FBI countered that such formalities would obstruct the bureau's work.[102] Attorney General Biddle stepped in and clarified the matter: if the violation was of an extremely minor character or due to excusable ignorance, he said, the arrested alien was to be immediately released; if the violation was willful but not serious, the arrested alien should be released with a sound warning. Only in cases serious enough to be held for a hearing board could an arrested alien be held for a warrant to be issued by the attorney general (although decisions regarding the later disposition were generally handed down by the Alien Enemy Control Unit).[103] Eventually, the FBI's zeal for investigating cases based on petty evidence prompted Roosevelt, in April 1942, to humorously write Hoover to ask: "Have you pretty well cleaned out the alien waiters in the principal Washington hotels? Altogether too much conversation in the dining rooms!"[104] Given that Hoover was not known for a sense of humor, it is not surprising that no record of Hoover's response survived.

Attorney General Biddle, however, continued to free arrested internees as quickly as possible. On 22 August 1943, he announced the creation of a twenty-two-member panel known as the Special Alien Enemy Hearing Board to facilitate transferring internees from army camps to INS camps, and from there, presumably, to freedom. Groups of four to eight members of the special board made periodic visits to army camps and detention centers to conduct hearings, eventually moving 4,120 internees to INS-controlled Fort Missoula (Montana), Fort Lincoln (North Dakota), Santa Fe (New Mexico), Seagoville, Crystal City, and Kenedy (Texas). While Biddle's motives may have been somewhat humanitarian, he admitted to *The New York Times* that German military prisoners were arriving in America by the tens of thousands from the battlefields of North Africa, and it was important "to provide internment facilities for Axis prisoners of war being brought to the United States."[105]

In an evident effort to be forthright with the public and at the same time calm the many hundreds of thousands of loyal American enemy aliens living in the United States, Biddle announced, three months later, in November 1943, that since Pearl Harbor only 14,738 dangerous enemy aliens had been arrested—"fewer than half of 1 percent of the 938,000 persons classed as enemy aliens in this country." Moreover, their cases were reviewed quickly and less than a quarter were interned. Specifically, 6,854 were released unconditionally; interned: 3,771; released on parole: 4,113; 1,444 were released after hearings before an alien enemy hearing board; and 5,410 after hearings before United States attorneys.[106]

CHAPTER SIX

THE CAMPS

Meanwhile, plans moved ahead for the construction of federal detention camps. On 22 March 1942, the Army's provost marshal general (PMG) ordered nine permanent alien enemy internment camps, plus a camp reserved only for families, with planning to begin on fourteen more. These INS internment camps should not be confused with the prisoner of war (POW) camps, which were maintained by the PMG's office, or with the War Relocation Authority (WRA) centers, which housed Japanese and Japanese-Americans evacuated from the West Coast after Pearl Harbor. The enemy alien program was separate from the others and was under control of the Army and the Immigration and Naturalization Service. At first, the INS Border Patrol was not enthusiastic about guarding enemy alien camps. Border Patrol officers were mostly tough, silent, almost heroic men trained to patrol more than eight thousand miles of American borders to prevent the smuggling of goods and aliens into the United States. It was dreary work, woefully underpaid, and often hazardous. The head of the patrol was the highly respected Willard F. Kelly, who argued strenuously against using his men for anything but their primary mission, but to no avail. He was overruled by the Justice Department, and the patrolmen went to work. Temporary and permanent camps were created from former Civilian Conservation Corps (CCC) camps, migratory worker camps, and sections of existing military bases at such places as Chaffee, Arkansas; Lordsburg and Roswell, New Mexico; Crossville and Forrest, Tennessee; Clark and Leonard Wood, Missouri; Livingston, Louisiana; McAlester and Stringtown, Oklahoma; Fort Lincoln, North Dakota; and venerable old Ellis Island, New York. German internees were also held in St. Paul, Minnesota; Tampa, Florida; Cleveland, Ohio; Detroit, Michigan; Opelika, Alabama; Tallahassee, Florida; and Waycross, Athens, and Atlanta, Georgia. The enemy alien incarceration program had taken on a life of its own.

Each camp had a distinct population: men only, single women and childless couples, or family groups including children. Germans (and Italians) were interned in at least forty-six locations during World War II, largely at the following camps:

Camp Kenedy, Texas (operated by the INS). Germans and Japanese, large contingent from Latin America. Mainly men.[1]

Camp Seagoville, Texas (INS). Single women, South Americans, some German and Italian families.[2]

Camp Fort Sam Houston, Texas (Army). Germans and Italians, largely men.

Ellis Island, New York (INS). Germans and Italians.

Camp Fort Stanton, New Mexico (Army). Primarily German seamen.[3]

Camp Fort Bliss, Texas (Army). Germans and Italians, only men.

Crystal City, Texas (INS). Families: Germans, Japanese, Italians, aliens from Latin America, Indonesians.[4]

San Pedro Immigration Station, California (INS). Germans and Italians, only men.

Camp Sharp Park, California (INS). Germans and Italians, mostly men.

Camp Fort McDowell, Angel Island, California (Army). Germans and Italians, only men.

Seattle, Washington, Immigration Station (INS). Germans and Italians, mostly men.

Camp Fort Lewis, Washington (Army). Germans and Italians, only men.

Camp Fort Missoula, Montana (INS). Italian seamen.[5]

Camp Fort Lincoln, Bismarck, North Dakota (INS). German and Italian civilians and merchant seamen, only men.[6]

Chicago, Illinois, Immigration Station (INS). Germans and Italians, only men.

Gloucester City, New Jersey (INS). Adult males and females.[7]

Camp Stringtown, Oklahoma (Army). Germans, Latin Americans, only men.[8]

Camp Fort Forrest, Tennessee (Army). Germans and Italians, Latin Americans.

Camp Fort George G. Meade (Army). Germans and Italians, merchant seamen, only men.

The majority of aliens arrested in New York, New Jersey, or along the rest of the East Coast were taken first to Ellis Island. Ellis Island Reception Center, with its cavernous hall and many rooms, offices and examination stations, had, since 1892, welcomed millions of immigrants to America. Now, it held people whose loyalty was in question, and served as the final departure point for those to be deported or repatriated. From here, the deportees, repatriates, and expatriates would board the famous humanitarian ships, the Swedish ships S.S. *Gripsholm* and S.S. *Drottningholm*, the S.S. *Winchester Victory*, and the S.S. *Aiken Victory* for the journey to Europe. Stranded seamen, aliens from Latin America, diplomats, German aliens from the U.S.—came and sometimes left. The man in charge at Ellis Island was Philip Forman, the INS chief of detention and deportation.

Ellis Island was a perfect prison—easily guarded and reachable only by boat. It could hold a large group of people for a limited time. In addition to the reception hall, Ellis Island had lots of nooks and crannies, a barber shop, music room with piano, a canteen, store, hospital, and bathrooms with long rows of showers, toilets, and washbasins. On the second floor was the large dining hall. Families were assigned to individual rooms, and single men and children slept in barrack-type halls.

During the first two years of the war, Ellis Island was used primarily as a transit and holding camp. However, by January 1943, the population of German internees had stabilized at about 350 enemy aliens and their dependents. Upon arrival each internee was given a pair of American army shoes, khaki socks, shirt, and underwear. To purchase additional items from the canteen store, each received $3.00 per month in scrip. The government also allowed those who wanted to work at camp maintenance jobs to do so for an additional ten cents an hour. Religious services were available, though irregular, with Lutheran services offered in German every other Sunday. Catholic services were held whenever a German-speaking priest arrived. Food was satisfactory, as were movies, athletics, and other entertainment. Ellis Island had a reading room and small library with some six hundred German and five hundred English books donated by the German Red Cross, the YMCA, and private individuals. Even the elected camp spokesmen, Ernest Kerkhof, and later Heinrich Dammann, conceded to Swiss inspectors that conditions could be worse.

Despite the strange new surroundings and the myriad difficulties involved in adjusting to a regimented, diverse society without personal privacy, the records disclose a surprising number of courteous letters of thanks to Forman. One, written by the spokesman for the people of Room A on 12 April 1942, thanked the authorities for "the opening of our 'roof-garden,' the improvement of our playgrounds, the showing of moving pictures, the weekly distribution of smoking material for our needy comrades and most recently, the very satisfactory change in our meals which we feel, can also be much credited to your Chef-cook, Mr. Battista."

In another letter to Forman, internee Joseph De Martin wrote "to express to you my gratitude for all the courtesies I received here during my two months here. From the censors to the guards and the people in the dining room—all were very kind to me. When a man suffers, every little act of kindness is of great comfort to his spirit. Please accept, sir, my sincere thanks, to you and all your people."

Also acknowledging changes for the better (or hoping to curry favor with the authorities), the spokesman for the German detainees in Room 206, Dr. A. G. Schickert, conveyed his group's gratitude for "the very great improvement of the meals served to us. The variety of the dishes as well as the appetizing trimmings served with them, such as a slice of lemon with yesterday's mackerel, were equally appreciated. I feel sure that the continuation of this program will greatly contribute toward maintaining the full contentment of our group."[9]

There were a few disciplinary problems, but they were minor infractions: some fights, an unauthorized telephone call, an occasional attempt to smuggle a letter past the censors. The only legal action of note during the entire period involved three German aliens who had been arrested in New York for failure to register with the State Department as active enemy agents. That was a violation of the law and made the German agents criminals, unlike the majority of the internees. Their trial was held at Ellis Island. Two of the three, Otto Bremer and Günther Gibbe, were found guilty and were sent to the penitentiary. The third man was found not guilty, and dispatched to join the large group of internees awaiting shipment to an internment camp or return to Germany.[10] Ellis Island was used to the last.

To assure Germany that the internees were being well cared for, Washington encouraged Swiss inspection teams to make regular visits to each camp. Accompanied by representatives of the U.S. State Department (Bernard Gufler, Parmely Herrick, and Whitney Young) and the Justice Department (Willard F. Kelly), the Swiss representatives (W. Weingärtner, W. C. Bruppacher, and others) spent several days and sometimes weeks at each camp investigating the quality of food, sleeping conditions, representation, sports, discipline, religious services, hospital staff, and the attitude of the camp commander. Internees were often personally interviewed by the visiting Swiss teams, and no item was too insignificant to be noted in their reports to Germany. Following their visit to Camp Forrest, Tennessee, in April 1943, for instance, the Swiss carefully noted that the camp commander, Colonel Russell S. Wolfe, "was from an old family in Charleston, South Carolina, descending from the English," apparently aware that the race-conscious Germans would be interested in such trivia.[11] Lengthy reports were forwarded to the German authorities, and all complaints by the internees were written up in detail. Other Swiss inspection teams looked after the interests of the Italians, and Spanish teams looked after the Japanese.

Many others who were arrested along the East Coast were held at the U.S. Immigration Station near Gloucester City, New Jersey. Located only a few miles from Philadelphia and Camden, Gloucester City was a grimy industrial Irish community despite its famous colonial roots. A large Victorian house on South King Street had been converted into an INS detention facility and was used primarily as a transit camp for internees. New internees arrived in twos and threes to await their moment before a hearing board. Others were released on parole or shipped elsewhere after hearings. The average number of internees held at Gloucester City Detention Station at any one time was about twenty-five men and twenty-three women. By all accounts, it was a comfortable and friendly place. Unlike the other camps, women had their own spokesman: Miss Ina Gotthelf, and Alfred Sohnius represented the men, all under the benevolent administration of INS officer Adolph Schiavo. Women were issued a pair of shoes and a dress, men shoes and work pants, plus two free packs of cigarettes each week for both. The internees could earn eighty cents a day making handicrafts and were allowed to keep up to ten dollars at a time. Anything more was held in an account. Many activities kept the internees occupied: daily classes in Spanish and French, gin rummy and poker on Friday evenings, and Catholic or Protestant services on Sunday. As in all camps, internees were entitled to regular visitors, although strict rules of nondiscussion and message censorship applied. Medical care was especially good at Camp Gloucester, which had access to a number of large urban hospitals nearby when an internee needed help. The Swiss inspectors were most impressed by Camp Gloucester's meals (an average dinner might be lamb roast with gravy, potatoes, green beans, cooked onions, fresh pears, bread, and coffee), and attributed everything to the INS camp directors, Thomas D. McDermott and Adolph Schiavo. "They are the right men at the right jobs," the Swiss inspectors reported to the German government.[12]

Internees from the Midwest were usually held in Chicago until their hearings were completed and their status decided. Women, normally no more than a dozen at a time, were taken to the Convent of the Good Shepherd, 1126 Grace Street, on the city's North Side. The convent took up much of a city block, with offices, classrooms, and a visiting room on the first floor, and a large living hall with eighteen available beds on the second. By all accounts, the convent was comfortable enough; food was plentiful, sunlight and fresh air ample, and religious services sufficient for even the most devout Catholics. Since the convent maintained no canteen, one of the sisters shopped daily for any items that the women requested. The detainees were held between six weeks and several months before being transferred to a permanent internment camp or sent to join their husbands at Seagoville or Crystal City. A similar women's camp had opened in Los Angeles.

Men were held at 4800 South Ellis Avenue in Chicago, in a large three-story private house with a rose garden. When inspected by the Swiss authorities in December 1942, the transit house held twenty-four Germans and one Japanese in a comfortable, airy, building; they received good food, unlimited mail, and books and newspapers. There wasn't much to do: the twenty-five to thirty detainees rotated chores, such as scrubbing the floors, kitchen duties, and tending a small outdoor garden. Every few days someone from the YMCA dropped by to check on their needs and distribute a few dollars to needy inmates. The Swiss inspectors were impressed; they found that the internee representative, Frank Kleinmond, and the INS official in charge, W. R. Wilson, though in normally adversarial positions, were good friends and poker buddies.

Smart-aleck Eberhard Fuhr, handcuffed to his brother, was brought to this Chicago detention facility from Cincinnati by two federal marshals in March 1943 (see chapter 5). "We were welcomed by fellow Germans, a Hungarian, a Rumanian, an Italian, and a German priest attached to the Holy See. There were no criminals." Armed guards patrolled the grounds, but security wasn't especially tight—as evidenced by Eberhard's one-time prank of sneaking out to get a beer. Young Eberhard turned eighteen while at the South Ellis Avenue facility, and demanded that he be allowed to register for the draft, internee or not. In the end, the INS administrator gave in, although the army managed without him. In July 1943, five months after arriving in Chicago, Eberhard and his brother Julius were transferred to the INS family camp at Crystal City, Texas, where they were united with their parents and younger brother.[13] The boys, both notorious pranksters, spent the next two years playing football, chasing girls, and taking care of their parents. The Fuhr family lived in a four-room multifamily unit, with cooking facilities and a small garden, until April 1947. At night, the brothers left their parents in their "little apartment" and slept in the nearby barracks.[14]

Those arrested west of the Mississippi were generally sent first to Seagoville. Seagoville was a modern federal minimum-security women's reformatory, taken over by the INS in March 1942 to intern mainly women aliens. Seagoville was, perhaps, the most civilized of all the internment camps. It had been built to resemble a small college campus: a quadrangle of seven two-story brick buildings, paved walkways, a theater–multipurpose building, and an "industries" building with sewing machines, arts and crafts, looms, and so forth. Lest the internees be lulled by Seagoville's domesticity, a high wire fence surrounded the camp, with an ominous white stripe marking a "kill zone" ten feet before the fence. The rural prison was built to hold four hundred inmates, although the wartime population often ran much higher. In addition to women enemy aliens, Seagoville housed married couples, children, and a number of German and Japanese diplomats and their families from throughout the hemisphere.

Latin Americans

Less widely known is that Seagoville also received alleged spies from Latin America, Central America, and the Caribbean, hereafter called Latin

America in this study. The State Department had long maintained surveillance over America's enemies resident in these areas. In 1941, the Office of Strategic Services, "Wild Bill" Donovan's clandestine OSS, ordered its Latin America section to investigate the level and commitment of pro-Nazi sentiment. Their alarming reports fill ten reels of microfilm. Considering that it was 1941, and America was balanced on the edge of war, the news was not good. "Brazil's vast untapped natural resources and strategic position," noted one report, "make it a desirable area of exploitation for Germany." Another report cautioned that "a dangerous condition exists in South Brazil and in neighboring portions of Argentina and Paraguay. . . . There are about a million persons of German descent in a total population of about five million. . . . Since 1939 the Nazi agents have undoubtedly made great headway in perfecting the organization of these Germans into politically regimented groups and possibly into groups with some military power. . . . German funds in Brazil are known to exceed twenty million free dollars." These funds could be used to buy the support of unscrupulous politicians and to purchase arms and equipment. In Guatemala "three Ministers of President Ubico's cabinet are known to be pro-Nazi, and possibilities for a palace coup exist." In Peru "there is a potential threat of Fifth Column activities . . . and the German minority exercises a disproportionately large influence over the economic life of Peru." The OSS reported from Bolivia that there had been an actual Nazi plot to seize the government the previous 19 July (1940) involving the German minister and Bolivian army leaders. The pro-Nazi fascist group, the Falangists, were also pouring into Latin America after Franco's successful civil war in Spain.[15] Similarly alarming reports came in from nearly every country in Latin American and the Caribbean. The State Department seemed to have real reason for concern about the possibility of Axis sabotage in the Western Hemisphere.

The actual numbers are small, but nonetheless sobering. Argentina held an estimated 50,000 German citizens, or *Reichsdeutschen*, of whom approximately 2,000 were members of the Nazi Party. In Brazil, of the 80,000 *Reichsdeutschen*, about 1,700 were members of the party. In Chile, there were 7,000 *Reichsdeutschen*, of whom 600 were official members of the party. The numbers in the remaining South American countries do not include residents of German descent, *Volksdeutsche*, who often numbered in the hundreds of thousands. While many belonged to German cultural organizations and subscribed to German-language newspapers, there is little evidence that they were of immediate danger to the hemisphere. Despite the known presence of shadowy *Abwehr* (Intelligence and Counterintelligence of the German High Command) and *Sicherheitsdienst* (Security Service) agents, it does not appear that the Nazis succeeded in interesting a large part of the German minority in any country, except perhaps Argentina. In the words of Louis De Jong, a historian of Germany's Fifth Column activities in World War II, "The Third Reich got no more organizational hold on the large mass of the hundreds of thousands of 'Germans' living in South America than on the few million living in the United States."

But Mexico was another story. The popular government of President Lazaro Cárdenas, in office since 1934, was unlike most regimes in Latin America: it had been legally elected, its military had been tamed and if anything, leaned toward the Left, and while Mexican politics were polarized as they were in most nations of the decade, fascism was not a particular threat. However, Berlin recognized the opportunity to establish a German presence in Mexico—since it was uncomfortably close to the United States—and supported such organizations as the Sinarchistas, Spanish Falangists, and a group of local Mexican Nazis called the Gold Shirts. They were surprisingly successful in some areas of Mexico, particularly in stirring up anti-Semitism. As in other countries, anti-Semitism was cloaked as a campaign to rid Mexico of "foreigners" (read: "Jews")—Europeans who had arrived in Mexico during the 1930s and took the few jobs available. This hatred of foreigners rose to a fever pitch—helped by lavish German funds, bribery, and the stimulation of native xenophobia. By the mid-1930s, there was open ridicule for the Jews in the daily newspapers. Restrictions tightened around Jewish-owned business and spilled into the private lives of Jews. In December 1937 the Mexican Senate threatened to expel nearly 20,000 Mexican Jews, especially those originating from Germany and Poland, although no such deportation ever occurred.[16] As Nazi activity continued to increase in Mexico, J. Edgar Hoover became alarmed. In June 1938 Hoover made his concerns public; *The New York Times* carried Hoover's shrill charges about Nazi spying in nearby Mexico,[17] and by September 1939 he was convinced that "the German [residents] in Mexico are allegedly in possession of 25 bombers . . . and 250 German pilots, many fresh from the Spanish Civil War. . . . It has been alleged that 8 German submarines are presently operating out of Vera Cruz, Mexico."[18] It turned out no such armament existed. If there was a serious embryonic Nazi spy ring in Mexico, its numbers never amounted to anything.

To help deal with the problem of Nazis in Mexico and Latin America, British Secret Intelligence agents came to New York in the summer of 1940. They opened a large, well-funded office in New York to collect information on enemy activities in the Western Hemisphere, and, if possible, to neutralize Hitler's efforts. To do so, Britain's new intelligence office circumvented American law by encouraging Hoover's FBI to extend its operation to Latin America and to befriend sympathetic foreign government officials. Headed by the famous spy William Stephenson—a Canadian millionaire known as "Intrepid"—the British intelligence office immediately set about counteracting German espionage. In the words of historian

Ladislav Farago, "It was the opening blow in the secret war waged with unprecedented bitterness and cunning, thousands of miles from the actual theaters of war. Not until a year later was the concentrated assault on German agents successful in completely demolishing the *Abwehr's* once promising Mexican outpost."[19]

Many Latin American communities had little sympathy for the viewpoint of North America, which saw World War II as a moral crusade against Nazi evil. While their governments may have declared war on Germany, many admired and valued the Germans living among them, and trade relations with Germany, Nazi or not, were deemed important to their economies. Indeed, many Latin American countries did not consider anti-Semitism necessarily objectionable and pro-fascist sympathies were widely expressed.

On the other hand, sometimes these Germans were too outspoken in their pro-Nazi sentiments and racial concerns. In one curious episode, German-born and Nicaraguan-born wives awaiting passage at the port of Managua to join their Nazi husbands, who had already been deported to the United States, became involved in a racial quarrel. According to *The New York Times*, the row began when a Mrs. Walter Hascke, German-born, attempted to persuade the Nicaraguan-born women to remain in Latin America. "Germany will soon win the war," she warned, and in obvious reference to Nazi Germany's racial policies, she threatened that "you will not be admitted to Germany and your marriages will be annulled." Another German-born wife, Mrs. Erich Puschendorff, "refused to associate with or be housed with half-breeds, and all other German-born members of this party feel the same."[20]

Nicaraguan-born Mrs. Herman Eggner retorted: "If your remarks are intended to cast slurs upon Indian or Spanish blood, remember that our ancestors were possessed of a high civilization when yours were wallowing in mud flats and caves." Nicaraguan officials separated the groups into two buildings to await the ship that would take them to internment camps in the United States.[21]

The issue of hemispheric security aside, America's real reason for trying to isolate and often literally kidnap German and Japanese in Latin America, including many who were citizens of those nations, was more calculating. Washington wanted to build up a reserve of internees to trade with the enemy. By mid-1942, the United States watched in horror as Japan captured more and more territory and, with it, more Americans. Washington foresaw an increasing number of its citizens falling into enemy hands and saw its only chance to retrieve them in giving up an identical number of Japanese. The government had learned from the 1941 Japanese Consulate break-in that Tokyo considered American Japanese to be cultural traitors; thus, America looked to Latin America to provide a ready reserve of Japa-

nese, and Germans, to be used in future exchanges. U.S. Secretary of State
Cordell Hull put it bluntly. He told President Roosevelt, "In exchange for
the Americans in enemy hands, we have to send out Japanese in the same
quantity" and urged the president to continue this effort until all Japanese
throughout the American Republics were removed "for internment in the
United States."[22] An internal State Department memo is even more
straightforward: "Inherently harmless Axis nationals may be used to the
greatest possible extent. We could repatriate them, we could intern them
or we could hold them in escrow for bargaining purposes."[23]

There is a third possible reason for the State Department's pressure on
Latin America: the elimination of business competition. Nelson Rockefel-
ler and Adolf Berle, who both ran offices supervising counterintelligence
efforts in Latin America, repeatedly expressed concern over German corpo-
rate expansion in "America's Backyard." According to historian Max Paul
Friedman at the University of California at Berkeley, and an expert on the
topic, some German nationals from Latin America who spent the war years
in a Texas internment camp simply were business competitors for American
interests in the pharmaceutical or airlines industries. Many were forbidden
to return to Latin America by the American authorities even after the war
ended.

Ultimately, Latin America's cooperation came largely as the result of
undisguised diplomatic pressure.[24] Of particular interest to Washington
were areas of Latin America where large pockets of enemy citizens or sympathizers resided or served in diplomatic missions. The issue came up the
month following the attack on Pearl Harbor, at the meeting of ministers of
foreign affairs of the American Republics held in Rio de Janeiro 15–28
January 1942. Among the many topics of political cooperation and military
preparedness was the issue of internal and hemispheric security. After agreement that the Latin American republics were in grave danger of internal
espionage by the Axis powers, the Rio conference rushed to meet the
problem head-on. Resolution XVII ("*Subversive Activities*") reaffirmed the
commitment of all governments concerned to "maintain and expand their
systems of surveillance." What followed was three pages of restrictions on
Axis nationals. For example, all enemy aliens were required to register with
the Latin American authorities; they were limited in internal travel and
change of residence, and, of course, forbidden to have guns, explosives,
radio transmitters, or dangerous propaganda. To keep Germans, Italians, or
Japanese from attaining the protection of citizenship in their host country,
the naturalization process was to be slowed down. If they had already
achieved citizenship, any act of espionage would automatically nullify that
citizenship.[25] Although the final resolutions were somewhat more cautious
than the United States would have preferred, the Latin American nations
gave way to intense American diplomatic and FBI pressure, and bribes, and

agreed to cooperate. The conference commissioned an additional confer-ence study on the matter. Unofficially, Latin American governments were responding to increased anti-alien prejudice in their own countries due to unemployment and heightened nationalism. There was also a welcome opportunity for Latin American governments to seize alien-owned prop-erty, from huge plantations to successful factories.

The arrest of Germans in Latin America took several forms. Sometimes an alien like Heinrich Kruse in Costa Rica received a simple postcard from the authorities placing him under house arrest. Walter Klein, whose story will follow, was picked up when he was ordered into a military jeep that pulled up to him on the street. Whatever the method, Axis aliens in Latin America, save Argentina, should not have been surprised when it hap-pened. Most of the Latin American republics had declared war on Ger-many, because of opposition to Germany, or due to pressure from the United States. Within months government newspapers questioned the peaceful intentions of Germans living in their midst. To whom did they owe their allegiance? By June 1942, newspapers in a number of Latin American countries published blacklists or proclaimed lists to isolate Ger-mans and German organizations. For example, on 28 June 1942, Costa Rica's leading newspaper, *Diario Costa Rica*, announced, "Patriotic Costa Ricans should not deal with people or businesses on the proclaimed list. Do not buy from enemies of democracy; the money you spend will be used to attack you. We must economically wipe out the crimes of the Gestapo. War is death. Stand with them or totally against them. [signed] Directiva de Accion Democratia Costarricense." There followed four col-umns of names, totaling 340. Among the many Germans and Italians were such major German businesses as AGFA Film and Hapag-Lloyd Steamship Lines, both in San Jose. This was serious. Similar blacklists appear in, among other countries, El Salvador, Ecuador, and Guatemala.[26]

Guatemala is a good case in point. Starting in 1942, German citizens in Guatemala were isolated, gradually arrested, and shipped to the United States. On 7 January 1942, one of the first groups of arrested Germans left Guatemala for New Orleans, and went from there to Camp Blanding, near Jacksonville, Florida; on 13 April 1942 a group of sixty-two people went to Camp Stringtown, Oklahoma. More arrived at New Orleans as shipping space became available. On 16 January 1943, 141 Germans left Guatemala to be interned in Camp Kenedy in Texas, and another batch of 67 left Guatemala on 23 October 1943 for the same destination. Germans were also arriving from Chile, Bolivia, Peru, and Ecuador. When the United States had a sufficient number for an exchange, the internees were shipped to Germany. For example, 117 Germans from Guatemala were assembled on 29 July 1942 in Stringtown and sent to New York, and from there, aboard the *Drottningholm*, via Goteburg, Sweden, to Pienemunde, Germany. Others were included on every humanitarian journey to Europe of the *Gripsholm* and *Drottningholm*.

The trip on the high seas was miserable. Whether Germans, Italians, or Japanese, the aliens were transported on such dilapidated ships as the *Cuba*, *Etolin*, *Florida*, *Acadia*, USAT (United States Army Transport) *General Ernst*, USAT *General Gordon*, USAT *General Meigs*, USAT *General Randall*, SS *Imperial* (Chilean), USAT *Madison*, SS *Matsonia*, USAT *Puebla*, *Shawnee* (Atlantic Gulf and West Indies Steamship Company), and the USAT *Colonel Frederick C. Johnson*.

The *Etolin*, for example, was an old oil-burning steam vessel built in 1913 and long in service by the Alaska Packers Association. Conditions were wretched, despite a new coat of gray paint with the flag of the United States and the word "Diplomat" painted on both sides. Hammocks hung in three tiers, one on top of the other, and pipes crisscrossed the holds of the ship where the internees slept. No light entered the area below decks. Like the thousands of refugees and soldiers transported around the globe, the internees ate their meals directly out of cans while standing at makeshift tables made out of long wooden boards which were hung from the ceiling with chains. There were no chairs throughout the ship. The bathrooms were quite primitive. Only saltwater was generally available, and then only enough for a light wash. The number of passengers on any transport varied from a few dozen up to four hundred.

Life aboard an army transport ship was even worse. The *Colonel Frederick C. Johnson* was a good example:

> The one-time Hudson River vessel, converted to troop carrying, failed miserably when men, women, and children were involved. The enemy aliens occupied two holds. The women and children were quartered in the afterhold, a space approximately fifty by forty feet with bunks in tiers of four. Lacking guardrails of any kind, those bunks were exceedingly dangerous for small children. . . . To enter the only latrine on the ship for their use, the women and children had to go through the men's quarters. Scheduling use of the latrine by both sexes, plus the necessary frequent closing of the area for cleaning, posed extremely unsatisfactory conditions. Drinking water was unavailable between 9 P.M. and 7 A.M., and during the entire voyage there was no fresh water for bathing or washing. . . . Atrocious neglect characterized the medical care of the internees. The ship lacked both medicines and medical supplies.[27]

The only saving grace for aliens aboard these ships was that the journey lasted no more than ten to twelve days.

When the internees arrived in New Orleans they were sprayed for lice and put aboard a riverboat and taken up the Mississippi. They landed at a train station where they were often united with their husbands or wives and taken west to Camp Kenedy or Crystal City, Texas.

The internment of plane- and shiploads of often bewildered arrivals was legalized by the INS, which declared nearly 5,000 Japanese, Germans and Italians, to be "illegal immigrants." "Compounding the bizarreness of the program," recalled INS Inspector Jerre Mangione, "was the Machiavellian device that was contrived to legalize their detention by the Immigration Service. This consisted of escorting the Latin Americans over our borders, then charging them with 'illegal entry' into the country." Far from secret to the American public, who were supportive or at least, indifferent, news of such transfers appeared in the newspapers.[28] Only the nativist American Legion seemed to have objected to the program, despite the logic of maintaining hemispheric security and collecting enemy aliens for possible future exchanges for American personnel. In an angry letter to Secretary of State Cordell Hull, American Legion official Francis M. Sullivan thundered that "the Legion condemns the practice of importing into the United States aliens from other countries for detention in enemy alien relocation centers and requests its discontinuance at once!"[29] The files contain no other letters of objection.

On more than one occasion, a number of the "dangerous" Germans and Japanese turned out to be simple "impoverished peasants who had been paid to act as substitutes for others." Facts indicated that certain Latin American governments simply "cleaned house" and shipped northward their troublemakers and unemployed noncitizens. When it occasionally came to the attention of the State Department before Ameria went to war that groups of normal German tourists en route from Latin America to Europe contained trained espionage agents, Washington felt that it was wiser to hold the spies rather than repatriate them for possible reassignment. The commander of the enemy alien internment camp at Fort Lincoln, I. P. McCoy, explained the situation this way: "Suppose you saw a man in Guatemala who owned a ranch with a mountain-top from which vital American shipping could be watched. Suppose this man had a strong German background and was under suspicion as a possible enemy agent. Would you pick him up and be sure, or would you let him go and risk the possible loss of many American ships and many American lives?"[30] In the words of another INS camp commander, "Only in wartime could we get away with such fancy skullduggery."[31]

On more than one occasion, the State Department even pretended to guarantee safe passage to German citizens who were traveling home, only to instead intern them in the United States, usually at Seagoville or at the immigration station at Algiers, Louisiana.[32]

Several cases are illustrative. Walter Klein, born in 1906 in Eiserfeld bei Siegen in Germany's Westphalia region, set out to make his fortune. In

1924 he settled in Haiti, where he worked in various German and English cotton, coffee, and textile factories. When Germany declared war on the United States days after the Japanese attack on Pearl Harbor in December 1941, Klein knew that it was only a matter of time before he was picked up by *some* government—the Haitian (in whose country he was a foreigner), German (who might want to induct him into the army), American (who might feel threatened to have German citizens living so close to the United States), or even the French (Germany's enemy, whose language and customs were the foundation of modern Haiti). One day, on the way to the dentist, a jeep pulled up and it was "suggested" that he get in. As it turned out, Klein had been picked up by the Haitian authorities. He was taken to a primitive internment camp in Fort National in Port-au-Prince. It was a loose arrangement, Klein remembered with amusement, where everyone could sneak out at night to drink (including the commandant) as long as they were back by 6 A.M.

After four months, in April 1942, a large American ship arrived to bring the detainees to the United States. The rumor was that they were to be exchanged for Jews trapped in Germany. Discipline on ship was the strictest military, and their greatest fear as they sailed across the Gulf of Mexico were the German U-boats known to prowl there. To everyone's relief the American ship made it safely to New Orleans, where they were registered, searched, and placed on buses for Camp Kenedy, Texas. Judging by the formidable fences and elaborate security measures, Klein knew he had been pulled into a major government detention program from which there was no immediate escape. In a humorous moment, as the Germans from Haiti were searched yet again, this time by the experienced INS border guards, one of the new arrivals seemed to be stuffed with money. He had sewn American dollars into the linings of his coat, suit jacket, shirt collars—even his neckties produced money! After the paperwork, the Germans from Haiti were assigned bungalows, fed enormous meals, and thrown into the general population of recent internees from Nicaragua, Colombia, Guatemala, and the Caribbean. Thus began three years of imprisonment in Texas, which ended with his ultimate exchange to Nazi Germany.[33]

Heinrich Kruse had a similar story. Heinrich was a farmer and dairyman. That's what he loved to do. He worked for his cousin, Willi Neuhaus, in the little North German village of Barnsdorf. His cousin also had substantial land holdings in Costa Rica and was a naturalized citizen. Neuhaus was impressed enough with the hardworking Kruse to appoint him manager of one of his plantations. Heinrich and his young wife, Clara, moved to Central America, learned Spanish, and became citizens of Costa Rica in 1939. Their only child, Reinhard, was born a Costa Rican citizen. But despite their adaptation to local culture, the Kruse family remained fiercely German. At this distance, like most German exiles living in Central and South

America, they could be swayed by dramatic propaganda from the Fatherland, without suffering the deprivations and fear experienced by those who lived there.

It was not until February 1943 that Germans were rounded up in Costa Rica. About 150 were arrested, including both Heinrich Kruse *and* his cousin, Willi Neuhaus, citizen and landowner. The group was jailed in a miserable old army barracks, where they slept on the floors and huddled to keep warm. After some weeks, they were intimidated into going to internee camps in America. Even before this group left Central America, their plantations and landholdings were nationalized by the Costa Rican government, lost to them forever.

The group was placed on an American ship and transported up the Pacific Coast to San Diego. From California, Heinrich, Clara, and young Reinhard were taken by train to the hot, dusty town of Uvalde, Texas, and nearby Camp Crystal City. Cousin Willi was shipped to the equally inhospitable Camp Bismarck, North Dakota.

For the next year, Heinrich worked on the prison farm that supplied the vegetables for a camp population of more than 3,000. His boss was a congenial American agriculturist named Carl Vandervort, who became instrumental in the Kruse family's life. Their year at Crystal City was uneventful; Heinrich tended the vegetable farm, and Clara kept young Reinhard occupied and their little bungalow tidy. Now, more than fifty years later, neither Clara, in her nineties, nor her fifty-seven-year-old son Reverend Reinhard Kruse, both living in Philadelphia, remember much about their year in the Texas camp.

This tranquil situation ended February 1944. A camp-wide announcement was made that a number of inmates had been selected for exchange to Germany. The camp rumor was that they were being exchanged for American prisoners of war being held in German POW camps. "We had no choice," both Kruses recall, "but returning to Germany was fine with us." Within days the Kruse family, together with a large group of fellow internees, were loaded onto a night train, which took them from Crystal City to New Jersey. From there they embarked on the *Gripsholm* for Lisbon, Portugal; then they traveled by train across Spain and France to the German frontier, where the exchange took place. Finally, they made it "in a hop" to Barnsdorf, where Heinrich quickly found work on local farms. Despite the war that raged around them and the ruinous postwar years that followed, the Kruse family continued to live a quiet rural life.

But shortly after the war ended, they began to dream of emigrating back to the United States. Maybe life there wasn't so bad after all. Their major impediment was the lack of an official sponsor—a serious problem. A sponsor had to guarantee the immigrant a job and a home for one full year, in addition to half the cost of the immigrant's return fare if the experiment didn't work. Where could they find such a benefactor? Carl Vandervort, the farm manager at Camp Crystal City. Their letters eventually found him working his own farm in Arkansas, and to their delight, he volunteered to become their sponsor. In 1950, the Kruse family immigrated to Arkansas, where they lived and worked for several years. In 1955, Heinrich and his wife Clara became naturalized American citizens. Heinrich died in 1983; Clara is alive and active and their and their son Reinhard is today a highly respected Methodist minister in Philadelphia.[34]

A classified report issued by the War Department's Military Intelligence Division lists the exact number of German, Japanese, and Italian internees brought to the United States from other American Republics. Of the 6,610 individuals listed, 4,058 were German, 2,264 were Japanese, and 288 were Italian. By the middle of 1945, 3,204 of them had been returned to Germany as part of larger exchanges, or to Latin America. Half a year after the war was over, there were still 820 internees from Latin America in American camps.[35] For the next two years, some were shipped south, others went to Germany, and a surprising number overlooked the hostility of being arrested and taken north and chose to remain in the United States.

There is no way to evaluate the number of genuinely dangerous German and other Axis citizens rounded up in Latin America and the Caribbean. In retrospect, it appears to be quite small. A larger number were devout German nationalists, even wild-eyed, but not necessarily dangerous. Berkeley's Max Friedman claims that only a fraction of those brought to the United States, perhaps no more than 3–5 percent, were Nazi agents who might have threatened America's security. The remainder were picked up because of baseless accusations, business competition, or the opportunism of Latin American regimes and individuals who took over their property. Only after both the Departments of State and Justice had investigated these arrivals and concluded that too few could be proved dangerous was the program finally halted in mid-1944.[36] While the premise of the government's action was to "preserve . . . the integrity and solidarity of the American continent from subversive activity," the government actually possessed evidence on only about 140 of the 5,000 total internees brought to America.[37]

Interestingly, a total of eighty-one Jews were among the groups of Germans to arrive from Latin America. Most Latin American countries did not round up Jews in particular, but they did not release them if they were found in custody. Only Panama and British Honduras, governed by anti-Semitic officials, proved eager to include Jews in their roundups. Those Jews who were refugees from Nazi Germany, or seemed in any way suspicious, were sent to the Balboa Detention Center in the Canal Zone for several weeks of U.S. Army interrogation. Afterward, they joined the other Jews and their families who were dispersed to Seagoville, Stringtown, Camp Blanding, Florida, and Fort Ogelthorpe, Georgia. The latter two camps, Blanding and Ogelthorpe, were run by the Army for Axis POWs and Nazi sympathizers and were dangerous places for the new Jewish arrivals. Equally dangerous for the Jews was the INS quarantine station at Algiers, Louisiana, where most were held pending their transshipment to other camps.

It took the efforts of the American Jewish Joint Distribution Committee, the National Refugee Service, Catholic groups, the American Civil Liberties Union, the Jewish communities of Dallas, New Orleans, Chattanooga, and Nashville, and finally, influential groups within the State Department itself, to untangle the bureaucratic red tape and combat the anti-Semitism that incarcerated eighty-one Jews from Latin America in hostile enemy internment camps in the United States. The majority were paroled in mid-February 1943 and allowed to resettle wherever they could find sponsors. Those who chose to serve in the U.S. military could get their status changed. The rest were liable for deportation at the end of the war.

On 29 November 1943, the Justice Department lifted parole supervision over the Jews, and they were released on a case-by-case basis. The last Jews in internment were set free in early 1946. Of the eighty-one Jews interned from Latin America, two voluntarily returned to Latin America, four died before they were released, and seventy-five chose to remain in the United States.[38]

America's effort to keep the program, and Washington's involvement in it, under wraps is described in a 1943 State Department memo, originating in the Division of American Republics, that "it is undesirable for the written record to show that the initiative came from us."[39]

"And it worked, too," says Dr. Alex-Edmund S. DaHinten, a German-Guatemalan professor currently developing and implementing public policy for the Minneapolis–St. Paul Metropolitan Metropolitan Council.

> Since I was a little kid in Guatemala, I heard references to Germans being caught by the U.S. and sent to concentration camps in Texas. When I started traveling through Central America, German–Nicaraguans, German–Cost Ricans, German–Salvadorans, etc., asked me if my family was sent to Texas, and told me stories about themselves, or their parents or grandparents being sent to Texas. The fact was very well known in the German Central American communities. But when I would talk about it with people here in the U.S., they were incredulous.[40]

After the war ended Washington didn't know exactly what to do with these these people from South America. In fact, unlike enemy aliens arrested in the United States, who were listed as internees, the Germans and Japanese from the Caribbean and Latin America were called detainees—as though they were en route somewhere before being stopped by American authorities. Dismissing the fact that they were, in essence, kidnapped, *The New York Times* concluded, on 6 January 1946, "The fact that force may have been used to bring alleged Nazi sympathizers to the United States for internment during the war is no reason for releasing them. . . ." The official *50th Anniversary History of the Seagoville Federal Correctional Institution*, published in 1990, astonishingly claims that these families "left their home countries to enjoy the freedom of America."[41]

CHAPTER SEVEN

LIFE IN THE CAMPS

The population of Seagoville—whether South American spies, diplomats in transit, or enemy aliens arrested in America—hovered around seven hundred. Single women lived in dormitories, and couples lived in sixty prefabricated one-room houses, dubbed "Victory Huts" by their manufacturer. The first commander of Seagoville was the well-liked Joseph O'Rourke, who would later be transferred to Crystal City. The next was a government psychiatrist, Dr. Amy N. Stannard. By several accounts, only her psychiatric skills enabled her to deal successfully with the irascible German spokesmen, Franz Wirz, Hans Ackermann, and particularly Fritz Stangl, whose daily complaints and demands became legendary.

The spokesmen for both the German and Japanese met regularly, and their comments (usually complaints) were passed to Dr. Stannard. They always seemed to find a problem. The early complaints usually concerned food. On one occasion, the Germans demanded more chicken, which, at the current price of thirty cents per pound, the budget couldn't afford. Then they asked for fresh figs, celery, and rhubarb, which unfortunately were not on the local market. Once in a while, their requests were reasonable. When the internees called for an increase in their milk ration of one pint per person per day, Dr. Stannard agreed and raised the amount to one quart for children to the age of eighteen, pregnant and nursing mothers, and those on special diets. The Seagoville camp, unlike most of the others, included a trained dietitian on its staff. Miss Marian Brooks, by all accounts a "beautiful blonde," made certain that the food served to the approximately seven hundred German and Japanese internees, who ate in separate mess halls, conformed to their ethnic tastes. An average menu for the Germans at Camp Seagoville, this from June 1943, was as follows:[1]

Breakfast	Lunch	Dinner
Stewed prunes or one-half grapefruit	Beef stew	Spaghetti
Bran flakes	Potatoes	Steamed string beans
Toast-Oleo-Syrup	Cabbage	Cold pickled beets
Coffee/Milk	Bread-Oleo-Syrup	Raw carrots
	Pudding	Bread-Oleo
		Syrup
	Tea/Milk	Tea/Milk

In the words of a staff member at Seagoville, "Miss Brooks is one of the main reasons why no one ever thinks of escaping from this place."

Dr. Stannard encouraged meetings with the spokesmen and the council of seven internee representatives, one from each of the seven buildings, called the Family Camp Committee. Together they thrashed out a long list of acceptable camp rules and discussed issues where no policy yet existed. However, most meetings were complaint sessions that saw the German internees make clear their disagreement with the censorship of outgoing mail, the absolute prohibition of the display of Nazi flags, the movie schedule, visiting speakers, the requirement that internees give advance notice if they intended to throw a party in their rooms at which alcohol would be served, etc. Good psychiatrist that she was, Dr. Stannard listened patiently, calmed the more demanding spokesmen, and tried to help where she could.

To relieve the boredom, men were put to work on maintenance and administrative jobs, and women organized plays, performed ballet and theatricals, and maintained an extensive library with nearly 3,000 books in Spanish, English, Japanese, and German, donated by the YMCA and the German government. There were open-air evening concerts and songfests. Many of the internees were linguists and artists and offered a variety of courses for the studious, ranging from Italian, German, English, and Spanish, to stenography and decorative woodworking. Seagoville also boasted a weaving room where prisoners could learn to make drapes and rugs, and a modestly equipped garment factory where they could learn, teach, or engage in dressmaking.

Unfortunately, camp jobs were often distributed by friends of the Nazi spokesmen. Many internees found that the best jobs went to the Bundists and the pro-Nazis. For instance, Alfred Heitmann, the one-time employee of Standard Oil who was described in chapter 5, was a German nationalist but did not find Hitler appealing. When offered repatriation to Germany, his wife had convinced him to reject it. Now he found himself outside the ruling clique at Seagoville. The worst jobs available were sent his way, when he was allowed to work at all. For most of the next three and a half years he was bored, mystified as to the circumstances that had brought him to Seagoville, Texas, and angry. Caroline, his wife, became an object of camp rumors. She left Germany in 1938 and became a permanent resident alien in America. In effect, she had broken with Hitler's Germany and was seen by many as a traitor. She was whispered to be an FBI informant. The Heitmanns' food was tampered with; BBs were found in their dumplings and gingerbread cookies. Both were excluded from certain areas of the camp. Caroline's single social outlet became her friendship with the Princess Stephanie von Hohenlohe, and they could often be seen taking their daily walks around the camp, arm in arm.

Children in most camps knew nothing of these adult matters. They played games with each other and pranks on the grown-ups. They ran through the carefully tended flower beds. Buck Rogers, Tom Mix, and

American movie stars were their heroes. They scribbled cryptic messages to one another on hidden areas of the bungalow walls. School was mandatory, but there were, in essence, three schools: a German or a Japanese school taught by internees, and a general government school. Most children—certainly the German children—attended only their national ethnic school. Fifty years later, Alfred Plaschke still recalls that his father, Rudy, taught mechanics and shop, Erich Schneider and Walter Steiner taught art, Hermann Koetter taught history, Franz Wiegner, math, and Mrs. Agnes Bock gave piano lessons. "Those were the days when kids studied and sat quietly in class," he recalls, "especially since the teachers knew our parents." Textbooks were shared; there were exams and homework assignments, graduation ceremonies and diplomas. But the schoolchildren were like schoolchildren anywhere: they stared wistfully out the windows, sent notes, experienced puppy love, and played marbles at recess. What they really wanted to do, however, was explore the camp or work at an odd job.

Anyone who worked on an official camp job, child or adult, was paid ten cents an hour, in addition to the $3.00 a month that the INS issued for basic necessities to all internees in every camp. Generally, everything was paid in printed coupons so the prisoners couldn't pool their cash to, say, bribe a guard or buy a bus ticket. It was a surprisingly adequate amount in those years, considering that coffee cost thirty-six cents per pound, cigarettes twelve cents a pack, a quart of milk eleven cents, beer ten cents a bottle, hand soap or toothpaste ten cents, and so on.[2] The few dollars they received in coupons or tokens became especially critical when the Treasury Department announced, on 23 March 1943, that the 1941 law freezing Axis assets would now apply to the internees as well. Each internee received a two-page financial report form (TFR-30) to list all assets—which the Treasury Department now froze. The only options to pay rentals, taxes, or investments was either by obtaining a license from the Treasury Department or by turning over all financial affairs to someone who was "not a national of a blocked country."[3] If the internees did sign their assets over, that person could make the money available to them through the camp commandant. Even refund checks from items returned to Sears Roebuck or Montgomery Ward could not be sent to the internees directly; they had to be deposited in the internee's bank account, to be frozen with the rest. From there, if arrangements had been made to circuit the funds to the camp commandant, it would be made available to the internees. For those who had no outside money or who didn't trust or understand the system, money now became very tight in the camps, and some internees saw their property, businesses, and belongings outside of camp evaporate in bankruptcies and lost business opportunities. Spokesman Fritz Stangl, a difficult character in the best of times, now bombarded Dr. Stannard's office with protests and veiled threats. The Treasury Department remained firm.

Life continued at Camp Seagoville. Morale rose and fell as mail came from friends and relatives in the United States and abroad. War news meant different things to different people. Those loyal to America celebrated each Allied victory, while the German nationalists and Nazis among them were despondent at the same news. Dr. Stannard continued her regular meetings with Fritz Stangl to hear complaints about camp rules against the spreading of rumors, lighting fires on the camp picnic grounds, the limit of three beers per day to a rowdy Mr. Meuser, and a request to show respect for the memory of President Franklin Roosevelt. At the same time, Dr. Stannard was also listening patiently to the spokesman for the Japanese internees at Seagoville. The problems from hundreds of people, Germans and Japanese, American-born children and kidnapped Nazis from South America, never seemed to end.

Yet whatever the problems, many Seagoville internees wrote glowing letters to friends and relatives about their treatment. The camp censors maintained a file of them for Dr. Stannard entitled "Bouquets and Brickbats." Here is a sampling:

[E]ach one gets $5.25 every month and we can pick out what we want. Very good underwear. Many of the internees have perhaps never in their lives been able to afford such clothes. The administration really does everything to make life bearable for us. The same is true of the food and medical care. . . .

Elli Donath, 15 November 1944

You have been here and know that I am rather pampered than persecuted. And while I profoundly detest being deprived of my freedom, I am treated in a correct and humane fashion by the detaining authorities.

Karl Wecker, 18 December 1944

We are very contented here. The lovely things that they told us about Seagoville are far exceeded by the actual facts. . . . One does not feel like an internee here. . . . We have two rooms with central heat and much entertainment.

Heinrich Hoelscher, 20 December 1944

I must say that with very few exceptions, the Americans here are very reasonable and show that they have understanding for our personal problems and that their hearts are very often located on the right side.

Else Schreiner, 4 February 1945[4]

Sometimes a problem arose that neither Dr. Stannard nor the internees could solve. The worst of these came near the end of the war. In late April

1945, with the conflict in Europe nearly over, the War Department did something that many former internees remember with anger to this day. Their food was cut back dramatically. "Due to the nation-wide shortage of food supplies," the directive read, "ration allowances are to be revised, effective immediately. Fresh meat, eggs, milk and milk products, fats, fresh fruits, and coffee are to be sharply reduced." Spaghetti, macaroni, cereals, salads, and vegetables would pick up the slack. Fatty meat appeared on the tables, and boiled cabbage became a staple. There are several theories about why this occurred: The first claims that food was truly running short, given the stupendous amounts of food required by the American armies across the world; the second theory states that it wasn't a shortage of food, but rather a shortage of farmers, as boys were drafted for the military. However, the 25,000 internees across the country, and the 380,000 German prisoners of war in more than 120 POW camps, had a less charitable theory. The Allies had entered Germany, and thousands of American POWs and interned U.S. citizens were liberated and safe. There was no reason to pamper the Germans in the United States any longer, since their treatment could no longer affect the health or survival of imprisoned Americans. While the Geneva Convention requires that prisoners receive rations equal to those provided for troops in base camps, the government now concluded that "equal" did not mean "identical." "The provisions of the Geneva Convention are satisfied when the rations furnished internees and prisoners of war are equal in nutritional quantity and quality."[5] The internees did not agree.

Meanwhile, new internees continued to arrive, while others were transferred to other camps in efforts to break up cliques or ship troublemakers elsewhere. Some prisoners left Seagoville for a more distant destination: they were returned to Germany to be exchanged for Americans in enemy hands—the Exchange/Repatriation Program.

The exchange program began in March 1942, after an exchange of diplomatic notes between Washington and Berlin hammered out specific details for the return of each other's citizens. Thousands of American businessmen, diplomats, students, tourists, and prisoners of war were trapped in Nazi Germany, and most, Washington hoped, could be exchanged for internees held in the United States. Government files make it abundantly clear that this exchange program was a major reason (next to the primary need to round up the most dangerous foreign elements in American society) for the entire internment program. Germans and German-Americans were often arrested randomly to be held for later exchange, and for the same reason German diplomatic personnel and their families anywhere in the hemisphere were shipped with all their belongings, voluntarily or not, to the United States. Once in internee camps, they would be held until passage space became available on the famous Swedish humanitarian ship *Drottningholm*. When necessary, additional space was chartered aboard the *Gripsholm*, *Acadia*, the Portuguese ships *Nyassa*, *Serpa Pinto*, or others, with the expenses shared by both countries. Every item was spelled out between the United States and Germany: the tight security and secrecy, the number of suitcases allowed (three), the size of the Swedish or Portuguese flags to be painted along the ships' sides, a long list of items that the enemy diplomats could take (personal and household effects, clothing, art objects, and kitchen utensils), and a list of things they could not (including autos, cameras, typewriters, professional instruments, photographs, and documents or papers of any kind). It was even ordered that personnel to be exchanged could not leave with more than one carton of cigarettes.

For its part, the German government pledged a similar exchange of American citizens in its care, although Berlin often failed to honor its promises. When things went as planned, the ships would meet in Lisbon or Lourenco Marques, Portugal, or Goteborg, Sweden, or Marsailles France, where lists and manifests were checked and double checked; then both groups, each numbering about six to eight hundred people, would change ships as planned.[6] By the end of the war 4,656 Axis aliens from twelve Latin American nations had been sent to the United States for detention, internment, or repatriation. Of this number, 2,242 were exchanged during 1942, and 2,414 remained in custody in the United States for later exchanges.

German diplomatic personnel were repatriated first in three transatlantic exchanges during the spring of 1942. Next, Berlin and Washington turned their attention to a second category: nonofficial German citizens from Latin America. Finally came the third category: German citizens who were enemy aliens in American camps, followed by those Germans who were not in camps and who lived relatively normal lives. Anyone who wished to do so could return to Germany.

On several occasions—perhaps as a show of good faith or possibly to threaten Germany with choking waves of millions of returned citizens—the State Department proposed to repatriate every German alien in the United States if Berlin would do the same with Americans caught in Nazi Germany.

Incoming foreign or domestic internees arriving at American transit and permanent internment camps were asked about their desire to return to Germany or Japan. Most were dazed, hungry, and frustrated at being unable to convince the authorities of their loyalty. Crying children were everywhere. Many longed for the safety and familiarity of their homelands. Conditions at one temporary camp, Dodd Field Internment Camp at Fort Sam Houston, Texas, at San Antonio, were described by one internee to the authorities on 30 April 1942, as follows:

1. Food is very bad, although we see the gradual improvement quite recently.

2. We are living in tents, four to a tent . . . which on rainy days is surely unpleasant. Some of the tents are leaky, and we had to exchange 3 out of 5 so far.
3. We have been issued winter clothing . . . but some of our newcomers did not even receive that.
4. Showers are provided for, but heaters being very inefficient, we lack the [*sic*] hot water nearly all the time. As to the drinking water, there is not even a single faucet near our living quarters.
5. No allowance or spending money has ever been provided by the Army. Some of us are entirely destitute and are depending upon the goodwill of friends for necessary things, like tobacco, etc.[7]

When given the opportunity to return to Germany or Japan, forty-two enemy aliens at Crystal City stepped forward, including dependents (and often American-born wives and children). Twenty-six requested to be returned to Germany, sixteen to Japan, and one to Italy. The Plaschke and Schneider families were among them. So was young Eberhard Fuhr, although he had little familiarity with Germany, and certainly had no intention of fighting in the German Army; he had fallen in love with a fellow internee, Millie, whose family had had enough of the United States. For whatever reason, their requests were shelved until February 1944.

Outside of the camps, the government placed newspaper announcements addressed to the enemy alien population at large: "FREE TRIP TO GERMANY! BE REPATRIATED NOW! AT NO COST! ONE WAY!" The vast majority were not interested. The State Department even contacted random German citizens in the New York area by telegram, informing them of available space aboard the *Drottningholm*. Most answered that "illness" prevented them from leaving at this time or that they were loyal to America and would never consider going back to Germany. Only twenty-two German citizens from the New York area volunteered to leave on a mid-July 1942 voyage. To prove to Germany that the United States had done its best (and that Germany should do the same), the State Department even included the letters of rejection along with the shipboard lists and manifests.[8]

On the West Coast, enemy aliens passed through any one of a number of small transit camps. There was Camp Tuna Canyon, thirty miles from the coast and seventeen miles from Los Angeles, within sight of the Sierras. The camp was a former CCC facility, with wooden barracks divided into two-man rooms, a small hospital, kitchen, showers, and so forth. While the camp was capable of holding 320 people, it was somewhat off the beaten track and seldom contained more than six Germans and thirty Japanese. On rare occasions, the number rose to fifty or seventy-five. Despite the small number of internees, the camp had all-day canteen and a 50-by-50-

foot swimming pool. The few people there kept busy by working in the camp garden or maintaining the property. A doctor visited daily, and on Sundays a Protestant clergyman came by to offer services in English. The tiny population nonetheless boasted two spokesmen, Dr. Heinz Hoffmann and his deputy, Peter Josef Walter. This little group of internees, living comfortably though prisoners nonetheless, was under the control of INS Inspector M. N. Scott.[9]

In the South, internees often went to a small transit camp, far less appealing in climate and living conditions, called the Immigration Detention Station in Algiers, Louisiana. Located directly across the Mississippi River from New Orleans, almost within sight of the French Quarter, Camp Algiers was a three-building former INS quarantine station built to contain about 240 people. The camp population fluctuated as groups of Germans, Japanese, seamen, and imports from Latin America arrived and left for other camps. Among the more interesting internees who passed through Algiers and on to Seagoville was the Fritz von Opel family, related to the von Opels of automotive fame, who had overstayed their vacation in America after Germany declared war on the United States. However many people came and left, several groups seemed to remain in Camp Algiers throughout the war—some defiant and vocal anti-Nazis who had gotten caught up in the internment system, a small number of German Jews from Latin America, and a small, obdurate group of hardened Nazis. There was plenty of cat-calling and taunting from both sides. "Can you imagine?" says Frank Meyer, "kids from both our groups were bused daily to the same schools. All the same we managed to have fun, and I was the class valedictorian of 1945. Man, the Nazi side was furious!" Meyer is today a physician in California.

The camp was under the command of Raymond Bunker. Camp Algiers had several kitchens for family meals, and the single men ate together in a small dining room. There was no canteen. A U.S. Public Health Service doctor made a daily stop at Algiers, and on Sundays a Baptist minister delivered a church service in English. The internees worked on camp maintenance, and the women and families did handicrafts that they were able to sell through stores in nearby New Orleans. Considering the Delta heat and mosquitoes, most internees were grateful to be transferred to Seagoville or Crystal City as new arrivals appeared. Swiss inspection teams found nothing particularly out of order, but they were unimpressed with the run-down conditions.[10]

The most impressive camp was in Texas.

CHAPTER EIGHT

CAMP CRYSTAL CITY, TEXAS

The Crystal City, Texas, camp for families was the largest and probably the most interesting internment facility. Crystal City was a scruffy little town created at the turn of the century by wealthy Mexican-Americans and Anglos to hold seasonal Mexican farm laborers for use on surrounding vast vegetable farms. Located about a hundred miles from the Mexican border, forty miles from the isolated town of Uvalde, Texas, and several hundred miles from San Antonio, the Crystal City migratory labor camp was taken over by the Farm Security Administration during the 1930s and by the Immigration and Naturalization Service in December 1942. At the time, the camp was already quite large: forty-one three-room cottages, several service buildings, and one hundred and eighteen one-room "Victory Huts." The temperature hovered around 120 degrees Fahrenheit from June through September, and the mosquitoes were even worse than the omnipresent scorpions. Despite these hardships, Crystal City was considered by most internees to be the most tolerable camp in the system, largely because men who found themselves shipped there could bring their families as "voluntary internees." Although many of the adult males at Crystal City were foreign-born, generally German and Japanese, "practically all the children and many women" internees, the government publicly acknowledged, were American-born and raised.[1] The camp was capable of holding in excess of 3,500 people. In the middle of nearby Uvalde was a six-foot statue of Popeye—which still stands today—a reminder that Crystal City sits in the middle of the winter garden area of Texas, and bills itself "the Spinach Capital of the World."

Alfred Plaschke arrived by Greyhound bus with his parents after almost a year at Seagoville (see chapter four). He recalled the shock of seeing the camp for the first time. "We thought we'd been brought to the end of the world, especially after beautiful Seagoville, with its brick houses, green grass, and paved streets. Suddenly, we saw nothing but dry, hot, flat desert, with rows and rows of plasterboard and tarpaper shacks, dirt streets, and guard towers at each corner of the fence. The desert mesquite and cactus came right up to the edge of the fence. Did I mention 'hot'?"

The INS originally planned to house West Coast Japanese at Crystal City, but quickly found itself warehousing an additional 2,100 Japanese nationals from Latin America, mostly from Peru, and German and Italian enemy alien families as well.

German internees were the first to arrive: thirty-five German families, totaling 130 internees, arrived from Ellis Island and Camp Forrest, Tennessee, on 12 December 1942. The flow continued for weeks. The new arrivals found no provisions for themselves and their families, and, in fact, were pressed into service to help build the camp they were to occupy. There was plenty of understandable grumbling, especially when some of the internee-workers were ordered to help build similar structures at Seagoville. On one occasion their anger erupted into a thirty-day work strike. As a rule, German internees came from nearby Camp Kenedy and Seagoville, Texas; Stringtown, Oklahoma; and Ellis Island; and the Japanese groups generally arrived from Camp Livingston, Louisiana, and Lordsburg, New Mexico.

When finished and occupied, Crystal City teemed with life. It was a city, with arrivals and departures, births and deaths. On average, the population at Crystal City hovered around 2,800 internees and reached a peak of 3,374 in December 1944, which included 2,371 Japanese, 997 Germans, and six Italians. From its inception through 30 June 1945, there were 155 births (all were American citizens), 138 internees released or paroled, and seventy-three transferred to other facilities. In addition, 954 Germans were repatriated to Germany, and on 3 December 1945 1,200 Japanese were repatriated to Japan. Only seventeen from both groups died—all from natural causes, except for three accidents: two Japanese girls who drowned in the pool (the mother of one of the girls, ten-year-old Sachiko Tanabe, was so distraught that she attempted suicide with sleeping pills), and a German boy who was crushed by a truck.

By 1 July 1943, the camp had expanded substantially and now consisted of 290 acres, 694 buildings, 519 of which were added after 1942, and an authorized strength of 161 administrators, INS guards, supply clerks, medical personnel, maintenance crews, and educators. By the end of the war the camp employed some two hundred additional craftsmen and laborers. Like most of the other internment camps, administration was carried out through seven divisions: headquarters; supply; internal security; internal relations; maintenance, construction and repair; education; and medical. Joseph O'Rourke, a popular border patrolman from Camp Seagoville, commanded Crystal City Internment Camp for much of the war. Unlike a number of small camps that were more easily hidden from the public eye, the local Crystal City newspaper reported on the camp from time to time.[2]

As a rule, the majority of the camp's internees were Japanese from the West Coast or South America and about eight hundred Germans from places as far as Bolivia, Costa Rica, Guatemala, Nicaragua, Peru, and the Dominican Republic. Inexplicably, the camp also contained three hundred Indonesian sailors seized from a Dutch ship that had landed in New York. Camp officials segregated these sailors from the remainder of the camp. They were interned at Crystal City for "protective custody" for the duration of the war. The adult Germans and Japanese did not often interact, except at work in the hospital or in the bakery. The children, on the other hand, played and swam together, built kites, and congregated together in school functions. As various exchanges took place during the war, the number of internees changed. In the summer of 1945, there were 2,548 Japanese, 756 Germans, and twelve Italians. By the end of 1946 all Japanese internees were released. Next released were the few Italians who had been adjudged especially dangerous and held in camps. Only the Germans remained behind barbed wire.

The camp offered six different types and sizes of family dwellings, from single rooms for childless adults, to three-room cottages, containing 360 square feet, a few with indoor baths and toilets, for larger families. While families often had individual cottages, privacy was at a premium. Most people added porches and gardens themselves, often using stolen lumber. A number had cats, dogs, or locally captured pets. Meals were eaten family-style at home or cafeteria-style at a common mess hall. Some tarpaper dwellings came equipped with an icebox, cooking utensils, bedding, and furniture supplied by the government. Most of the vegetables and meat consumed by the internees came from the farm located outside the camp, maintained by aliens under the guidance of a local Texas rancher. The farm's cows provided the dairy products, and teams of internees took turns delivering the 2,500 quarts of milk required daily by the 1,600 children; other internees delivered the precious daily ration of blocks of ice for each house—an item more valuable than gold when the temperature hit 120 degrees Fahrenheit in the summer.

Up to sixty internees a day (out of a population of, say, 3,000) were treated at the eighty-bed camp clinic, usually for imaginary or camp-related problems. Five doctors, including two Japanese women, were on duty or on call; they delivered some 155 babies during the course of the war. In fact, according to a Justice Department memo, Crystal City had "the lowest incidence of disease anywhere in the United States."[3]

The camp issued plastic token money, much like casino chips, to the internees to buy food and clothing. Each adult over fourteen years of age received $5.25 a month, children from six to thirteen received $4.00, two- to five-year olds got $2.25, and youngsters from six months to two years received $1.25 monthly. The Plaschke family, for example, with two parents and two boys under fourteen years old, received a total of $18.50 per month in plastic tokens. Moreover, after April 1943, the internees at Crystal City, as elsewhere, were offered the opportunity to work for an additional eighty cents per day. Each ethnic group operated its own canteen store— the German General Store and the Japanese Union Store—which began with such necessities as soap, shoestrings, tennis shoes, handkerchiefs, candy, cigars, canned goods, soft drinks, and beer. Within a short time, the stores handled thousands of different commodities, and long rows of homemade grocery carts were parked in front of both stores every morning. The two prison stores earned an astonishing combined gross sales of $200,000 yearly.

The government saw to their spiritual needs. Every courtesy extended to the internees, the government reasoned, might be reciprocated to the unknown number of American citizens who were held in Nazi jails and concentration camps. Moreover, if these internees were ever to be purged of their fascist sympathies, religion might be the best available replacement. Regular Catholic Mass was conducted every few days in German by a local priest named Peter Johannes Weber, and Lutheran Pastor Karl Heuer drove in from San Antonio once a month—although only a small percent of the internees attended either service. To provide entertainment, however meager, there were periodic movies (often the same ones), and like every camp, Crystal City maintained a small library of books donated by the German Red Cross, War Prisoners Aid of the YMCA, and private sources from relatives or local townspeople.

The camp received a steady stream of official visitors. Nearly every month, there would be another junket from Washington to "size up the situation" at Crystal City. For example, on 29 April 1943, an intelligence officer (Lieutenant J. D. Harris) from the Eighth Service Command in San Antonio, arrived to discuss undisclosed confidential matters with INS Commander O'Rourke. On 13 May 1943, it was Mr. Bell of the Alien Enemy Control Unit in Washington. Then, on 16 August 1943, a representative of the Bureau of the Budget, Robert E. Wood, bustled in on a fact-finding tour. INS Commissioner Harrison and assistant Evelyn Hersey included Crystal City on their sixteen-camp whirlwind tour between 26 October and 19 December 1943. The State Department's Mr. Benninghoff, together with a representative from the Spanish Embassy, made a surprise visit in mid-December 1943, to assess conditions of the Japanese internees. Six weeks later, the Japanese internees were visited by the director of the National Japanese American Student Relocation Council. Even the supersecret Office of Strategic Services (OSS) made an appearance at Crystal City, when F. C. Kempner and R. L. Salzman quietly arrived to interview certain unnamed internees. When the niece of the king of Sweden, Mrs. Elsa Bernadotte Cedargren, visited Crystal City on behalf of the International YMCA on 17 February 1944, poor O'Rourke must have wondered when he was supposed to find time to run his camp.

Everyone was encouraged—required in some camps—to work. Crystal City offered a number of choices. The Germans usually refused to farm, considering "stoop labor" beneath them. The slack was taken up by the Japanese, many of whom had been truck farmers in California. Japanese internees also worked in the camp sewing program, making sheets, pillows, even hospital nurses' uniforms for use in the clinic. A small tailor shop was run by Japanese from Peru. The German men were usually found in the machine shop, making camp furniture, teaching metal and woodworking to the older boys, or working in the motor pool. Whatever the job, the pay was the same, ten cents an hour. German women generally declined to work outside of the home. Mail service was unregulated, but strictly censored for anti-American remarks, escape plans, or war information. The German internees even maintained a volunteer fire department. In many ways, camp life mirrored normal society. There is no record of any escapes from the camp during the entire war. ("Where would we have gone?" Plaschke asks.)

On 25 February 1945, Anna Flechsel wrote the following letter to her sister Mathilda in Larchmont, New York:

> If you think that treatment and food are bad here then you are mistaken. This is not New York, but Texas. Here is quite another kind of people. The whole staff from top to bottom is always friendly. I have often thought it would not be bad to stay in Texas for good. . . . The people here are not at all like there. And our food is good and there is plenty of everything. Rather two years here than half a year at Ellis Island.[4]

At the beginning, Crystal City, unlike most camps, did not permit radios or newspapers. Someone at INS headquarters, the rumor went, feared that the inmates might contact nameless saboteurs in nearby Mexico. It was not an entirely groundless fear, considering Mexico's recent anti-Semitism and Nazi influence. Whatever the reason, the internees were forced to rely heavily on themselves for entertainment. They formed a band, choir, and a sophisticated theatrical group. There were concerts and plays, and, for the Germans, evenings in the "Vaterland Cafe" playing cards, singing, or drinking beer. Dances were held regularly for young people and schoolchildren in order to simulate a normal social life. For the more athletic, there were sports of every variety, including intermural baseball and basketball games between the Germans and Japanese.

German camp news appeared in a five to six-page weekly mimeographed newsletter called *Das Lager* (*The Camp*) that kept the population (and the authorities) informed of all goings-on. *Das Lager* contained camp schedules, soccer scores, poems, and occasional pleas to parents to control their noisy youngsters in the movie auditorium or keep them from running through the pretty Japanese garden in front of the hospital building. The newsletter was filled with chatty camp news, such as camp officer O'Rourke's complaint (in the 29 January 1944 issue) about people cheating on their hourly wage cards; in another issue (15 January 1944), the camp spokesman, Heinrich Johann Hasenburger, demanded a referendum on his leadership—everyone was urged to vote their support for him.

Das Lager, like most camp newspapers, often contained cryptic messages and mysterious combinations of numbers purported to be soccer scores. An example of such a suspicious article appeared in the 22 July 1944 issue. After denouncing rumormongers for whatever reason, the article informed the camp population that a meeting of "the informal council" had considered "the denunciations" and found "the charge" to be groundless. There is no way to determine either the recipients of the messages or their meaning. One can only wonder.

Since most men who were arrested brought their families along, a federal school was established for the more than three hundred school-age youngsters.[5] The Crystal City school began with significant problems: there were no school activities or traditions, past grades, or transfer records. Moreover, the students resented being there. They were strangers to their teachers and to one another. Yet within a very short time, due largely to dedicated teachers from local Texas communities and from within the camp, and a government-approved principal named Hugh Parks Tate, the Crystal City Federal High School soon boasted an admirable curriculum—impressive enough to satisfy the visiting accreditation teams of the Texas Education Agency. In addition to the usual reading, writing, and arithmetic, students learned history, zoology, English, botany, and Spanish. Physics and chemistry were not offered, however, due to budgetary restrictions. They also did lots of singing and enjoyed plenty of athletics. The school had a student council, drum-and-bugle corps, pep squad, honor society, an annual yearbook humorously called "The Roundup," and even a senior prom. A school football, baseball, or basketball game, made up of two Federal High School teams, since there were no visiting high schools, nonetheless drew a thousand spectators and was complete with hot dog vendors and a half-time pep rally. Participants still recall the March 1945 Ping-Pong tournament when the Japanese beat the Germans, or the miraculous half-court shot which saw the *Northstars* win over the *Saints*, 27-25. The biggest baseball game of the 1944 season took place in November, pitting *The Teachers* against *The Girls*—resulting in a humiliating 14–6 defeat for *The Teachers*.

The enrollment during the term 1944–1945 was 144 in elementary school and 186 in high school, with more Japanese students than Germans. Forty youngsters graduated from elementary school and sixty-six from high school during the two terms 1943–1944 and 1944–1945.

After school, both the German and Japanese communities were allowed to maintain additional classes to educate their children in their native language about national customs and politics. Herr Kriechbaum, a German from Costa Rica, administered the German school. Nostalgic current memories clash with the official records, which insist the these classes were occasionally taught by rabid nationalists who imbued Nazism or Japanese politics into their students in the face of the unaware American authorities.

The kids spent the hot Texas afternoons exploring the camp, cavorting in the large water reservoir that the sympathetic camp commander converted into a swimming pool, and playing on the tennis courts, baseball diamonds, and volleyball courts that filled vacant lots all over camp. There was even a Boy Scout troop. The older kids seemed to get into mischief. Art Jacobs, a youngster at the time, remembered that some of the seventeen-year-olds who worked in the photographic lab used to switch padlocks on the door. At closing time the official unknowingly closed up with the internees' lock, allowing the boys to enter the building at night to pilfer materials. On the way out, the internees replaced the padlock with the original one. The next morning the official would unlock the padlock, not knowing the difference between the locks, but always wondering how the material was being used so quickly. The Japanese kids were less troublesome, although they believed that the German kids were better treated by the authorities. The children who grew up in Crystal City agree that they remember no incidents of friction between the German and Japanese kids. None. "The only times we clashed was in sports," remembers Gerd Erich Schneider, whose father was arrested in Houston with Plaschke and Koetter. "Football—us against the Japanese kids—was the only real conflict. If the score was going against us, we brought out the Fuhr boys. Man, they were big!"[6]

Typical of the era, most of the boys took on nicknames such as "Fang" Fehrenbach, "Romeo" Bosmann, "Porky" Akiyama, and "Hollywood" Sawamura. "Crystal City had a lively, almost cheerful atmosphere," said Jerre Mangione, special INS camp inspector for the Justice Department. "Except for the barbed-wire fence around it and the absence of passenger vehicles, it resembled a thriving southwestern town, complete with a school, hospital, a bustling community center, a bakery, and other stores. . . . From the distance, in the black of night, the flood-lit compound looked not like a prison, but like a magical city. . . . The illuminated camp could be seen from the Mexican border."[7]

Magical or not, Camp Crystal City is today remembered with fondness only by its children. It was the last of the Immigration Service camps to close down (other than Ellis Island), holding stray Latin Americans, repatriates, and others whose cases were pending in the courts, until 27 February 1948, two and a half years after the end of the war. "Looking back," says Plaschke, "it seems only us kids had any fun there; for us, it seemed like a perfectly average childhood. We weren't aware of the political tension and shenanigans in the grown-up world."

More than one participant disagrees with this idyllic picture of a child's life in Camp Crystal City. Young Othilia (Tillie) Reseneder, whose father Jacob was arrested in February 1942 (see chapter four), hated every minute of it. "My sister and I lived in a one-room hut, which had room for just a bed, one dresser, and a chair. My mother and father lived in another one-room hut. Before I went to bed at night, I would sprinkle my bed with water because it was so hot." She hated being forced to line up three times a day to counted, she says. "Whistles blew, and no matter where in the camp you were, you had to run back to your hut and stand out in front of it and be counted." Tillie remembers that armed guards were omnipresent. "Once I sprained my ankle, and they took me to San Antonio to get it x-rayed. Here I was, eleven years old, walking down the streets of San Antonio with two big guards with guns. I was very embarrassed."[8]

The Jacobs family in the Bronx, N.Y., 1939. *Courtesy of Arthur Jacobs.*

May Day celebration at Camp Crystal City, Texas.

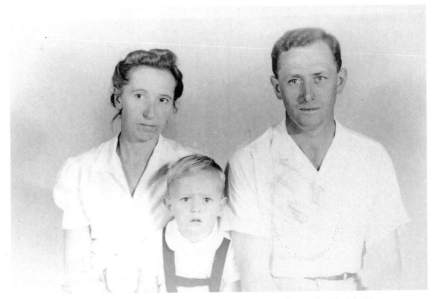

FBI photo of the Kruse family at Crystal City Internment Camp in Uvalde, Texas.

In front of the hospital in Seagoville, Texas, 1942.

The view of house six and house four as seen from the Industry Building, Seagoville, Texas.

A German social hall in Crystal City. Note the musicians consist of one Japanese girl, one German girl, and one German man. *Courtesy of Arthur Jacobs.*

The men of the 1945 Crystal City Internment Camp Band. *Courtesy of Arthur Jacobs.*

The student body and faculty of the German school at Internment Camp in 1945. *Courtesy of Arthur Jacobs.*

An aerial view of the Crystal City Internment Camp in Uvalde, Texas, 1944–45. *Courtesy of Arthur Jacobs.*

The arrival of German internees at Camp Kenedy in Texas.

The Swedish humanitarian ship, SS Gripsholm. It was used for various transports throughout the world including the return of enemy aliens back to Europe.

New arrivals at Enemy Alien Camp.

Departing German detainees giving the Hitler greeting to accompanying
German POW's.

A group of Fort Lincoln Players during New Year's Even, 1941 in Bismarck, North
Dakota. Martin G. Dudel (far right, back row) was an internee. *Courtesy of Deborah Ann
Lincoln.*

Handing out and
receiving food.
*Courtesy of Deborah
Ann Lincoln.*

The barracks in winter. *Courtesy of Deborah Ann Lincoln.*

CHAPTER NINE

NAZIS AND TROUBLEMAKERS IN THE INTERNEE CAMPS

Life in the camps clearly had a darker side. At Crystal City, most issues of *Das Lager* contained a streak of pro-German propaganda, and occasionally, anti-Semitic jokes. The newspapers at the other camps, such as *The Latrine*, from Camp Forrest, Tennessee, and the *Bismarck Echo*, from Fort Lincoln, North Dakota, were largely the same: camp.news, upcoming programs, and occasional Nazi propaganda. Camp Forrest's *The Latrine* (the only camp newspaper written in English rather than German), had a more comic masthead, but contained occasional propaganda and an anti-Semitic joke or two (i.e., issues of 17 April 1943 and 1 May 1943).[1] Certain copies at Crystal City contained particularly blatant material, especially those published during the reigns of Kurt Hasselhorst as the editor of *Das Lager* and Heinrich Johann Hasenburger as the spokesman for the Germans at Crystal City. Both were strident Nazis, and a number of issues contained patriotic drawings, slogans, and a large dollop of support for the Fatherland. The jargon was reminiscent of the National Socialists, and the masthead drawings, which changed every issue, were often military and political in style. Blurbs about conditions in Germany were one-sided, and a 1943 Christmas visit by the camp children to the German prisoner-of-war camp in Huntsville was trumpeted for two issues. Political holidays like Hitler's birthday on 20 April were celebrated with speeches in the camp auditorium, community games, and, at evening time, a songfest around a bonfire. Judging by the newspapers, there is little question that there was a strong Nazi undercurrent at Crystal City as there was at most of the other internment camps. At the same time, it must be remembered that the newspapers did not necessarily reflect the attitudes of the internees which, in some cases, were democratic and loyally American despite their bewilderment at being incarcerated. The INS *Final Report* about Camp Crystal City didn't mince any words: "Pro-enemy sentiment is in the majority, and under this daily influence, typical American boys and girls have been changed in heart, attitude, and behavior." However, surviving participants today dismiss any such influence on their lives.

The reasons for rising Nazism in the internment camps are unique to the interned enemy alien experience. First, these people were usually committed nationalists when they arrived. Most had deep pride in their German roots. The FBI may have too often confused Nazism with the patriotic feelings that many immigrants retained for their homelands, but the nationalist fervor for Germany was genuine enough. The fear and anxiety arising from their arrest in the middle of the night, chaotic decisions, followed by banishment to a distant internment camp was often enough to push German patriotism to support for the Nazis. Another reason was the working-class roots of the internees; their traditional hopes for the future had long been the very fertile soil for national socialism. The average age of the men in the camps was thirty-nine—the age when men had careers and businesses or artistic skills; instead, they were sitting in camps watching everything disintegrate. Their anger might well direct them to Adolf Hitler. They were also being hardened by the events. Nazism, which might have seemed absurd in their living rooms before their internment, now seemed reasonable when fueled by bitterness.

Not only were they now living behind barbed wire, but the German internees found themselves at a cultural disadvantage. Unlike their Japanese fellow inmates, the Germans had never been in the minority before and found it difficult to relax. After all, Americans of German ancestry make up a huge percentage of the population. German words pepper the English language, and their influence is evident in every facet of American life. In contrast, at Crystal City and Seagoville, they were a small group in a largely Oriental world. Nor had the German internees any experience in community self-government, something that every Japanese community took for granted. The Germans in America may have spent their evenings or weekends at local cultural centers or beer halls, dancing, singing, and listening to occasional political speeches and travelogues. But there was no attempt to govern the members of the community, something that Germans in America generally resisted in any case. In fact, membership in German-American societies had declined steadily in the late 1930s and 1940s, especially as members found that the relationship was largely one-sided: Germans were asked to support the organizations, but the organizations were not there when the Germans needed help. Indeed, many internees grew to resent their local and regional German-American societies (even more than they resented the American government). They felt that they had been victimized by groups that wanted their support and membership dues but provided little help when the Feds singled them out. Some wondered if they hadn't been thrown to the wolves by real Nazis in their midst to distract the authorities. This dislike for their German-American societies became clear upon their release after the war: few ever returned to watch the travelogues or attend oom-pah-pah evenings at the community beer halls. In contrast, the Japanese had a different view of their community. It was their source of cultural nourishment as well a safe haven in an otherwise unfriendly country. They brought their community structures with them from Japan. Thus, Japanese internees, while no less angry or frightened than their German fellow internees, had somewhere to turn, and their loyalty continued unbroken after the war was over. Overall, the Germans were more rootless, and more vulnerable to bad leadership. Due to these many pressures and frustrations, German internees showed a marked shift toward Nazism as the war progressed.

As far as camp control was concerned, the American authorities actually could do little. The camp may have been under American authority, but it was run by the spokesmen who were elected by each of the several nationalities in the camp. Often, they were aggressive and bad-tempered types, trying to impress the others by irritating the Americans with endless complaints, requests, and protests. Sometimes the internees couldn't agree on a single spokesman, and on one occasion poor Commander O'Rourke had to contend with two or even three. The first two groups of German internees arrived from Ellis Island and Camp Forrest, Tennessee, in December 1942, and each had its own spokesman. A third group of arrivals from Camp Forrest brought yet another. None of the three would yield. An election was held to settle the controversy, but it produced Hasenburger, so difficult and pro-Nazi that he was ultimately given seventy-two hours' notice and transferred with his family to the INS detention center at Algiers, Louisiana. The last two spokesmen, Baron Georg von Falkenstein, a recent arrival from the detention camp in Algiers, Louisiana, and Willy Boeck, were more cooperative with authorities.

But there were troublemakers aplenty. Usually they were part of the Nazi clique, but problems also arose from the numerous German nationalists, opportunists, followers, and some innocent people who were very angry at their treatment by the American government; for many, it had been their government as well, and it had turned on them. Some people were claustrophic and developed "barbed wire fever." Whatever the origins, the camp chief internal security officer, E. D. McAlexander, chief liaison officer, Larry Elwood, and chief surveillance officer, Gerald P. David, had their hands full. Hardly any week went by in which the Germans were not up to something. Choosing, at random, the month of March 1943, there was a spate of thefts and vandalism. The camp authorities spent much of their time tracking down children who damaged fourteen bags of concrete by cutting them open with shovels (22 March); other children who sneaked into the prohibited east area and opened the reservoir valve to flood the fields (20 March); and still others who threw refuse into the canal (18 March). On 24 March, a group of children were chased out of a construction site and later proved to have broken into the carpenters' tool boxes and carried off tools. Then there was construction material missing. Lumber, Sheetrock, and screening were in very short supply at Crystal City, and it wasn't long before the internees were stealing from the camp construction projects and eventually from one another. Warnings were posted everywhere, with few results. Finally, the guards conducted mid-morning raids. On 10 June 1943, Guard Darrel Canion, Matron Ruth Pitts, and Construction Superintendent John Keller went to Triplex 24-A, where they found Karl Steimle hiding two pieces of Sheetrock, twelve inches wide and eight feet long. Next, they raided Triplex 15-C where Rudolf Plaschke was found hiding ten pieces of eight-foot lengths of lumber. No one could explain how the materials had come to be there.

Social problems marred camp life as well. One morning in March 1943, Mrs. Germer was shopping in the German general store when she spied three cans of olive oil hidden under the counter. She became crazed, accusing the clerk of putting all the good stuff away for himself and of creating a black market. According to the complaint filed against her by the store manager, she called him "a dirty dog." That did it! The manager took the matter to the German Council, which unanimously decided that the store should be off limits to Mrs. Germer until further notice and that Mr. Germer should do the shopping. Mr. Germer, however, agreed with his wife, and turned in his tokens and ration book and pledged never to shop in the general store again. After three weeks, the Germers reconciled with the community, although they never forgave the store manager for hoarding olive oil.[2]

Another situation involved the German internees as a group, questioning the camp authorities. On 9 April 1943, Mr. N. D. Collaer, who ran Crystal City Camp prior to O'Rourke's arrival, had another of many tedious and frustrating meetings with Karl Kolb, perhaps the most nazified of the lot. This time Collaer had called the meeting. He heard that there had been a mass resignation of members from the Council of German Internees the night before and, fearing internal camp unrest, wanted to learn the facts from Kolb, the council leader. His concern was not idle. Resignations from the chief carpenter, the assistant head of the internee education division, the internee in charge of billeting and employment, and another in charge of maintenance were potentially serious events. "What happened last night, Herr Kolb?" Collaer asked. For eight full pages of the stenographic record, Kolb danced around the questions. Was he being questioned as the spokesman of the German internees or as an ordinary internee? How could he speak as the spokesman when there was clearly an ordinary internee inside that person? And vice versa. Mr. Collaer was firm. "Certain it is," the American assured Kolb, "that I shall not permit you to dictate the terms under which the officials of this facility conduct investigations!" Twelve pages of the transcript later, Kolb was declared "uncooperative," escorted to the custody of the chief surveillance officer, and was not allowed to communicate with anyone for the remainder of the day. There was little else the authorities could do to punish civilian internees. The resignations were never explained, but nor were they troublesome to the authorities.

Within days, the Germans were at it again. A delegation from the Counsel of German Internees protested that the American staff should not appoint the internees to camp jobs, but should give the responsibility to the council, which knew the internees best. Next complaint from the Germans: Ordinary internees should not have free access to visit the commandant; appointments should be made by the internees through the council. On 21 April, following an evening of celebration on Hitler's birthday, complete with a swastika flag, a number of the German internees felt brave enough to demand the removal of the two American flags in the camp, one of which hung on the wall of the recreation hall and the other on a flagpole in the middle of the camp. A formal letter was handed to Collaer, signed by five German Council members. "We believe that the flag of the Detaining Power does not belong inside of an enemy alien internment camp, and the German internees of this camp are unanimously against keeping the flag in its present place within the enclosure of this camp." The complaint closed by saying that "As this matter has been brought to your attention on previous occasions . . . we kindly beg you to take the necessary step so that this unpleasant question will not have to be brought forth again, and also that new groups coming here will not have to raise this issue any more."[3] A second complaint to Mr. Collaer concerned their own German flag. It seems that after their celebration on the twentieth, they left the swastika flag displayed in a prominent place in the recreation hall, and three unidentified guards, "during the check period on the evening of said date, removed the swastika and destroyed it."

After discussing the matter with his superior, the INS commissioner in Philadelphia, the firm and courteous Collaer offered the following suggestions. First, the guards should not be punished. "These men are not disciplined as are our career employees. Most of them are rugged individualists, many of whom have held public office and are somewhat inclined to feel that their views regarding the way the job should be handled are entitled to consideration." Second, "I shall bend every effort to prevent misunderstandings among the level-headed people of this community, but there are many whom it will not be possible to reach." Third, "it will probably be a week or two before it will be possible to effect the removal of the [American] flag and flagpole." And finally, during that time, "it would be well for the Central Office to formally announce the extent to which emblems having a political significance may be displayed in meeting places at these facilities and the extent to which patriotic celebrations should be permitted."[4]

The American flag was moved outside of the camp gate to the flagpole in front of the administration building, and nothing more was heard about it. More than likely, there was a fifth point as well, an unspoken one: "I request a transfer from this madness." N. D. Collaer left soon afterward and was replaced by the more indulgent O'Rourke. Collaer was promoted to acting assistant commissioner for alien control, and stationed at the INS headquarters in Philadelphia.

As the months behind barbed wire passed, tension among the internees intensified dramatically, as did the strain between the American authorities and their increasingly hostile prisoners. Tempers flared regularly in the Vaterland Cafe, and drunkenness and fights were almost commonplace. By Christmas 1943, charges reached INS headquarters in Philadelphia that a violent Nazi subgroup had become dangerously powerful at Crystal City. An organized group of club-wielding hoodlums roamed the camp, perhaps on orders from Bund leader Fritz Kuhn, and O'Rourke was unable to bring them under control. There were reports of unauthorized innumerable distilleries, one of which actually blew up in early December (O'Rourke apparently accepted their explanation that they were making marmalade). A number of German internees protested that spokesman Hasenburger had received only 149 votes out of 631 but had nevertheless been given the position and created a virtual dictatorship over the group. Several charges were made to the Swiss inspectors that on Hasenburger's orders, entire families were periodically "excluded from the community" for unpopular opinions, refusal to obey orders, or refusing repatriation if offered the opportunity. Such community punishment was silent but dramatic. The family would receive no food at the general store, the butcher shop, or the mess hall; they could not use the laundry or be waited on in the barbershop, and they could not attend any meeting or festivity. When a Mr. Gebhard, for whatever reason, refused to do camp duty, the spokesman ordered the entire family "excluded." After four days of starvation, the family was hospitalized by camp authorities. Other potential dissenters in the population got the message.[5] To the relief of the American authorities, Hasenburger requested repatriation with the first group in February 1944.

Even with his departure, however, the small number of troublemakers continued to disrupt life in Crystal City. In 1944 the 1 May celebration erupted into fistfights, and two men's faces were injured when they were struck with heavy beer steins. A drunken internee, George Kreuzer, pulled a twelve-inch kitchen knife but was calmed by the new spokesman, Georg von Falkenstein. The following week brought another problem: the German Council voted to "exclude" certain families, over the objection of the moderate von Falkenstein. Then came the theft of a two-pound can of coffee from a storehouse that triggered a camp-wide investigation. In August 1944, a drunken George Kreuzer threatened to throw hydrochloric acid in the face of Mrs. Anna Vogl if she ever dared to walk by his bungalow again. According to spokesman von Falkenstein's report against Kreuzer, he also "attempted slander of the lowest kind against Mrs. Vogl, who has always conducted herself orderly and properly in the camp." Perhaps von Falkenstein was too moderate for the tension-ridden camp because on 17 September, 496 German internees gathered in the auditorium and by a bare 51 percent majority, elected a new spokesman, Willy Boeck. The problems, however, didn't cease. There were more drunken brawls involving Kreuzer and his drinking buddies, Karl Lechner and Joseph Schurwerk, rocks thrown through windows, threats against von Falkenstein, and an attempt by the three to overturn a housetrailer, together with its sleeping inhabitants. By the end of the year, 1944, the camp guards were being called every few days to break up shoving matches, drunkenness, and threats, real and imagined. One morning, the guards received a call from the clothing store to remove internee Kurt Plath, who had angrily pushed his way into the tiny store before it was his turn to enter. He claimed he had been waiting outside since 6:30 A.M., and as the door was about to open at 8:30 A.M., a gaggle of ladies arrived and pushed in front of him. He was only trying to be first in line. The year closed on a report of a "flasher" who jumped in front of Mr. and Mrs. Louis Karch as they walked home after attending a camp movie. According to the report, "On the way home we were approached by a young man of the Japanese race—his clothing was disarranged, and his sex organ was exposed. We observed this man running toward the Japanese section. My wife is certain as to the race of this man, but would be unable to identify him with any degree of accuracy."[6] No line-up was planned. So closed 1944.

One can only imagine what must have gone through O'Rourke's mind when he received a letter, on 19 January 1945 from INS headquarters suggesting a propaganda film about the wonders of Crystal City. "I believe that we can safely say that Crystal City is considered to be one of the best, if not the best, internment camp ever operated by any country and, because of the children of various races, there is a wealth of excellent pictorial material available there." Among the suggestions for shots the film might include were: the signpost at the entrance of the outside area and one of the flag flying over the camp; the watchtower, mounted guards and guards in automobiles patrolling the fence, the sequence ending with a view of the front gate with guards examining cars entering or leaving the area; new internees arriving by bus, of the welcome given to them by other internees, perhaps with views of camp residents lined up at the fence to greet them, of the band playing as the internees enter the community house to be checked in; the houses and streets within the area, with special emphasis on flower and vegetable gardens around some of the houses; the canteen and the grocery store showing customers purchasing food and supplies; followed by shots of a housewife preparing the food in her kitchen and of the family gathered around a table for their meal; internees at play, listening to their orchestras, watching Punch and Judy shows, attending motion picture shows, playing tennis, soccer, and basketball; a German classroom showing students standing stiffly next to their chairs until their teacher has entered and given them permission to be seated; German students doing gymnastics under the supervision of one of their teachers; the glee club performing and the German adult-education program in action; the hospital, with internees receiving dental treatment, clinical treatment, children's and infant's wards, and nurses looking after a newborn infant or child; and a final view of Old Glory being raised to the top of the flagpole.[7]

The film in fact was made. In 1945 the INS produced *Alien Enemy Detention Facility*, an engaging twenty-one-minute movie, in black and white, which displayed the best sides of the Crystal City experience. The film is dramatically narrated and filled with the patriotic images of the day. It is available in the National Archives Motion Picture Division under the file number 85.0001.

In sharp contrast to Crystal City, Fort Lincoln, North Dakota, was a "rough" camp. The fort's facilities were long outdated, having been commissioned at the turn of the century. The camp was isolated. The winter weather was intolerable. The German seamen lived in a ten-acre compound within a fifty-acre camp. A ten-foot cyclone fence surrounded the entire camp, topped by barbed wire, which formed the first barrier against escape. To prevent tunneling the fence continued three feet into the ground. A white stripe several feet within the barbed wire fence marked the ominously named "kill zone," within which the guards were allowed to shoot at anyone who approached the fence with the intention of escaping. In addition, there were guard towers, floodlights, tracking dogs, two-way radios, and a system of super-sensitive microphones attached to the fences to detect the tiniest tampering.

The compound occupied by the Axis seamen was a self-contained little village. There was a bakery, a garage, machine shop, butcher shop, school, radio-repair shop, woodworking shop, hospital, tailor shop, shoe-repair shop—all operated by the detainees.

Unlike the other camps, Fort Lincoln was supposed to be cloaked in secrecy, although the reason for this is unclear. Perhaps due to an overzealous INS commander, the camp tried to be very hush-hush. The citizens of local Bismarck cooperated, although many other internment camps were openly discussed in their nearby towns, as sources of revenue or as evidence that internal enemies really existed. As the war progressed, however, Bismarck's curiosity triumphed over its paranoia, and rumors and gossip about the camp abounded. Articles appeared in the *Bismarck Tribune*, albeit infrequently, about goings-on out at the camp: new buildings, changes in the camp routine, daily menu, even the number of loaves of pumpernickel bread baked daily. In fact, knowledge of the camp was commonplace and both the town and the camp benefitted from the employment of each others' carpenters, plumbers, and mechanics. On the other hand, the presence of Japanese internees, whether from Peru or California, was another matter, and local ire against them was public and sometimes explosive, resulting in occasional isolated cases of vigilantism. Although a 1946 article of internee life by the *Bismarck Tribune* boasted that "the very existence of the camp was a top secret and the voluntary censorship code prohibited reference to it, directly or indirectly," such does not appear to be the case. On only one point were the locals apparently unaware: "the existence in the camp of a large number of Germans from Latin America was unknown to but a few residents of Bismarck."[8]

The German merchant seamen at Fort Lincoln (and the two camps for seamen at Stanton and Missoula) were different from internees at the other camps. Many of the early German internees (called detainees before Pearl Harbor) had been employees of U.S. oil companies like Standard Oil. While German U-boats prowled the Atlantic in 1941, sinking thousands of tons of American and British shipping, employees were laid off to be re-hired when the seas became safer. Other German merchant seamen arrived in New York when their ships were chased into U.S. harbors by the British navy. Most lived comfortably in New York for eighteen months, enjoying the safety and temptations of the big city. A number even expressed a desire to become American citizens. However, once America went to war in December 1941, they all became enemy aliens and were interned without hearings or judicial recourse. They were more frustrated than embittered.

Fort Lincoln was different for other reasons as well. Since the detainees/internees were seamen rather than civilians, their camp's routine followed naval habits and traditions. The first tradition of the navy—indeed, of most military institutions—is that officers live better than enlisted men. The same was true at Fort Abraham Lincoln. The men lived in prefab CCC-type barracks with gas heat, a latrine and washbasins, double-deck Army bunks, and Spartan conditions. The Germans and the much larger group of Japanese alternated the use of the mess hall, where food was prepared with the detainees' national tastes in mind. At the same time, ships' officers enjoyed many of the same luxuries they did aboard their ships; they lived in small single-bedroom cottages, surrounded by gardens, in a separate section of the camp. Officers' meals were often cooked by chefs and served by stewards, and each of the three camps holding detained seamen—Fort Missoula, Fort Stanton, and Fort Lincoln—had at least one orchestra or lounge band.

The INS was especially concerned about Nazism among the seamen, sometimes with good reason. Unlike the internees at other camps, the seamen had traveled more widely than most internees, were better disciplined, and many were familiar with machinery, engines, radios, tools, and maps. The merchant navy seamen also had money. Enlisted men received their monthly salaries of $8.00, and officers received $10.00—enough, if pooled, to bribe a guard or buy a railroad ticket to freedom. Oil company employees, although also sailors, were different: When they first arrived most carried paychecks in their pockets, all drawn on German banks. On 14 June 1941, Washington froze all Axis funds in the United States, leaving some seamen essentially penniless. Politics was indeed a particular problem at Fort Lincoln. A small but unknown number of internees were devoted citizens of Germany and fascist Italy. For example, the weekly camp newspaper, *Bismarck Echo*, was written in German, and while the majority of any issue contained primarily the usual sports and movie schedules and information about new arrivals and departures, there was always a strong element of Nazi sentiment. There were poems to Hitler, a celebration of Propaganda Minister Goebbels's birthday, and news about German prisoners of war interned in America. Some of the humorists among the seamen renamed the camp *Friedrichsruhe* (Friedrich's Rest) after the country villa of Germany's nineteenth-century chancellor and founder, Otto von Bismarck.

Despite their strong political views, the sailors were viewed by the Justice Department not as Fifth Columnists or dangerous enemy aliens, but as unfortunates who, through no fault of their own, had to be held in the United States until they could be returned to Europe. Taking advantage of an unusual opportunity, the U.S. government encouraged the men to experiment with democracy. Camp spokesmen received periodic votes of confidence from the camp population, and a camp panel, composed of three ordinary seamen and three officers, punished violators of the rules. The internee admistrators generally cooperated with INS authorities, even if the rank and file were often mistrustful.

The seamen who arrived at Fort Lincoln were followed by Germans from Latin America and German-American internees. Each group had its own spokesman. The seamen were represented by Captain Otto Trautmann, the German civilians by Dr. Gerhard Sprenger, and the Germans from Latin America by Joachim Marggraff. The American INS camp commander, Ike McCoy, had his hands full. Fort Lincoln's population peaked in April 1942 with 500 Germans and 1,200 Japanese.

The men played athletics at every opportunity, usually soccer and fistball. Since work was not compulsory, and the summer months were brief, most of the men spent their days getting suntans. The most popular indoor sport, winter or summer, was poker. Many passed the time by making pets of local critters: gophers, mice, snakes, squirrels, doves, cats, and dogs. One man used his cat to treat his rheumatism and was often seen walking the grounds with the feline draped around his neck or tucked inside his shirt. During winter, the men built a forty-foot ski slope and a skating rink for the camp's two ice hockey teams, the "North Dakota Bombers" and the "Bismarck Lightnings." There were theater groups and songfests, boxing matches, and intriguingly, a roaming storyteller. The camp sported a 300-seat movie theater, a substantial library, and a wood shop.

Both the Germans and the Japanese maintained their own canteens, with shelves stocked with toilet articles, tobacco, writing stationary, and candy. Later in the war, McCoy allowed the sale of wine and beer to boost morale. The internees could keep the canteen profits and use them to buy musical instruments, athletic equipment, and books or magazine subscriptions for the camp library. Religious services were available: weekly Catholic Masses were provided by a Dr. Schmücker in German, and Protestant services were delivered in both German and English by Pastor Möller from Bismarck. The Japanese internees had their own Buddhist and Shinto priests to lead their services. Despite such amenities as good food, a German beer hall complete with wall murals of Bavarian scenes, an eighty-acre garden, a farm with cows, pigs, and chickens, a bakery that turned out a hundred loaves of German pumpernickel and fifty loaves of rye bread every other day, an ambitious sports program, a 5,400 volume library, and two movies each week, a constant stream of complaints continued. Fort Lincoln was masculine, political, isolated, and brooding. Consequently, security was especially tight.

The entire population of 1,600 men was counted at the changing of each of three shifts of border patrol guards, and the men could not resume what they were doing until a release whistle announced that the count had been completed. No shift change could take place until all the detainees—changed to "internees" after 7 December—were accounted for. A surprise bed-count at the midnight shift change was not unusual. Two guards of the twelve-man shift patrolled inside the fence with tear-gas guns, while the remaining ten patrolled outside with rifles and shotguns. The border patrolmen brooked little nonsense from rebellious internees and, according to one report, "occasionally used their gas guns to break up reluctant poker parties."[9] Apparently, when the authorities said "lights out," they meant "lights out!"

If caught attempting to escape, standard punishment was thirty days in the camp stockade. After escaping from the camp, an internee might be shot by a trigger-happy guard or citizen. Despite the difficulties and the very real danger in trying to escape, internees seem to have had tunnels underway all the time. Every few weeks the guards stumbled onto a tunnel in some stage of completion. One tunnel that ran from the mess hall basement to a point well outside the fence was discovered when a truck loaded with concrete blocks drove over it, and caved it in. Guards foiled another attempt when they found a pile of clay-covered clothes—the guard dogs sniffed the clothes and identified the men. Sometimes they almost made it out before being caught: Hermann Cordes and Albert Gregeratzki tunneled forty-five feet, well past the wire fence, and, still in the tunnel were headed toward a clump of trees before a guard patrol outside the fence heard muffled noises and laughter coming from underground. A few shots into the ground sent Hermann and Albert fleeing back to the tunnel entrance, and they received thirty days in the stockade.

On 12 June 1941, twenty-eight-year-old Johann Marquenie tunneled out and set off a manhunt that would have done justice to the likes of Dillinger. One hour after a routine night check revealed Marquenie's empty cot, more than fifty border patrolmen, state penitentiary guards, city and county police, and railroad detectives were on his trail. Marquenie, the third officer from the German ship *Clio*, was finally captured three days later, rowing down the Missouri River about forty-five miles southeast of the camp. He had been living on chocolate candy bars and fig cookies that he had stockpiled back in camp. When Marquenie was asked why he escaped, he said he had "no particular reason"—he just wanted "to be alone."[10] In approximately five years of operation, only seven internees escaped from Fort Lincoln, and all were caught without incident—though one eluded capture for three months and was finally picked up in New Orleans.[11] ("At Crystal City, and Seagoville too," Plaschke recalls, "the guards were pretty informal and treated us well. Us kids would often chat with them up in their towers.") At some camps, inmates feared the anger of the local population more than the camp authorities. But not at Fort Lincoln. In the end, 3,950 men passed through Fort Lincoln, 2,150 Germans and 1,800 Japanese. The camp closed officially on 1 March 1946: fifty Germans were repatriated to Germany, and the rest were shipped to Ellis Island.

Other types of disciplinary problems also troubled Fort Lincoln. Between March and October 1944, for example, nearly twenty men were marched to the stockade for the following violations: seven internees were punished for violating curfew in the camp canteen (each received five and a half days under arrest), one for drunkenness (five days), two for refusing to peel potatoes (fourteen days each), one for trying to smuggle a letter past the camp censor (five days), three for refusing to work (three and a half), one for brawling (four days), and so forth.[12] A more humorous disciplinary problem concerned snoring. Apparently, the noise in the barracks after the lights went out at 10:00 P.M. reached intolerable levels. Martin Dudel, at Fort Lincoln before his parole in April 1942, remembered in his diary that "the two worst snorers were finally bunked in a room together; they were so resonant that the first man to fall asleep was the only one to sleep at all that night. Life became so difficult for them that finally one upended the other's bed and grabbed him by the throat. The other snatched a board and chased his assailant around the compound."[13]

Each internee at Fort Lincoln received the standard $3.00 per month in scrip, so most were anxious to volunteer for the contract labor to civilians that earned them an additional ten cents an hour. Work was generally harder at Fort Lincoln than at most camps, largely due to the remote location and often inhospitable weather. Work inside the camp included jobs in the kitchen, hospital, laundry, bakery, tailor shop, shoe-repair shop, camp offices, machine shop, chicken coop, garage, and the like. Outside of camp, internees were assigned jobs, under guard, with the Northern Pacific Railway Company or with the INS or Park Forest Service; during the summer months they were farmed out to places as far as the U.S. Forest Service Camps at Warland or Troy, Montana, or to half a dozen Forest Service camps along the Priest River, Idaho. During the brutal winter weather, most men stayed indoors and played poker.

Jerre Mangione, the INS camp inspector who had earlier likened Camp Crystal City to a "magical city" in the desert darkness, was far less enthusiastic about Fort Lincoln. To him, Lincoln seemed "dreary and listless," a general gloom accentuated by the flat landscape. The camp also had a significant number of troublemakers, although the no-nonsense INS camp officer, I. P. McCoy of the Border Patrol, conceded, "I guess if I were in an American internment camp over in Germany I'd be raising the same kind of hell." At the end of his inspection, Mangione remembers that he "was glad to leave Fort Lincoln. Of all the camps I visited and would be visiting in the months to come, it was the grimmest reminder that . . . the war had thrust us into the shameful position of locking up people for their beliefs."[14]

Fort Stanton, New Mexico, was the second camp for interned German seamen. In the camp population of approximately 650, there were eight captains, sixty ships' officers, 130 under-officers, and 450 sailors representing the following ships and lines:

Norddeutscher Lloyd: *Columbus, Eisenbach, Leipzig, München, Hannover;*
Hamburg-Amerika Linie: *Arauca, Odenwald, Cordillera, Friesland, Monserrate;*
Laisz, Hamburg: *Karin;*
Friedrich, Hamburg: *Pauline Friedrich.*

Fort Stanton was a curious camp. The internees were sailors but not military types. They sailed on the best-known German lines. As such, they were answerable not to the camp authorities but to their ship captain. The official American camp commanders were Lawrence K. Stallings and Ammon Tenney, but to everyone's mind, the German sailors were ruled by the iron discipline of interned German Captain Wilhelm Daehne of the *Columbus.* The seamen responded only to Captain Daehne's orders, and those of his men; the American authorities could bellow or reason but to no avail. Eventually, the Americans simply gave in. Fortunately, Captain Daehne never directed the men to act against camp security.

Most of the men at Fort Stanton were older; about fifty of the men were over fifty years of age, many were in their sixties. One ship's officer was seventy-six years old. Unlike other camps, they were treated less harshly by the authorities, probably due to the persistence of their spokesman, Captain Daehne, the Swiss inspectors, and to the influence of their powerful German employers. For whatever reason, the men could listen to the radio, watch movies twice a week, and attend classes in an extensive prisoner-created "university." The prisoners built their own sports field and tennis courts and could swim in the camp pool. They were issued two clean bath towels and hand towels every week. The men also received gifts and food parcels from the YMCA, German Red Cross, and the companies that employed the men. Apparently anxious to avoid irritating the great German shipping lines, the Swiss authorities even contacted sailors' relatives in Germany to request that they write more often. The German crewmen were granted the recreational privilege of hiking in the hills of the Fort Stanton Reservation, and the camp canteen sold bottled and draft beer, consumption of which resulted in arguments between the internees. As far as the amenities were concerned, the Swiss inspection teams declared Stanton to be the among the best civilian internment facilities in the United States.[15]

Yet there was a small group of troublemakers, and each Swiss inspection reported a variety of fights and attempted escapes. On 3 September 1942, for example, four men from the *Columbus*—Willy Michel, assistant engineer, Bruno Dathe, watchman, Christel Crantz, assistant electrician, and Hermann Runne, boilerman—made a break. Border patrol guards noted their absence at the breakfast head count and alerted the local authorities. Roadblocks were erected, and a horse detail was dispatched to search for their trail. A local rancher discovered the escaped internees bathing in a canyon stream near Ruidoso, New Mexico, and went to alert local townspeople. A group of armed citizens captured the internees, reportedly shouted obscenities at the Germans, tied ropes around their midsections, and forced them to march toward Ruidoso. Fortunately, border patrolmen arrived and took custody of the internees. They were brought back to Fort Stanton and spent thirty days in the stockade.

Reinhold Poielski didn't make it past the fence and got ten days in the stockade.

Horst Werner Benesch and Walter Brincker were still awaiting punishment for a failed escape when Swiss inspectors passed through the camp on 5 September 1944.

In mid-1944, the attitude of the INS guards seemed to turn against the German sailors. Perhaps it was because the internees lacked respect for the guards or because the news from the war front revealed the existence of concentration camps, or because of exasperation with periodic escapes, but numerous internees reported guards who threatened to kill them, escapees who were severely mistreated by the border patrol guards, and lots of abusive language.[16]

Fort Stanton experienced other problems as well. On at least one occasion an internee was treated for violent psychotic behavior. Fort Stanton was also the only camp that experienced an epidemic, when trichinosis appeared in seventy-five sailors from the *Columbus* in May 1942. The American army rushed in four additional doctors, a pathologist, zoologist, seven nurses, and fifteen male attendants. All but one of those stricken by the intestinal parasites recovered: the lone death was thirty-year-old Heinrich Renken, cook's helper aboard the *Columbus*. An investigation traced the trichinosis to pork purchased from a standard U.S. military supplier; the disease did not appear elsewhere.

There was much political violence in camp as obdurate Nazis sought to dominate their anti-Nazi fellow internees. The authorities tried hard to isolate the anti-Nazis in camp and transfer them to Fort Lincoln, North Dakota. In November 1942, the first group of thirty-five anti-Nazi crewmen were shipped to Fort Lincoln, and additional groups were regularly transferred in 1943. In 1944, the last group of ninety-two anti-Nazi internees was transferred to Fort Lincoln. Despite these efforts to separate the two groups, several deaths occurred that may have been linked to politics: internee Hermann Neuoff was found hanging by the neck on 18 March 1944 (despite ample evidence of murder, the coroner's jury certified his death to be a suicide), and Otto Zeitsch, who was beaten to death on 13 May 1944. No culprits were found in either case.

The internment camp at Kenedy, Texas, was located in a town of about 2,900 people fifty miles southwest of San Antonio. Kenedy was the site of a former CCC camp, which closed when the nation went to war. Its closing was a severe loss for local businesses, so when the city fathers learned that the federal government was searching for a site to locate an enemy alien internment camp, the Kenedy Chamber of Commerce shifted into high gear and offered their town. Their patriotism was applauded and Camp Kenedy became official in February 1942. Workers hurriedly erected more than two hundred prefabricated huts, each of which could house five or six persons, to accommodate an anticipated eight hundred to two thousand internees. Barbed wire enclosed the detention area, and guard towers and powerful searchlights were placed in strategic positions. Anticipating the arrival of the first internees, the carpenters, electricians, plumbers, and other workers frantically built a dining hall, kitchen, hospital, headquarters building, quarters for officers and nurses, warehouses, and latrines. Kenedy was reserved for men only and was largely made up of Germans and Japanese from Latin America, and some Japanese from California.

On 23 April 1942, the entire town turned out to see its new neighbors. In keeping with local security measures, only authorized personnel could take photographs. According to the dramatic report in the *Kenedy Advance*, a blacked-out train arrived and disgorged internees in groups of twenty—including Walter Klein from Haiti (see chapter six)—flanked by four border patrolmen and soldiers. Several of the travelers appeared sick and required transportation, but the remainder trudged across the grassy area between the train and the camp. The Germans were described as being "young and smart-looking," the Japanese as "small, unshaven, and insignificant-looking people." The Japanese—almost all from Peru—claimed that the officer in charge, Aubrey S. Hudson, discriminated against them when he assigned them old CCC structures, while the Germans received newly constructed quarters. The charge was substantiated the following month during the first routine inspection by the Spanish consul, Jose Maria Garay, and a State Department official.[17] As if to challenge the new construction as well as the mettle of the authorities in charge, a devastating hurricane struck Camp Kenedy in the middle of the night. No one was hurt, although buildings were demolished, electric wires downed, and gas mains broken. Local workmen were mobilized, and the camp was rebuilt with the aid of the Japanese internees but without the help of the Germans. Led by an old German sea captain, they stubbornly refused to do anything not covered by the Geneva Convention of 1929. They maintained this stance for most of the war. Japanese internees from Latin America and the Carribean, on the other hand, were leaderless and dispirited and hoped to improve their situation by cooperating.

Walter Klein remembered his first view of his new home at Kenedy: a nice, little bungalow, 180 square feet, furnished, but without window glass. Four people lived in each bungalow. Elsewhere in the camp was a canteen, large washhouse, hospital, and a small store. Meals included plenty of food, although the internees ate little and much of the food was wasted. The German internees had the opportunity to work outside of the camp (the Japanese were unwelcome by the community), but Klein and most of his friends refused to work for—in his words—the "enemy." Instead, Klein took a job in the twenty-four-bed hospital. The director was a local physician, but Klein claimed adamantly that the real director was a German doctor, Georg, from Santo Domingo. In addition, the hospital had an American nurse and three orderlies, two Germans and one Japanese. There were occasional minor sicknesses, which Klein believed were caused by boredom and too much time to think. A few internees who died of natural causes were buried at a camp cemetery outside of the fence.

As at other camps, security was strict and straightforward: roll call twice a day, at 9 A.M. and 4:30 P.M. The men lined up on the hot unpaved streets as camp officials scrutinized the ranks, using picture albums with snapshots of the internees to help with identification. At night, guards conducted three or four bed checks. Watchtowers, spotlights, barbed-wire fences, an alarm system, and guards on horseback around the outer perimeter completed the security measures. Only one internee, a German, ever managed to escape, and he was swiftly and easily caught.

Kenedy maintained a library that held 1,323 books in English, 270 in German, four in Spanish, and one in French, films in English and Spanish, and numerous monthly magazines, all donated by humanitarian organizations. German seamen received additional packages of books, writing paper, and toilet articles from their employer, North German Lloyd Bremen. The internees organized classes to teach one another foreign languages, stenography, and other skills. One of Walter Klein's bungalow-mates began a stamp collection by sending away for stamp ads and retrieving envelopes from other internees. Protestant services were offered every second Sunday in German by Pastor Fritz Sandner from Guatemala, and Catholic Mass in German was offered almost daily by Father Hubert Michael Kueches from Puerto Rico. Attendance was high at both.

The INS considered Kenedy to be a transit camp, as opposed to the more stable Crystal City or Fort Lincoln. One major difference between Kenedy and most other camps was that the size and makeup of the population changed greatly as groups arrived and left. The number of internees often rose or fell by two or three hundred. A representative breakdown from June 1943 was as follows:

> 588 Germans from South and Central America representing Bolivia, Colombia, Costa Rica, the Dominican Republic, Ecuador, Guatemala, Haiti, Honduras, Nicaragua, Peru, and El Salvador;
> 18 enemy aliens from the United States;
> 28 assorted other nationalities; and
> 19 Italians
>
> Total: 653

Several months later the population soared to nearly a thousand, and plunged soon after to 630.

From the beginning Kenedy was a bit quirky. Subject to the unremitting south Texas heat and occasional tropical storms, it had a reputation for being the dumping ground for troublemakers from other camps. Escapees, in particular, were brought to Kenedy; the most celebrated hero was Alfred K. H. Fengler from Fort Lincoln, who had slipped away from a Northern Pacific Railway work site and was nabbed three months later enjoying life in New Orleans. The first officer in charge, Aubrey Hudson, and his replacement, border patrolman Ivan Williams must have been driven to distraction by the endless number of disciplinary problems. In one case, a Johann Wagner from Peru was sentenced to three days in the stockade after being warned three times against wearing short and indecent (*unanständige*) pants. In another case, Emil Belz and Alfred Bauer spent three days in jail for refusing to fill out some administrative forms, while Max Effinger and Max Gast served their three days for getting caught making alcohol out of fruit juice.[18]

The German seamen were usually behind most camp problems. They were hefty men, disciplined and obedient, but when unsupervised generally reverted to hard-drinking, rowdy behavior. Many spoke English. Moreover, most had visited Germany not long before the war led to their internment and strongly supported Hitler. Every camp that held German seamen had the same experience—they were a constant source of annoyance and sometimes outright danger. This was not true of the Japanese, particularly early in the war. The Japanese were largely leaderless, often more Peruvian or Brazilian than Japanese. Few had recently visited Japan, and fewer still had a worshipful stance toward Emperor Hirohito. As the war progressed, however, a minority of Japanese internees began to behave like the Germans and protest any camp policy or decision that they disagreed with.

These factors combined did not make for a happy camp. When the internees were noncooperative, the camp authorities responded in kind. A visiting Swiss inspection team in June 1943 listed the problems. Everything seemed to be in short supply, missing, or broken. Coffee, tea, chocolate were not to be had; meat was seldom served; only three washing machines worked, allowing each internee to wash only five items of clothing per week. The free razor blades promised by the authorities were ten weeks in arrears. The wash basins were broken. The beer was declared undrinkable, being the same low strength as in the U.S. military (3.2 percent). Cigarettes in the camp canteen sold for two cents more (fifteen cents per pack) than the same cigarettes at Camp Fort Meade (thirteen cents) and three cents more than at Seagoville (twelve cents); underpants at Kenedy cost sixty-five cents, as opposed to only sixty cents at Meade.

The disgruntled internees simply broke the rules as they chose. In addition to the usual fistfights and brawls, they refused to work in the kitchen, two men continued wearing those "short and indecent pants" despite repeated warnings, and two roommates continued an intermittent punching match over one's playing of his radio after lights out. In this case, both men received three days in the stockade, which was reduced to one day following a lecture about the rules from the German camp spokesman. Even a Catholic priest, Pfarrer Albert Woelk, was in a fistfight with one Heinz Schubert over an undisclosed matter. Both received five days in the cooler, later reduced to three after a routine lecture from the camp spokesman. Commander Williams must have wondered what the next months might bring.

One memorable disciplinary case was that of Herbert Reckefuss, who stole and drank the sacramental wine from the camp chapel and ended atop the main administration building, singing bawdy ballads. An investigation revealed that he had help from Teodor Nicolini (previously arrested for wearing short and indecent pants), and both received three days in the camp stockade. A final example of Kenedy's disciplinary problems concerned Emil Betz and Heinz Koeller. They had found an Esso road map in the glove compartment of one of the guards' cars and were packed and ready to leave for Mexico when they were caught. Thirty days in the cooler, later reduced to eight. To complicate the life of the already overworked camp director Ivan Williams, the last four men—Reckefuss, Nicolini, Betz, and Koeller—met in the stockade and decided to go on a hunger strike. They went hungry from 16–20 June 1943 and quit only when Williams agreed to send them all back to Germany at the first opportunity. He promised with gusto.

On the positive side, Camp Kenedy created a giant sports event that was equaled at no other camp. For eight days, between 1–8 May, the camp held the "Olympiad Camp Kenedy 1943," which boasted a dazzling array of events: from tennis, soccer, handball, and shot put, to Ping-Pong, high jump, and, on a closely watched circular track within the camp fences, a three-kilometer run. There were single events, team events, and contests that pitted German against Japanese internees. There were even special events for older men (over fifty years of age). For the Germans, the Olympiad harkened back to the glory of the 1936 Olympics in Berlin, combining propaganda with a welcome distraction, and offered prizes to the winners. Camp athletes competed for handmade belts and billfolds, pounds of coffee, chocolate bars, pens, tobacco pouches, and hams. Commander Williams himself donated several dozen packs and cartons of cigarettes for prizes. Between events there were parades, beer and bratwursts, comedy soccer matches, a South American Caribbean band, movies, phonograph record concerts, and speeches from Williams and the camp spokesman. A good time was had by all.[19]

Overall, despite occasional incidents, the camps were relatively quiet places, with their populations generally divided along generational lines. As the war progressed, most camp populations also divided themselves into moderate Nazis, dedicated Nazis, and neutrals. Walter Klein claims that his Camp Kenedy was nonpolitical, although he admitted that a Nazi flag stood on the camp stage, with the American flag on the other side. ("It must have been supplied by the Red Cross, since none of us had such a flag," says Klein.) The real Nazis, he claims, were a group of twenty-four German-American enemy aliens who spent two months at Kenedy, at the end of 1943, until they could be transferred to another camp. They flew a large swastika flag over their section of the camp, proselytized to everyone, distributed Nazi literature, and occasionally terrorized the camp. "We Germans from Haiti and South America were appalled, and happy to see them leave."

As the end of the war approached, the populations divided themselves into two additional categories: those who wanted to be repatriated to Germany as early as possible and those who intended to remain in America after the war.

In camps with both Germans and Italians, such internal issues were submerged in nationalistic hooting and cat-calling. In these camps with mixed national groups, there was plenty of friction. According to inspector Jerre Mangione, "the Japanese . . . behaved as though the other two groups didn't exist. The Germans and the Italians, on the other hand, expressed open contempt for the Japanese, whom they regarded as an inferior people, but they also had a low opinion of one another. Their general incompatibility sometimes resulted in fisticuffs." Said one Italian seaman, "If, God forbid, the Axis powers should win the war, there would soon be another war between the winners."[20]

Most often the malcontents were close to the camp spokesman, and they spent their time writing endless complaints to the Swiss inspectors and American authorities. Some troublemakers were loners who hatched plots to provoke the camp administrators or extend their political control within the camp. A few, like Bund Führer Fritz Kuhn, who had been convicted in New York on charges of grand larceny in 1939 for misappropriating Bund funds, were considered genuinely dangerous. After his release from Dannemore Prison in 1943, his American citizenship, granted in 1934, was revoked (on the grounds that it had been obtained fraudulently). He was shipped to Crystal City. When he arrived in camp the other internees largely avoided him, mostly out of fear of damaging their own cases. A few claimed to have deeply resented his presence. He was a criminal, having been convicted of embezzling party funds, and the other internees wanted the public to understand that they were not like him. Kuhn spent most of his time strutting about Camp Crystal with his small group of ardent supporters. After several months Kuhn was sent to Camp Kenedy where, according to camp commander Ivan Williams, he joined:

> the fanatical Nazis who had been members of the German-American Bund. The convinced Bundists liked to dream up "complaints" to present to the camp authorities, mainly to enhance their prestige with fellow Bundists. One persistent complaint demanded that the internees be issued pajamas. The more fanatical of them kept inventing new Nazi holidays, with mass meetings, demonstrations, and displays of Nazi emblems.

Camp commanders forbade such activities, to the general relief of the majority of other internees. "For many of the interned Germans, it is the first time they have had any direct experience with hard-core Nazis, and they find they have little in common with them," Williams observed.[21] Later, Kuhn was transferred to Fort Stanton, New Mexico, for disciplinary reasons. He remained there for the rest of the war. In September 1945, Kuhn was declared to be "dangerous to the public peace and safety of the United States," put aboard the *Antioch Victory*, and deported to Germany.[22] His wife and son, Walter, had already been repatriated in early 1944. After a brief reunion with his family, Kuhn was arrested by American authorities in Germany as an "undesirable" and confined. He later escaped and lived on the lam in Germany for several years. Kuhn died an unrepentant Nazi in 1951 in his native Munich.

At Seagoville, the presence of a strident and disruptive Nazi named Mrs. Theolinda Zillmer-Zoser so offended other internees that in June 1943 they appealed to the Swiss authorities (in vain) to have her moved to another camp.[23] On other occasions, as with the case of the notorious Nazi internee Karl Kolb, internees' behavior was indeed so disruptive that they were transferred from camp to camp.

The removal of one such troublemaker concerned a man named Diebel, from Camp Stringtown, located in the southeast corner of Oklahoma. A Nazi demonstration broke out, which brought down the wrath of the camp authorities. A rowdy group of some twenty-five internees gathered at the camp gate to bid farewell to their comrade, chanting "Heil Hitler" and giving the outstretched arm salute. Then they broke into party songs and were well into inflammatory speeches before the army guards dispersed the group back to their barracks. The officer in charge of Stringtown's 450 internees was a leathery old veteran named Lieutenant Colonel Bertram Frankenberger. He intended to stop all such nonsense in his camp, and believed that the Nazis best understood strength. His response was posted on the camp bulletin board:

> Effective this date the following internees, for having taken part in a demonstration on July 30, 1942, considered wholly unwarranted, disgraceful conduct, disrespectful to United States officers of the law, and infractions of camp discipline and good order are deprived of privileges and restricted to prescribed limits for a period of thirty days. They will be quartered and messed separately. They will in no way exchange or receive articles of any nature from an internee or unauthorized person during their period of punishment.

Colonel Frankenberger's memo went on to list all the privileges that the named offenders would do without for the next thirty days. They were:

1. Mail
2. Radios
3. Camp exchange
4. Recreation room
5. Visitors
6. Magazines, newspapers, and all reading matter

7. Enter only squad room assigned and no other barracks or enclosure
8. Athletics
9. Lights out and in quarters by 8.00 P.M.
10. Deprived of ten (10) cents a day allowance
11. Deprived of all voting rights and of holding any type of office
12. Drawing on any personal fund for purchase[24]

The records do not indicate any further Nazi outbursts at Camp String-town.

The greatest danger to the internees did not necessarily come from groups of Nazis in camp but sometimes from the Americans in nearby communities. At the sizable INS camp at Bismarck, North Dakota, which held both Germans and Japanese, the antagonism of local residents toward the internees, in the words of an INS inspector, often reached "a perilous degree." Tension, especially involving the Japanese from the West Coast, was evident from the beginning. The arrival from California of the first 415 "Jap Aliens," in the parlance of the times, made dramatic front-page news in the *Bismarck Tribune* (right next to an anxious report about the desperate fighting on Corregidor in the Philippines). According to the newspaper, the special thirteen-coach Northern Pacific was "ringed by a cordon of federal immigration patrolmen armed with sub-machine guns, as the little yellow men scrambled out of the coaches, 25 at a time, to guarded trucks and rushed out to the internment camp to join the 400 Germans already there."[25] A later headline described camp life by announcing that "Facist [*sic*] Sympathizers Live Like Caged Animals."[26] The public hated the "traitors" out at Fort Lincoln, and when one of the German aliens escaped from the camp, townspeople swiftly formed a posse to hunt and kill him. "Fortunately, the border patrolmen were able to get to him first and return him to the camp unharmed," commented camp inspector Mangione.

Local residents' feelings also ran high near the INS camp at Santa Fe. Enraged by a local newspaper account of America's disastrous defeat in the Philippines, published together with the names of New Mexicans killed by the Japanese, the townsfolk went on a rampage against the internment camp. Armed with weapons ranging from shotguns to hatchets, a large group marched on the camp to kill all two thousand of its Japanese internees. They might have succeeded were it not for the camp's quick-witted commander, the near-legendary Ivan Williams, recently brought in from Camp Kenedy. Williams blustered, reasoned, and cajoled for more than an hour before the ringleaders called off the lynch mob. A year later, after Williams was reassigned to another camp, trouble broke out again. The new commanding officer at Santa Fe, Lloyd H. Jensen, begged the INS to make the barbed-wire fence a foot taller—not to prevent escapes but to protect the internees against local hostility.

At Crystal City, the situation was safer. Folks in the bordertown of Uvalde, forty miles away, hardly knew the internees were there. Most of the internees never saw Uvalde either. "I was at Crystal City for two years, and only saw Uvalde once," says Alfred Plaschke, "when I was driven into town to get fitted for glasses."

The total number of internees at all the camps fluctuated as new groups arrived and others were paroled or released. The number reached its peak at the beginning of 1944, with 9,341 aliens in custody, and dropped to 6,238 by the end of the year. At Fort Lincoln, for example, of the 3,950 aliens interned there more than one-half, or 2,188 internees (1,313 Germans and 875 Japanese), were determined by a local hearing board to be sufficiently loyal to be released. Nearly one hundred of these, motivated, perhaps, by patriotism or a desire to speed up their naturalization, joined the armed forces. Eleven others won their release after submitting writs of habeas corpus to the U.S. District Court in Fargo.

CHAPTER TEN

THE EXCHANGES

A sizable group at each camp, however, got their freedom in a different way: they were voluntarily or involuntarily returned home to Germany or Japan. Germany had an unknown number of American citizens in its hands whom it was willing to exchange. The two countries had successfully concluded several exchanges early in 1942, when three categories of internees were repatriated: diplomats, followed by German citizens from Latin America, and finally a small number of German enemy aliens. Every exchange was a substantial undertaking, considering the significant outlay of transportation in trains and buses required to move hundreds of people from camps across the United States to Pier F in New Jersey, and from a European port to a central discharge point. Guards and customs officials, nurses, sailors, and government agents were needed at both ends; and numerous German, American, and, most importantly, Swiss bureaucrats were involved in selecting those to be repatriated, juggling long lists of names, and solving thorny questions of citizenship. Still, it had all gone smoothly. Now, late in 1944, circumstances were developing which made possible another major exchange.

The war was clearly turning against the Axis: America and Britain had cleared North Africa, invaded Sicily and Italy, and they had landed on Normandy on 6 June to open the long-awaited Second Front. On the Eastern Front, the 900-day siege of Leningrad ended, the vaunted German army had been pushed back from Moscow, and ninety thousand survivors of the German Sixth Army surrendered to the Russians at Stalingrad. Even Hitler's generals realized that it was time to find a way out. By attempting to assassinate the Führer on 20 July, perhaps cooler heads were hoping to salvage a postwar advantage that such a humanitarian gesture as exchanging internees might accomplish. However, the assassination attempt had failed, throwing Hitler into a world of conspiracies, cruel retaliation, and imaginary secret weapons. Humanitarianism in Germany or America would not have played a decisive part. What then prompted another exchange?

The impetus appears to have come from the internees themselves. As early as 29 February 1944, the Legation of Switzerland wrote to Franz Wirz, the German spokesman at Seagoville, to stop his internees from badgering them. "The Legation is receiving an increased number of individual inquiries concerning repatriation," wrote the official, "and there is no mechanism for an exchange in the foreseeable future." A month later, Wirz received another letter from the Swiss pleading with the internees to stop writing. And in mid-October 1944, the Swiss Legation assured the new spokeman at Seagoville, Fritz Stangl, that "there is no development in the negotiations at present which would substantiate that an exchange will materialize in the near future." Suddenly, however, the Swiss reported a slender possibility: "The German government is not opposed to the conclusion of an exchange agreement."[1] Nor, indeed, were U.S. officials who very much wanted to clear the internee camps of undesirables, and rescue any remaining American prisoners in enemy hands before the closing days of the war permitted fanatics to turn on them. On 8 November, the State Department learned that the German government was amenable to an exchange, and events moved into high gear.

The internees wanted to leave the United States for a variety of reasons, many of them traveling to a country they may not have remembered or perhaps even visited. Some elected to leave after rediscovering their "Germanness" in the internee camps—drinking in the Vaterland Cafe or listening to the likes of Karl Kolb or Fritz Kuhn. Others left because they were outraged at the way they had been treated. A number claim that they were bullied into leaving—it turns out that some local hearing boards were tired of "coddling" the internees, and threatened them with outright deportation, a category which would prevent them from returning at a future date, unless the internees volunteered to be exchanged. So in most cases, the families of the repatriates volunteered to go along.

Emotions of the internees who were leaving were mixed over repatriation. To some the exchange was a heroic gesture by foolhardy nationalists and ideologues or an angry statement against the unjust treatment they had received. A number had lost homes or businesses to vandals or taxes and had nothing left in America. Those brought up from Latin America simply wanted to go back and pick up the pieces of their lives.

By 1944, the Plaschkes, for example, were fed up with three years of internment, and the loss of their house to foreclosure or vandals, and only wanted to go back to Germany—wartime or not. They never hid their feelings. Indeed, as early as April 1942, only months after being rounded up, they had told the authorities at their temporary internment camp at Fort Sam Houston, Texas, that they wanted to return to Germany.[2] So did Hermann and Gertrud Koetter. They were much relieved when they read their names among the 575 names on the posted lists. In December 1944, the Plaschke family—Rudolf, thirty-three, Berta, thirty-six and pregnant with a baby daughter who would be born on board the *Gripsholm*, Alfred, thirteen, Paul, eleven—and nearly one thousand other repatriates from camps around the country readied for the trip back to war-torn Germany.

Wilhelm Wartemann was fed up, too. Four of his children had been living on welfare at the All-Church Home in Fort Worth for the past two years; his wife Anna and infant daughter were on parole in Midlothian, Texas, living on $18 a month from the Swiss Legation; and he was re-arrested and returned to camp when his own parole turned sour in May 1942. Wartemann finally convinced the bureaucracy to reunite his family at Crystal City in October 1943. Three months later in December 1943, the internees at Crystal City were offered a chance to be repatriated to Germany, and the Wartemann family stepped forward with alacrity. Of the nine years Wilhelm had lived in America, the last three were years of hard-ship, frustration, and mortification. On 15 February 1944, the Wartemann family, numbering five children and their parents, were repatriated to Eu-rope aboard the S.S. *Gripsholm.*

Some younger men were enthusiastic about the adventure of going to Germany. The older internees were more cautious; many were devoted German nationalists rather than pro-Nazis. One concern among the men, both young and old, was the fear of being taken as spies if they were ever captured by the American army. Many were frightened about having to serve in the German army. Walter Klein, still a German citizen despite his years in Haiti, hesitated to be repatriated until a German government tele-gram from Berlin assured him that he would not be conscripted. Only after receiving that message did Klein step forward to join the next train trans-port to New York and the *Gripsholm*, bound for Barcelona on 2 May 1944.

From mid-1943 on, rumors flew at Camp Kenedy. Every week seemed to bring another possible scenario for their future. Notably, the rumors always included an erroneous theme: that the internees were going to be exchanged for European Jews. To the end of his life, Walter Klein believed that shiploads of Jews were being exchanged for the internees ("one to one," he recalled with amazement, as though the internees were far more valuable than their Jewish counterparts). From the first, there was a surge of takers. Each was interviewed by a camp hearing board, but for the early repatriates it was a pro forma meeting. Most longed to go home, and the hearing boards were just as relieved to see them leave.

The Koetters, Hermann and Gertrude, late of Lamarque, Texas, were asked which option they wanted to take: America or Germany? Their two boys, having risen to important positions in the U.S. Army despite their parents' incarceration, immediately telegraphed them at Crystal City: "Stay in the United States! No matter what!" Hermann reluctantly agreed and declined the opportunity to be exchanged. The authorities didn't approach him again.

At many camps, however, internees took advantage of the government offer. At Crystal City, the board processed 634 repatriates (out of a German population of 1,297) between 8 and 11 February 1944, and the authorities were grateful to note that most of the irritating camp Nazis were among them. At Fort Lincoln, 688 Germans and 525 Japanese filled out the necessary applications. Nine of the thirteen women then interned at Gloucester City, New Jersey, stepped forward to join the exchange. Similar groups at the other detention camps volunteered to return to Germany on the *Gripsholm*. Groups of internees continued to leave as shipping space to Europe became available. Each side sent the lists or categories of people it particularly wanted back. In November 1944 the State Department collected 207 internees: eighty-two from Crystal City, forty-two from Kenedy, twenty-three from Seagovillle, thirty-six from Fort Lincoln, fourteen from Ellis Island, four from Sharp Park, three from Fort Stanton, two from Priest River, Idaho, one from the Atlanta Penitentiary, and an unknown number of Germans living unhappily in Kansas City, Chicago, New York, Minnesota, and Detroit, and shipped them to Europe. They were joined on board by groups of returning German war prisoners, usually chaplains, physicians, veterinarians, and other noncombatants caught up on the battlefield.

Interestingly, as the departure time approached, a few repatriates had second thoughts. They reconsidered their decision but would not tell their countrymen; most said they were frightened of their fellow repatriates. Camp commanders and visiting hearing boards, imbued with war patriotism, were anxious to move them on and often refused to allow a change of decision. One who was turned back was Karl Eppeler. A former Bund member until its dissolution in December 1941, Eppeler had been denaturalized. His American citizenship, awarded in 1930, was declared null and void and he became an enemy alien. The FBI arrested him in mid-October 1942, and he was shipped to Ellis Island, Seagoville, and finally, Crystal City. His wife, whose citizenship was not annulled, followed Eppeler voluntarily. When internees were tendered notices of removal and asked if they wanted a hearing to reconsider the decision, forty-eight-year-old Eppeler said "no." Months later he changed his mind; he now wanted to stay in America, and a hearing was convened in O'Rourke's office. The main question was: "Why did you change your mind?"

Eppeler's first reason was that remaining in the United States would "keep him out of trouble." "According to what I now know," Eppeler said, "I see only one way to keep out of trouble in the future, and to make a living in the future, and that is by becoming self-sufficient, and the only way I can see that is right here."

When questioned further by O'Rourke and hearing board representative McCollister, Eppeler conceded, "I have been away from Germany for almost twenty-three years—I have no money." It was easier to make money in the United States than in Europe.

Another explanation for his change of mind concerned the requirements for parole. When first asked about repatriation, he was told that to remain in the United States he would have to sign an agreement to accept parole. "But before signing," said Eppeler, "I wanted to know what was on that parole. They would not tell me that. Only if I signed and a parole was granted, would I be advised of the conditions. You naturally get sort of careful what you sign." But, over the past months he had become more trusting and would sign a parole agreement.

The questioning now took an interesting turn.

Q. Do you think you could live in this country and have respect for it after the way your case has developed? How are you going to feel inside toward this country if you make it your home? You were a citizen; that citizenship was revoked, and you were interned. Have you formed any bitterness?

A. I don't think being mad is the same as bitterness. Don't you think a man who is born in this country sometimes has a gripe against the government—or a disagreement?

Q. Why do you want to be a citizen of this country again? Don't you feel in your heart that you have been grossly mistreated by this country?

A. Calling it "grossly mistreated" is putting it rather strong; but one thing I know: in times of war, things are done that in peacetime are not done. You have to take a more philosophical attitude than that.

Unable to provoke Eppeler into voicing his bitterness toward the government, which they could then use as the basis for rejection, the hearing board turned toward a common area of investigation for most internees: To whom are you loyal? They reminded him of his devotion to the Bund and turned the questions to his willingness to defend America against, say, Germany.

Q. In wartime, don't you think a man has to choose one side or the other? The fact that you were sympathetic to one would indicate that you would be in favor of one. Don't you wish one side or other would win?

A. I quit wishing long ago. I guess I am sort of a fatalist about this question.

Q. But you have a desire, of course, one way or the other. Isn't that true?

A. Not necessarily.

The Repatriation Board decided that Eppeler's evasive answers, history of fascist extremism, and late change of heart, did not present a compelling case for remaining in the United States. Moreover, he dwelled on his desire to prosper in the United States, but financial need is not an acceptable basis for permanent immigration to America. He was repatriated to Germany.[3]

When it came time to leave, hundreds, and at some camps, thousands, of curious internees gathered to watch the repatriates leave with suitcases and footlockers, and march toward the waiting buses to the trains. At Crystal City, a spontaneous celebration broke out, complete with a small group of marching Japanese children in their paramilitary uniforms and the entire camp population singing the German national anthem, "Deutschland Über Alles," many with their arms outstretched in the Nazi salute.[4] The 19 February 1944 issue of *Das Lager* lamented the camp's loss of 634 people and likened Crystal City to a ghost town. The population of Crystal City took another sharp dip in January 1945, when 575 German internees (out of 2,951) left for Germany aboard the *Gripsholm*. By the end of the war, some 4,450 Germans and their families had been exchanged.

Ten days after Germany indicated a willingness to resume exchanges, the State Department and the Immigration Service took over. Washington quickly dispatched a detailed, three-page list of directions to the INS office in Philadelphia. From the INS they went out to every camp. Internees were limited to three large footlockers, which would be searched, stored under guard for two to three days prior to departure, and transferred to sealed railroad baggage cars. Security was extraordinarily tight. From the start of the process "the Germans are to be held incommunicado from all contacts with other camp aliens. The Germans must not be returned to their old quarters. . . . [Moreover] every German repatriate will be given a light personal search or frisk for concealed contraband articles. Certain repatriates, designated by the security agencies, will be given a strip search."

There is no indication in today's records about what may have been in the baggage en route to Germany. In preparation for the January 1945 repatriation, the State Department issued a "List of Articles Which May or May Not Be Taken Out of the United States by German Repatriates." The Germans were able to take the usual items: personal and household effects, small antiques, art objects, baby carriages, German passports, and birth certificates. The list of "may not be taken out" was twice as long and included such diverse items as furniture, garden tools, electrical appliances, radios, gold, printed matter, binoculars, sketches, and, except for passports and birth certificates, documents of any kind."[5] It is difficult to imagine what the State Department feared the repatriates might do with contraband garden tools, printed matter, or personal sketches, especially in light of the restrictions on the number of suitcases allowed. Nevertheless, their baggage was strictly isolated, guarded, and searched.

Before leaving, the Plaschkes, like everyone else, spent all their tokens to buy items scarce in Germany—seemingly everything. The camp authorities tried to provide a range of basic necessities, especially stocks of winter clothing to help the returning internees face the cold, bleak conditions in Germany. They were allowed to take one item from each pile, and if a search of their luggage during Customs inspection turned up duplicates, all but one was confiscated. One wealthy German asked for an overcoat, and it was issued to him. However, during the inspection at the wharf he was found to have *six* overcoats, several doubtless for resale at home. He shrugged and smiled as the extras were repossessed. Other passengers were found to have everything from armloads of cigarettes, to boxes of buttons and safety pins, to leather shoe soles and parts of camp furniture.

Once aboard the train, guards would be stationed at the end of each car, with no visiting allowed from one car to another. The internees were not allowed newspapers. From Jersey City, the internees boarded buses—under guard, of course—to move to the next stage of their journey. Thus far, they had changed hands from the State Department, to the Immigration and Naturalization Service, to the Department of Transportation, and back to the State Department. When they arrived in Jersey City, they came under the protection of the Jersey City Police Department. At Pier F, where the Swedish *Gripsholm* was docked, the internees became the responsibility of the Customs Division of the Department of Treasury. Then they were turned over to the U.S. Navy and the Office of Naval Intelligence who provided security at the port of embarkation, and finally led up the gangplank into the hands of the Swedish authorities who controlled operations aboard the ship.

For the American authorities, the logistics were a nightmare. Every thirty to sixty minutes another train arrived in Jersey City. For example, at 8:15 A.M. train #1 delivered 200 German prisoners of war; at 9:15 A.M. train #2 brought 70 German POWs from Canada; at 10:00 A.M. train #3 appeared with 190 German men from Fort Lincoln, North Dakota, among them 32 "dangerous troublemakers." Then came trains #4 and #5 from Crystal City with a total of 421 men, women, and children, and three baggage cars each. At 11:00 A.M. train #6 pulled in from Fort Stanton, New Mexico, and Seagoville, with 182 German men and women, including "1 stretcher case, 9 insane cases, and 6 dangerous troublemakers." A cutter pulled in at 1:30 P.M. from Ellis Island with 89 German men, women, and children. Eventually, the *Gripsholm* and a backup ship, the *Letitia*, took aboard 952 repatriates, plus approximately one hundred border patrol officers, doctors, matrons, and medical attendants. There were "12 stretcher cases, 17 insane cases, 11 isolation cases."[6] The ships carried more than 7,000 pieces of internee baggage.

At the last moment the State Department included one hundred German nationals living in Mexico, as the Mexican government, for whatever reason, suddenly decided to participate in the exchange. These Germans were delivered to the American authorities at the Texas border town of Laredo, checked and double-checked, and turned over to immigration guards and placed on the Missouri Pacific Railroad. They were put in three coach cars, guarded, as always, and their baggage was placed in a sealed baggage car. The final words of instruction from the State Department to the agents on the scene were that "the German nationals must not, under any condition, have access to this baggage from the time they arrive at Laredo until the baggage is turned over to the Customs at Crystal City."[7] The Germans arrived at Crystal City, were searched and counted, and sent eastward to join the others on Pier F.

Most internees recall this leg of the trip train as absolute chaos; they remember guards everywhere, colored tags on their coats and baggage, denoting families, destinations, and those who were chronically ill or had mental problems. Each family found its tiny stateroom, piled its luggage where they could, and made its way along cramped corridors to locate friends or reach fresh air. The *Gripsholm* left on 7 January 1945, brightly illuminated and festooned with Swedish flags. Once at sea, the returning Germans found that the Swedish sailors were polite, the food was good, and the children had a delightful time playing while their parents relaxed, under blankets, on the deck chairs. The ship crossed the Atlantic unmolested, carrying another group of people to their new homes who remember being, alternately, anxious, angry, bewildered, enthusiastic, nostalgic, and hopeful. So began the exchange process of interned enemy aliens to the ruins of their homeland.

For the next three weeks, on their way to Marseilles, the young Plaschke boys roamed the ship, made friends here and there, and, imagining the ruined conditions in Germany ahead, kept a close eye on their few belongings. Everyone on board was in terror of U-boats. For thirty-eight-year-old Walter Klein, his seven-day *Gripsholm* voyage to Lisbon was spent dreaming of his hometown of Siegen. He consoled himself, sadly, by imagining that boatloads of Jews were traveling toward America in exchange, and were experiencing the same dread of the German submarines.

In return for the group being shipped to Germany on the *Gripsholm* in January 1945, America requested that Germany send back 850 American or Latin American civilians and sick or wounded American prisoners of war on the *Gripsholm*'s return voyage. In a surprising gesture, considering the State Department's inaction on behalf of Europe's doomed Jews, the American note added that "50–75 individuals of the 850 be selected from Bergen-Belsen and Auschwitz Concentration Camps and be given 'ad hoc' passports to make the journey." Emboldened by the approaching Allied victory, the State Department requested that Germany also include: (1) "all North American internees in Camps Laufen, Spittal, Biberbach, Wurzach, and Bergen-Belsen"; (2) "all South American and Central American nationals in Liebenau, Laufen, and Bergen-Belsen"; and (3) "all such nationals in Police hands"—estimated to be about 250 people.[8] There was no response from Berlin other than a routine acknowledgment of the diplomatic exchange. There is no evidence that Germany complied.

For its part, Germany sent the State Department another list of 750 specific German nationals it desired, in the traditional order of preference: (1) "German nationals from other American republics interned in the United States, and (2) German nationals formerly residents of the United States, now interned in that country." In most cases the United States was able to comply, but of the 750 persons requested by Berlin, twenty-nine refused repatriation, thirty-eight were considered security risks and ineligible to be returned (including Marianne von Moltke and several others who were currently in prison), and five could not be located.

The schedule of the main repatriation vessels was:

Gripsholm	19 June 1942	to Lourenco Marques
Gripsholm	2 September 1943	to Murmagao
Gripsholm	15 February 1944	to Lisbon
Gripsholm	2 May 1944	to Barcelona, Algiers, Liverpool
Gripsholm	23 August 1944	to Sweden
Gripsholm	7 January 1945	to Marseilles
Drottningholm	7 May 1942	to Lisbon
Drottningholm	15 July 1942	to Gothenburg
Nyassa	13 June 1942	to Lisbon
Serpa Pinto	3 July 1942	to Lisbon
Letitia	7 January 1945	to Marseilles

In May 1945, the war in Europe was over, and America turned to the Japanese. Shipping space to and from Europe eased, and the new president, Harry Truman, announced that the United States had no use for untrustworthy residents. Never one to mince words, Truman argued that if they were "bad news" before, they're "still bad news now." Though the European war was over, and German aliens were no longer enemies, Truman issued Proclamation 2655 on 14 July 1945, that "all alien enemies . . . within the limits of the United States . . . who shall be deemed . . . dangerous to the public peace and safety . . . may be required to depart therefrom. . . ."[9] In other words, any enemy alien considered dangerous during the war could now be repatriated, voluntarily or not. The first German internee deported was Fritz Kuhn.

Two months later, during the Latin American Conference on Problems of War and Peace, President Truman enlarged the repatriation program to include kidnapped enemy aliens (as defined below) from around the Western Hemisphere. Proclamation 2662 declared:

All alien enemies now within the continental limits of the United States (1) sent here from other American republics and (2) who are within the territory of the United States without admission under the immigration laws are, if their continued residence in the Western Hemisphere is deemed . . . prejudicial to the future security or welfare

of the Americas . . . [,] subject . . . to removal from the United States
to the lands belonging to the enemy government. . . .[10]

In other words, wartime deportees kidnapped from Latin America or anywhere in the Western Hemisphere would not be returned to their countries
of residence—clearly, Washington's attempt to dominate the Americas in
the postwar world. But what was to be done with thousands of legal and
illegal enemy aliens?

CHAPTER ELEVEN

THE WAR IS OVER

With the war coming to a close, it was important to remain flexible, and Washington delayed as much as possible a decision on a clear-cut policy. By mid-summer 1945, the government had decided on two basic plans for handling the internees: (a) release outright those deemed nonthreatening to American postwar concerns, especially if they were sufficiently cowed to challenge the handling of the internee program; and (b) maintain in detention those felt to be a continued threat to American interests. In late 1945, unable to delay any longer, the government began to release some of the 10,905 internees. But what to do with those who might still constitute some threat to postwar America?

President Truman decisively cut the Gordian Knot. On 8 September 1945 "the President of the United States by proclamation authorized the Secretary of State to order the repatriation of dangerous alien enemies deported to this country during the war." Also included was "any person who appears to be so clearly dangerous as to make his repatriation desirable . . ."[1] The future for the most dangerous aliens was deportation, whether it was called "exchange," "repatriation," or "expulsion." Curiously, Truman removed the issue from the hands of the Justice Department and transferred responsibility to the State Department, creating a string of legal complications. Most importantly, Truman's proclamations left three major questions unanswered: "Who among the thousands of enemy aliens in detention camps was dangerous and posed a threat to hemispheric security?" "To what country should these people be shipped?" and "What about U.S.-born spouses and children of aliens?"

These questions were discussed at the highest levels of the U.S. Army and Justice Department, giving rise to still more questions: "Are the internees to be shipped to the nations of their birth or to their countries of choice?" or "What is to be done with American-born dependents who are not in a position to support themselves financially?"

General Lucius Clay, commander of the American Zone of Occupation in Germany, was understandably reluctant to admit several thousand strong German nationalists—people who hadn't personally experienced the utter destruction of Nazism.

Where would the Japanese be sent? Since the 1941 consulate break-in in Los Angeles, the FBI was well aware that Japanese-Americans and Japanese residents in the United States were not trusted in Japan. They would not

be welcomed by the Japanese. Nor would they be welcomed by General
Douglas MacArthur, Japan's new benevolent ruler. The occupation was
surprisingly peaceful but would not have benefitted by the appearance of
several hundred outspoken Japanese nationalists.

Another problem concerned the Italians. What about those who were
interned prior to Attorney General Biddle's 1942 Columbus Day reprieve
and who had remained in custody?

At the same time, tension in America mounted as labor unions demanded every available job for returning GIs, and the army and the INS
wanted to redirect their manpower. Also, American towns were eager to
get their campground facilities back. The solution was provided by the
internees themselves: many simply wanted to leave. Washington encouraged—and, by some claims,[2] intimidated—groups of Germans, Japanese,
and Italians to be repatriated as shipping space allowed. One curious devia-
tion involved sending Latin-American Germans to Germany, giving rise to
the suggestion that American industrialists were trying to handicap their
business competitors in Latin America. A letter to the editor of the influential *Washington Post* on 5 October 1945 questioned this policy. In a rather
rambling polemic, a Roger Baldwin acknowledged the kidnapping program, and the current repatriation of German, Japanese, and Italian internees, but protested that German internees from Latin America were being
wrongly repatriated to Germany rather than to Latin America. "Many who
were residents of those countries for 5–30 years," who "have married na-
tives and raised families there" should not be returned to Germany. The
State Department was urged to conduct hearings among these misdirected
Germans, and abide by their choice.[3] Whatever prompted this outburst,
the issue never reappeared in the press.

Despite the temptation to overuse such a blanket warrant, only a limited
number of internees were ultimately plucked from their camp populations;
many of those took their cases to court and won. Internees deemed too
dangerous to remain in the United States were notified individually that
they were being expelled. Each such internee received a printed notice
stating that:

> based upon the evidence considered at your earlier alien enemy hear-
> ing or hearings, it has been determined that you should be removed
> and repatriated to the country of your nationality. . . .
>
> Prior to the issuance of a final order for your removal and
> repatriation you are entitled to a hearing before a hearing board
> appointed by the Attorney General . . . to present evidence to
> show that you are not dangerous to the public peace and safety of
> the United States. . . .[4]

Accompanying the removal order was an acknowledgment form ("I
have received notice of the determination of my removal from the United

States and repatriation to the country of my nationality") and request for a repatriation hearing ("where you may present evidence why the final order for your repatriation should be stayed"). Since involuntary repatriation was a dramatic and potentially abusable government policy, the Justice Department made an extra effort to investigate each case. For those who wished to present new evidence, a special repatriation hearing board came directly to the camps. (The blue-ribbon board was composed of C. Edward Rhetts, assistant attorney general, Edward J. Ennis, director of the Alien Enemy Control Unit, and John L. Burling, special assistant to the attorney general.) To avoid any later charges of peer pressure, internees were offered a final and private hearing at Ellis Island.[5]

By December 1945, deportation of undesirable aliens had begun, a process which continued until July 1947. Following a nine-day voyage by ship, the deportees arrived in northern Germany; there they were met by armed guards and transported in sealed cattle cars to established prisoner camps, such as Asperg, near Ludwigsburg, a high-security facility reserved for individuals—Nazis, war criminals, etc.—considered most dangerous. Postwar Germany was in chaos, food and clothing were in short supply, and high-security prison camps were miserable places to spend the bitter winter of 1945–1946.

But the repatriation was not done without a fight. In mid-1945 a group of twenty-four Crystal City internees organized a committee to try to halt the deportations and effect their mass release. They approached Kurt Mertig, chairman of the Citizens' Protective League (CPL) in New York, to hire a lawyer to take the matter to court where they hoped to test the constitutionality of the whole deportation program. The internees collected their remaining pocket change to provide $50 per person to challenge the government. Mertig approached the German internees in Fort Lincoln, Ellis Island, and several other camps to join the lawsuit. With $2,300 in his war chest, the group's lawyer, James J. Laughlin, met with Attorney General Tom Clark in September and asked that all remaining internees be released on parole. Attorney General Clark listened but regretted that nothing could be done at the moment. If cancellation of the process was not possible, the lawyer asked, perhaps individual cases could be reviewed in court. This request, too, was denied. Finally, the internees took the issue before the U.S. Court of Appeals—*Citizen's Protective League et al. v. Tom C. Clark, Attorney General of the United States*—and lost unanimously in May 1946. They were considered dangerous to the public, now and in the future. The court had spoken and the INS, in turn, acted quickly. District directors and the authorities at Crystal City were instructed to serve all outstanding removal orders except in the cases of Japanese nationals and in those cases stayed by court action. In addition, the current INS commissioner, Ugo Carusi, reminded the district authorities that "you should exercise such safeguards as appear necessary, including having the alien escorted under guard to and from places." However, trustworthy aliens awaiting repatriation in thirty days might be allowed to complete their affairs unguarded, but district directors were warned that "they should be paroled only under such safeguards as will assist their departure from the country or, in the event of their failure to depart, their removal by this Service to Germany." Only at Crystal City was the officer in charge instructed "to defer the serving of the orders until further notice since it appears likely that further litigation will prevent removals actually being effected."[6] The fate of more than five hundred German internees imprisoned at Crystal City, Texas, remained undecided.

INS Commissioner Carusi also answered a number of vexing questions:

Should the deportees or parolees be permitted to go to Canada?

Answer: Not until they produce evidence that they will be legally admitted.

Shall they be permitted to depart to other countries?

Answer: They shall be permitted to depart to any foreign country under the conditions related to legal entry.

May INS field offices grant extensions of stay beyond the prescribed thirty-day period?

Answer: Except in cases of unusual merit, extensions will not be granted, and mere failure to have secured a visa enabling the subject to depart to some other country will not be considered grounds for extension.

Where the head of a family is removed to an enemy country of his nationality, may his wife and children accompany him voluntarily at Government expense?

Answer: Yes. Wives and dependent children of enemy aliens who are removed will be allowed to accompany aliens being removed to Germany or other enemy country at Government expense.[7]

The Justice Department was firm: those internees deemed dangerous were declared "deportees". They could never return to United States except to visit. Those who volunteered to be exchanged could someday return. The first postwar repatriation began on 7 November 1945, when some three hundred internees were shipped from Crystal City to Ellis Island. The initial batch were all volunteers: (a) voluntary repatriates who were not deportable and who were apprehended in the United States; (b) voluntary repatriates who were deportable and who were apprehended in the United States; and (c) voluntary repatriates who were brought to the United States from the Latin American republics. The next group of deportations were involuntary. In total, the Justice Department deported about 495 German internees—318 from Fort Lincoln, 80 from Crystal City, 12 who were employed on (Fort Lincoln) Extra Gang No. 5, seventy-five employed on forest-service projects in the Spokane District, five from the Sharp Park Detention Camp, and five held in San Pedro.

In June 1946 a group of German internees from among the 220 awaiting deportation at Ellis Island returned to court. This time they argued that their deportation would be illegal because they had been denied lawyers and the right to cross-examine the government's witnesses. Another dead-end; they lost in federal court in August 1946, and again in the U.S. Court of Appeals at the beginning of 1947. Enemy aliens continued to be subject to government orders.

A handful of internees tried another route: they filed writs of habeas corpus claiming that they could not be deported as alien enemies since their native countries were no longer enemies. In January 1946, the effort backfired when a federal court ruled that the other internees aside, Latin American internees were "alien enemies" who could be detained and de-ported. Shortly thereafter, 513 Japanese (90 percent from Peru), 897 Germans, and 37 Italians from Latin America were given perfunctory hearings and shipped not to Latin America but to the Axis nations. Most were out-raged at having been first kidnapped, then brought to the United States against their will. Most had arrived in steerage, were detained for years, and now were being returned to war-devastated countries half a world away.

Some, like Alfred and Caroline Heitmann, hired local lawyers to battle the system. On 7 May 1945, the Heitmanns were shipped from Seagoville, their home for the past three and a half years, to Ellis Island. Upon arrival they contacted relatives living in Buffalo, who, in turn, hired the best local attorney to get them out. Whatever the lawyer did must have worked, because they were released on parole in one month. Without so much as a "farewell," the Heitmanns were free from internment but subject to travel restrictions.

Nearly one hundred other German internees won their release through an arrangement with the Justice Department to volunteer for the U.S. Army.

As the internees were paroled, exchanged, or released, the INS started closing down the camps and funneling the internees to those that remained open. The Kenedy Internment Camp, Kenedy, Texas, closed in September 1944, the Kooskia Internment Camp in Kooskia, Idaho, shut its doors in May 1945. The Seagoville Internment Camp returned to its original func-tion as a penitentiary in June 1945. After the war, the institution became a minimum-security prison for men, which it remained until 1980, when soaring crime rates and overcrowded conditions in the nation's penitentiar-ies forced it to upgrade to a medium-security prison, and, most recently, to a maximum-security prison. Little is remembered there about the war years.

Fort Lincoln, near Bismarck, North Dakota, closed its doors on 1 March

1946. It remained abandoned for more than twenty years. In June 1969 Congress voted to provide funds for a training center for Native Americans: today, the old Fort Lincoln is the United Tribes Technical College.

Formal detention operations at Fort Stanton ceased on 20 November 1945. The INS agreement with Fort Stanton to occupy the abandoned CCC camp required that the portable, prefabricated CCC-type barracks, most in poor condition after five years of continual habitation, be dismantled and transported to various INS facilities. Those structures not required by the INS were turned over to the Fort Stanton Hospital. The swimming pool was used by hospital personnel for some years after the war. Only the large laundry building, with a large swastika scratched on the second floor wall of the north side, still remains in operation to this day.[8]

Gradually, as cases were adjudicated and numbers decreased, remaining internees were moved to the last operational internment camp, Crystal City, and when that was finally closed, to the deportation station at Ellis Island. There they awaited the disposition of various legal actions on their cases. Eberhard Fuhr, near the end of his odyssey, remembers the dramatic change from Crystal City.

> At least at Crystal City we had a big perimeter we could walk around, so there was a certain feeling of freedom. At Ellis Island you were confined to this big room. It was a real, total bore. We did a lot of talking and a lot of card playing and a lot of waiting. I painted for ten cents an hour because I needed that for cigarettes, but above all because you needed to keep yourself busy. Otherwise you'd go daffy.[9]

One by one the camps were phased out—some long after the end of the European war in May 1945. In June 1945 there were 1,800 German and 3,500 Japanese enemy internees still behind barbed wire. "When V.E. Day came [in May 1945], we all thought our release was imminent," says Eberhard Fuhr, by then a two-year veteran of Camp Crystal City, "but nothing happened. When V.J. Day came [in September], we were sure our release was imminent—but only the Japanese internees were released. Soon the German internees from South and Central America were released—and we were still behind barbed wire."[10] As late as 14 March 1947, nearly two years after the end of World War II, Crystal City still held 108 German internees.[11]

These last internees were put to work dismantling the buildings in the now-vacant Japanese area of the camp. The prefabricated "Victory Huts" were shipped to border patrol camps and other federal facilities. (In fact, Eberhard Fuhr was at Crystal City long enough to dismantle his own building in February 1947, before being transferred to Ellis Island.) The last internees were largely discharged and sent home. Certain cases were shipped to Ellis Island. The camp officially closed the following year, in February 1948, and once again became a migrant labor camp.

Charlotte Maier (née Krause), now an elderly woman living in Munich, vividly remembers leaving Camp Crystal City early in the summer of 1946. Her father Albert, a physics teacher, had been arrested at the end of 1942— "for nothing at all," Charlotte angrily recalls. While both her parents were German-born, they were naturalized American citizens. Neither was connected with the German-American Bund. With her father's arrest, however, her mother had no choice but to petition the court in Chicago to join him at Crystal City with their three children. "Growing up in camp was not too bad for us children because we had friends from all over South America, a good school, and even music lessons. We were quite lost when we were released to return to regular public school. In June 1946, my father was notified that he was free to leave; our family received train tickets to our hometown, Chicago, and $50 each as 'start-up' money. That was it! Our lives changed as suddenly as they had back in 1942."

Princess Steph, the international hostess, spent the war years at Seagoville Internment Camp. At the end of the war, Seagoville was one the first camps to shut down, in June 1945, and according to her son, she was the very last person to leave. "Her detractors and enemies had managed to prolong her captivity to the final possible moment."[12] Not surprisingly, she managed to land on her feet, bruised but unbowed, and moved to Beverly Hills, California. Her son remembers that "when she arrived from Seagoville her most urgent desire was to burn all the clothes she had worn for the past four years. But the postwar world was one of global shortages so, instead, she gave them to a local Catholic charity to distribute." It wasn't long before she was back in New York's high society; however, when she found herself portrayed unflatteringly in the society columns, Steph moved to Philadelphia with her old paramour Lemuel Schofield, former director of the U.S. Immigration Service. From the early 1950s onward, Steph went through Schofeld's death, an Internal Revenue Service lawsuit for $250,000, suitors, social crises, and executive positions influence-peddling for the mass-circulation German magazines *Quick* and *Stern*. During the next decade, she arranged or conducted interviews with such notables as the Shah of Iran, President Kennedy, and Henry Kissinger. President Lyndon Johnson invited her to his inauguration in 1965. She later teamed up with Axel Springer, the German publishing mogul, and moved effortlessly among the great writers and millionaire publishers in Europe and the United States. Steph died on 13 June 1972, in Geneva, Switzerland, where her villa looked down on beautiful Lake Geneva.

The Krause family did not do nearly as well. They returned to Chicago with no place to stay, few friends, and barely enough money to survive. There was no work for a fifty-one-year-old physics teacher so his wife, Maria, went to work as a saleswoman in a bakery. The children, seven, eleven, and fourteen years old, had to work after school and during vacations to help the family survive. "Before the war Papa had a good job, and we owned our own home; who would have known that within a few short years we would lose it all."[13]

Fritz von Opel, brother of the famed auto manufacturer, spent the war years in Seagoville. Upon his release in 1946, he divorced his wife Margareta, and went to Africa where he opened a successful hunting and safari business.

Albert and Caroline Heitmann were paroled to Buffalo, New York, after three-and-a-half years of internment. Caroline had two sisters and a brother there; it was they who hired the lawyer who got the Heitmanns out of Ellis Island. But now they hit hard times. Jobs were scarce in 1945 with tens of thousands of former soldiers looking for work. Besides, who would hire a paroled enemy alien? Standard Oil did offer him a job, but it conflicted with the conditions of his parole. Thus began a string of jobs that ranged from grave digger in Buffalo, to foundryman, to plant maintenance at the Carborundum Company in Niagara Falls, New York. Albert remained at Carborundum until his retirement in 1979. He never became an American citizen. Caroline was also broken by the internment but decided to protect herself from any future trouble by becoming an American citizen. With a letter of support from Dr. Amy Stannard, her warden at Seagoville, Caroline was naturalized in 1946. Their only child, John, was born in 1948, and is currently a noted professor of the history of science at the University of Dayton (Ohio). "My parents never spoke about their experiences in the internment camps," John recalls, "it was simply too painful for them to remember."

The Lambert Jacobs family, arrested in 1944, were held in Crystal City from the end of April 1945 until 1 December 1945. They were shipped, with ninety-seven others, to Ellis Island. Leaving the camp was fine with Jacobs; he was ready to return to Germany. The past year had been a nightmare. This whole thing happened, he believed, because he wouldn't tell the hearing board that he would join with Britain and Russia to fight Germany. Now that the war was over, some nameless Justice Department bureaucrat recommended that he be shipped back to Germany. All Jacobs knew was that his name appeared on the next exchange list. A member of his final repatriation hearing board actually suggested that if he returned voluntarily, it would look better on his record; if he waited until he was forcibly repatriated, he would doubtless have difficulties later on. Jacobs, disgusted with the whole business, agreed. It was time to go home. Like the families of most internees, his wife and children, however reluctantly, joined him in the exchange.

Suddenly, a champion appeared on their behalf. Senator William ("Wild Bill") Langer of North Dakota, Republican member on the Senate Judiciary Subcommittee on Immigration, became sympathetic to their plight.

Motivated as much by a politician's periodic need for a colorful cause as by
the illogic of the deportation scheme, Langer introduced Bill 1749 in the
Senate on 21 July 1947. The bill called for a halt to all deportation proceed-
ings on behalf of 207 specific German aliens interned by the government
on Ellis Island, including Eberhard Fuhr, his brother Julius, and parents
Carl and Anna. On 24 July, the bill passed into law[14] and those internees
who had not volunteered to return to Germany knew the end was near. A
few weeks later new hearings took place on Ellis Island. Fuhr's hearing
lasted ten minutes. "From the first question on I knew it was over. The
guy asked rational questions. He didn't talk about submarines coming up
the Ohio River and stuff like that. It was obvious that it was geared not to
find fault but to find a reason why you should be allowed to stay in the
States."

"When I walked out I told my brother, 'We're out of here. This is all
over.' " Two weeks later Fuhr was called into the director's office. The
director told him, "You're free to go. We'll have your train tickets tomor-
row morning to go back to Cincinnati." Fuhr, now twenty-two, couldn't
wait. "When's the next ferry to the mainland?" "Twenty minutes," he was
told. Eberhard and his brother Julius couldn't stand confinement for another minute. They explained the situation to their parents, assured them
they would all be free and together in a matter of weeks and were on the
ferry for New York City. When Carl and Anna Fuhr returned to Cincinnati
they found their boys and little else. Their home had been ransacked by
burglars after their sons Eberhard and Gerhard had been taken away by the
FBI back in 1943. Their prewar friends shunned them. Who among them
may have turned them in to the FBI? However uncomfortable, even miserable, the Fuhr family chose to remain in the United States. They spent the
next years trying to come to grips with their five-year imprisonment. Carl
went to work in a bakery. He died in 1961. Anna died a year later.[15]

Tillie Reseneder, now Tillie Busse, says the the four-year internment
"ruined her life." "One of the reasons it still bothers me is I just feel I was
gypped and deprived of a proper education, and my freedom was taken
away. I didn't finish grammar school or go to high school."[16] Today, Tillie
is a home typist who lives near Easton, about fifty-five miles north of
Philadelphia.

While it is clear that the interned children were deprived of a traditional
rounded education, and that some subjects were neglected, graduates like
Art Jacobs and Al Plaschke went on to college and military training programs without difficulty. Both have since retired from the U.S. Air Force.
Jacobs retired from the faculty of Arizona State University. Eberhard Fuhr
graduated with highest honors from Ohio State University and later earned
an MBA at the University of Wisconsin. He worked for twelve years in
sales and marketing for Shell Oil Company. He left to join a decorative

lamination business and is now retired. Julius retired from the insurance business; Gerhard, who enlisted for service during the Korean War, sold real estate. Julius did not even mention his internment to his children until they were nearly grown. Brother Gerhard never fully recovered from the experience.

Alfred Plaschke, fourteen years old, had no choice but to go to Germany when his family was involuntarily deported in January 1945. He recalled how anxious his parents were about the conditions that would face them in the collapsing Third Reich, yet everyone was buoyed by the prospect of seeing long-lost friends and relatives. Arriving at Marseilles aboard the *Gripsholm*, the 600 repatriates were taken by Swiss trains to Montreux and across Switzerland to the Swiss-Austrian-German border town of Bregenz at the edge of Lake Konstance. The group had no papers or passports. Moments later they were escorted into southern Germany where a bored German official checked each name against the ever-present lists. The Plaschkes embarked on an odyssey to find their relatives that included their train being strafed by British fighters, huddling in a bomb shelter, being threatened by a Nazi official waving a pistol, and a twenty-kilometer hike in the dark. They arrived in Hamburg in time for a massive Allied bombing raid.

Alfred Erich Schneider, the painter and decorator who was arrested in Houston in late December 1941 (see chapter four), volunteered to be exchanged. The Schneider family of four left Crystal City and boarded the *Gripsholm* on 2 January 1945. Erich had come from Dresden before he emigrated to the United States in 1928, so it was to Dresden that he was now returned. The *Gripsholm* was too busy outrunning a mid-Atlantic hurricane to fear German U-boats, but made it to Marsailles intact. The passengers took the standard train ride to Montreax, Switzerland, and from there to the border city of Bregenz, and on to Dresden. The Schneiders arrived in Dresden on 10 February 1945—three days before the terrible fire-bombing. Somehow they survived. Then came the Russians.

What followed were months of terror and escape that would do justice to a spy novel. Clearly, eventual return to the United States would be much more difficult, if possible at all, from Russsian-occupied Dresden, so the family planned their escape to the American zone. First, father and sister bolted on 1 June 1946, and made it to freedom. Young Gerd Erich, then eighteen years old and American-born, tried to take the legal route and appealed to the U.S. Consul in Berlin. Instead, he ended up in a United Nations' Displaced Persons camp, and his mother was trapped in Dresden. After months of depression, Gerd Erich watched the tent flap suddenly open and there stood his pal from Crystal City, Alfred Plaschke. Alfred pledged to rescue Gerd Erich's mother from Soviet hands. Five days later he delivered. The Schneiders managed to book passage aboard an "old rust-bucket" named the *Marine Perch* and returned to the United States in 1948.

Erich picked up where he left off and resumed his painting and decorating job in Houston. Gerd Erich, known to all as "Sonny," became an electrician. He eventually moved his wife, three children, and a dog to Denver. In 1969, in need of a change, Sonny found the answer in installing domestic water pumps, which, in the water-starved mountains of Colorado, was more lucrative than pumping oil. He and his wife, Wanda, today live in Evergreen, Colorado.[17]

It didn't take young Plaschke long to realize that he wanted to go home to America, too. Alfred and his younger brother began to work on ways to leave Germany—without their parents. When American consular service was reestablished, the boys stood in long lines to prove that they were American citizens. They received their passports in 1947 but found that was only half the solution: they had to find a way to get home. While he waited, Alfred worked as an apprentice auto mechanic. Eventually, he got a job with the Waterman Steamship Company, cruised the world, and waited for his chance. Seventeen-year-old Alfred eventually made it to Mobile, Alabama, where he jumped ship, and caught a Greyhound Bus for Houston. He appeared at the door of the Koetter family, family friends from earlier years in Crystal City, and moved in for the next several years. Having little little business experience or education, Alfred joined the army. He liked the military so much that when his army enlistment was up, he turned around and joined the air force. The air force made him a communications expert, and he stayed in for twenty years. His brother meanwhile emigrated to Australia where he still lives.

Throughout Alfred Plaschke's life, his story has brought on several reactions: some, especially in the air force, reacted with suspicion, and several tried to block his access to security clearances and advancement; the second and by far the largest group, didn't believe him and accepted him as he was. It was the last type that made him the most angry—they didn't believe him. Because the entire German internment is relatively unknown, most former internees simply were not believed. The Fuhr brothers, and indeed, most of the other former internees, report the same reaction from people for most of their lives. "It is common knowledge that only the Japanese were interned, not Germans," Plaschke sneers. Once he discussed his past with a government personnel counselor and was told that he "was making it up." "In any case, I was (and am) an American citizen—born in the U.S.A.!"

Arthur Jacobs had an even tougher time when his parents were repatriated. His father was angry about the treatment they'd received and didn't hide his feelings. The family left overcrowded Ellis Island in January 1946 aboard the S.S. *Aiken Victory* for Europe. When they arrived in war-torn Germany, they were greeted by armed, suspicious U.S. soldiers who escorted these "American Nazis" across Germany in locked, dark, cattlecars with nothing to live on but bread and water. No one really knew what to do with the repatriates, and they were thrown in prison. Art Jacobs spent his thirteenth birthday in a cold prison cell in Asperg, together with high-ranking German military officers suspected of Nazi war crimes. Fortunately, an American officer and his wife took an interest in young Art and helped him return to the United States. In 1947, at the age of fourteen, Jacobs was back on American soil. Interestingly, both Jacobs and Plaschke spent their careers in the U.S. Air Force, Jacobs rising to the rank of major. Each tells of facing occasional curious questions about his early life behind barbed wire. In Jacobs's case, no one seems to have held it against him; technical educations, top secret clearances, and promotions continued to come his way. Plaschke, on the other hand, believes that his family's wartime intern-ment made promotions difficult.

Walter Klein of Haiti left Camp Kenedy with the first group of enthusi-astic detainees at the end of March 1944. One day during routine roll call, his name was read from a list of those approved to be exchanged; he had only three days to gather his belongings and say his good-byes. Then fol-lowed a train ride to New York, a hair-raising seven-day trip on the *Grips-holm* to Lisbon, Portugal, and a train ride to Madrid and Biarritz. At the French frontier the returnees faced the usual bureaucratic red tape with clipboards, long lists, inspections, and searches. Everything was double-checked before they were turned over to the German authorities. They spent eight days in France before a German train arrived to take them all to Saarbrucken. Eventually Klein was delivered back to his delighted family in Siegen where, despite the chaos of the end of the war, he managed to find work and return to the rhythm of small-town life. Money that he had managed to save during his two years at Kenedy was transferred to him by the American authorities without difficulty. All in all, Walter Klein believed he was treated fairly, and that, everything considered, he had a pretty good time in the process. Walter Klein died in Germany in 1980.

Wilhelm Wartemann, his wife, and five children, stepped aboard the *Gripsholm* in February 1944 in anger. The family had been split up for two years, and the Fort Worth refrigeration engineer felt that nine years in America was enough. Germany, they quickly found, was far worse, as they spent the next year living in a bomb shelter at the family farm in Wilhelms-haven, on the North Sea. In 1947, the two oldest children were able to locate a sponsor and emigrated to the area they knew best: Texas. The next child, Carl, emigrated in 1951, and in 1952 their parents followed. After three years in Galveston, the family moved to Houston. The youngest daughter, JoAnne, married in 1962, moved to Dallas where she and her three sons live today. Her father died in 1969; Anna is eighty-seven years old, and like most of the older Wartemann children, still crackles with resentment and bitterness at their wartime internment and repatriation.[18]

Some internees shrug off their internment. Four Germans from Fort Bismarck who joined the U.S. military to get out of the camps were as brave and valuable as any. Herbert Seifert returned to Germany in 1944 in an army uniform—twenty years later he was discharged as Master Sergeant Seifert. Edward Drewello returned to Germany in 1944 by way of army intelligence. Kurt Peters listened for enemy submarines for navy intelligence, and Ernest Pohlig saw Guam from the deck of a bullet-strafed ship. After the war, several went to school on the G.I. Bill. Interestingly, all four men, and numerous others, returned to settle in Bismarck. Seifert and Drewello worked in the local hospital (Seifert became a laboratory supervisor), Peters headed the public information department of a large utility company, and Pohlig became a licensed carpeting contractor. All were well liked by friends and neighbors.[19]

When the Koetters were arrested in December 1941, their two sons, Juergen and Gunter, were trying to get into the military. Little chance, they believed, considering their parents' record. Juergen appealed to anyone with government clout—the chief of U.S. Customs in Houston and even a rabbi in Galveston. To his astonishment, he received his draft notice in October 1942. "You must know someone in Washington," an officer marveled when Juergen received his top secret clearance even as his parents sat in an enemy alien internee camp as security risks. (To this day Juergen cannot name his benefactor.) In the army, he pursued electronics and was eventually selected to join a secret unit whose only designation was ANCPS-6. Next came advanced training in geophysics at the prestigious Massachusetts Institute of Technology (MIT), and on to Camp Murphy, Florida, where he became a member of the team that developed one of America's most secret weapons. Working with such luminaries as Professors Shery Wells from Yale, Jacob Millman from the City College of New York, and Howard Stabler from William and Mary, Juergen Koetter spent the war years working on projects so secret that he needed security clearances, badges, and loyalty oaths. His laboratory at Camp Murphy, Florida, was directly across the street from an element of the Manhattan Project. He continued to work on the radar project through the end of 1944 and into 1945, long enough to see his designs help win the war.

To add to the irony, his brother Gunter was also in the army and served as the personal aide to General Brewer.

After the war, Juergen worked for General Geophysical Company and eventually founded a successful construction company in Houston. Gunter became a well-known architect and lived in retirement in Houston. Tragically, both brothers died of cancer within months of one another in August and December 1996.

Eberhard Fuhr and his family never went back to Germany as planned, and his relationship with girlfriend Millie ran the course of adolescent puppy love. After his internment ended in 1947, Eberhard went to college at Gustavus Adolphus in Minnesota, graduated from Ohio State, and eventually went to work as a salesman for Shell Oil. He married Barbara Minner who, like Millie, was the daughter of an internee at Crystal City. Eberhard applied to become an American citizen and was naturalized in 1955. His brother Julius, widowed after a long, happy marriage, happened to meet an old girlfriend from Crystal City some years later while vacationing in Australia. Margie Eha had been among the German families brought to Crystal City from Brazil and was also widowed. They married and now live in Minneapolis.

Barbara (the wife of Eberhard) Fuhr's family did not fare well after their release from internment. Her father, previously a writer, was unable to pick up the threads of his career. He had not sharpened his skills in half a decade; literary styles had changed; and his reputation as a former "Nazi" internee made peddling articles to magazines quite difficult. Barbara's mother kept the family afloat by selling pots and pans at a department store. Her father was reduced to shoveling coal. Over the years, the German internees have not remained in close contact, unlike the Japanese internees, largely from Crystal City, who belong to numerous organizations and meet for yearly reunions.[20] Approximately three-quarters of the 9,000 aliens arrested and interned during the war went back to their old pursuits. Most felt displaced. America could never be trusted again. Whether former German or Japanese internee, they were embittered by their treatment, lost youth or education, lost home or business. A surprising number felt guilty and ashamed about their experience, despite the fact that the overwhelming majority were innocent of any crime or threat to security. They resented having a prison record. Overall, most internees and their families emerged from the experience damaged in some way.

Philosophically, everyone understands that a country has the right, even the obligation, to round up suspected traitors during wartime, and most former internees conceded that there were plenty of outspoken Nazis around (mostly in their camps). Nevertheless, most were baffled and angry about being pulled into it. "All I did wrong was mouth-off to a hearing board," says Fuhr. "That shouldn't get you five years in a prison camp—think of the effects alone of six years of poor education." Still, the experience yielded at least one benefit. Fuhr smiles as he looks up at his framed master's degree from Ohio State. "And, I wouldn't have met my lovely wife Barbara."

The former German internees all agree on several things, however. The first is their resentment of the FBI and Ennis's Alien Enemy Control Unit. The FBI, in particular, assembled the lists, collected the data, harassed the witnesses, made the arrests, and influenced the decisions of the hearing boards.[21] Countless landlords allowed the "federal agents" into any apartment they wanted to ransack, with or without a search warrant. J. Edgar Hoover's power and ability to manipulate public hysteria through judiciously timed newspaper statements was legendary.

Former internees all concede that there were certainly a number of German nationalists, even hard-core Nazis, loose in the United States. That was not in dispute. The closest estimate appears to be that between 15 to 20 percent of those Germans interned were committed Nazis. How many of those were dangerous to American security is unknowable. Yet today, no one claims to have taken them seriously: they were "blowhards" and "essentially harmless." As for the others, however, a large portion of those arrested seem to have been unlucky victims of Hoover's xenophobia and paranoia. Their names had simply ended up on the FBI's notorious Custodial Detention Index. Whether or not they were "dangerous" or "security risks" to the war effort is an open question; what is clear, however, is that sympathy with the enemy is not a crime in the United States so long as it is not translated into deeds or the visible threat of deeds. In the words of Eugene Rostow on the subject of wartime internment, "It is essential to every democratic value in society that official action, taken in the name of the war power, should be held to standards of responsibility under such circumstances."[22]

The wartime alien internment program broaches two basic constitutional issues: the arrest, removal, and confinement of persons without trial, pending examination of their loyalty; and the indefinite confinement of persons found to be disloyal. In a study undertaken by a Select Committee of the U.S. Senate in 1976, the government concluded that:

> The FBI's domestic intelligence jurisdiction went beyond investigations of crime to include a vague mandate to investigate foreign involvement in American affairs. In the exercise of this jurisdictional authority, the Bureau began to investigate law abiding domestic groups and individuals; its program was also open to misuse for political purposes. The most intrusive intelligence techniques—initially used to meet wartime exigencies—were based on questionable statutory interpretation, or lacked any formal legal authorization.[23]

While Congress failed to confront the problem of a rogue domestic intelligence service, the attorney general did not. By 1943 Attorney General Biddle was fed up with Hoover's excesses and in a directive on 6 July 1943 demanded that the director immediately abolish the Custodial Detention Index. The index was, in Biddle's words, "impractical, unwise, and dangerous." Moreover, there was "no statutory authority or other present justification" for keeping such a list. The attorney general concluded his directive to Hoover by stating that the FBI's system for classifying "dangerous" persons was "inherently unreliable," the evidence used was "inadequate," and the standards applied were "defective."[24] In other words, the program was unfair and had to be immediately closed down. The director did not comply. Unwilling to abandon the bureau's investigation-detention program and emboldened by his own power and independence, Hoover simply renamed the program. The CDI program no longer existed, technically satisfying Biddle's order, but a new program, called the Security Index, appeared in its place. (Five weeks after receiving the directive from his superior, Hoover memoed all special agents in charge about the name change. "Investigations of individuals who may be dangerous to the public safety shall be discussed as a 'Security Matter,' and not 'Custodial Detention,' " ordered Hoover. "The phraseology, 'Custodial Detention,' shall no longer be used to designate the character of the investigation, nor shall it be used for any purpose in reports or other communications." Years later, when faced with yet another "shut-down" directive, Hoover changed the name of the Security Index (SI) to the Administrative Index (AI)).

However reviled by former internees, the FBI was nevertheless invaluable to the overall security of the nation. It did fall within the legal purview of the FBI to locate, investigate and, armed with the proper warrant, arrest suspected spies and potential traitors. This the bureau did with hard work, forty-eight-hour work weeks, shoe leather, and courage. At the same time, a large but unquantifiable percentage of the 16,054 enemy aliens arrested by the FBI alone—5,422 Japanese, 7,041 Germans, and 3,503 Italians—between 7 December 1941 and 30 June 1945, were clearly innocent of any crime.[25] The grand total of enemy aliens arrested by the Justice Department, though not necessarily interned, was 31,275 (16,849 Japanese, 10,905 Germans, 3,278 Italians, with a few Hungarians, Bulgarians, and Romanians). The German internees came from practically every state. A demographic survey reveals that the majority came from states with significant German-American populations: 2,292 from New York; 756 from New Jersey; 388 from Pennsylvania; approximately 350 from the Southeast; 300 from Texas; 572 from California; 250 from the Northwest; and some 800 from Michigan, Illinois, Wisconsin, Ohio, Missouri, and Indiana.

In addition to their resentment of the Justice Department, another point on which many former internees agree is the perception of anti-European (anti-German) bias in the internment program. (It must be remembered that the Custodial Detention Program was separate from the War Relocation Program, the racially motivated internment of some 120,000 Japanese-Americans in 1942.) With regard to the CDI internment program for "dangerous" aliens, of the above-noted total number of aliens arrested during the war, 10,608 (7,041 Germans plus 3,503 Italians) were European. Ten thousand European aliens were arrested versus only 5,422 Japanese.[26] Actually, the number of European internees was far higher—more like

25,600—with the addition of aliens brought up from Latin America, interned seamen, and random Hungarians, Romanians, Bulgarians, and Czechs. The majority of the internees were aliens, although the program swept up several hundred German- and Italian-American citizens as well. After Italian aliens were "reprieved" by Biddle in mid-1943, German aliens became the government's only target group. Although Japanese-Americans were gradually released from relocation camps after the 1944 Supreme Court decision, *Endo v. United States*, and Japanese internees were released from enemy alien camps until June 1946, hundreds of Germans and other internees of European origin were held as late as August 1948. (Admittedly, many of those interned so long were locked in court cases of their own choosing, to fight repatriation, retain their citizenship, or regain their lost homes or property.) Internees also pointed to the option offered to Japanese in the relocation program of joining one of two combat units, the highly decorated 442nd Regimental Combat Team or the 100th Infantry Battalion, to prove their loyalty. Hundreds of Japanese-Americans in the relocation camps, however embittered at their treatment or that of their parents, nonetheless stepped forward. A large percentage gave their lives. No such program was made available to the German internees, perhaps because only a fraction were of military age.

Lastly, the internees (and the records) agree that the enemy alien internment program of World War II has been passed over by history.[27] Their experience had never been told. Even the former detention camps left no mention of the German inmates held there during the war. Today, the Crystal City camp is gone. In its place are a senior citizens' center, a public housing project, the municipal airport, and a city maintenance and equipment yard. Not until 1985 was the only memorial created and it was dedicated to the Japanese-Americans internees, designed by a former internee who is now a prestigious architect, Alan Taniguchi.[28] Regarding Ellis Island, the official *Ellis Island Source Book*, published in 1985, notes only that Ellis Island was used to detain "suspected alien immigrants."[29] At Seagoville, currently a men's maximum security federal penitentiary, the facility's recent fiftieth anniversary *Official History* passed over the war years almost completely. As if to symbolize the unimportance of the internment program to the history of the Seagoville Correctional Institution, the photographs of all seventeen past wardens are on display—only the space attributed to Dr. Amy N. Stannard, dutifully listed as having served from 1941–1945, is empty.

The National Archives' official history of internment available to the public, entitled "World War II: The Home Front," contains not a word about the arrest and internment of thousands of Germans; it chronicles only the internment of Japanese-Americans. The Smithsonian Institution National Museum of American History and the American Library Association received a grant of $40,000 to develop a (wonderful) traveling multi-media exhibition on internment called "A More Perfect Union: Japanese-Americans and the U.S. Constitution." Between May 1994 and April 1996, plans called for the exhibit to visit more than fifty libraries across the country. German-Americans are not mentioned. On 19 February 1976, President Gerald Ford officially revoked Executive Order 9066, proclaiming that "we know now what we should have known then: Not only was that evacuation wrong, but Japanese-Americans were and are loyal Americans."[30] No reference was made to any other ethnic group. Periodic media coverage to commemorate anniversaries of wartime events—all have omitted reference to the internment of Germans during World War II. As recently as 1987 and 1988, articles in *Time Magazine* and *The New York Times*, flagships of America's popular news, stated flatly that there were no camps for German-Americans. In fact, *The New York Times* was adamant, stating that "the government never came close to locking up German-Americans as security risks."[31]

Particularly galling to former interned German aliens are the government's efforts to reimburse Japanese-Americans while passing over the Germans. Over the past forty years, since 1948, Congress has enacted nine separate laws to compensate Japanese-American former internees—an admirable record, although only Japanese-Americans are specifically mentioned: American-Japanese Evacuation Claims Act (Public Law 80-886), 2 July 1948; Amendment to Claims Acts of 1948 (82-116), 17 August 1951; Benefits for Certain Federal Employees of Japanese Ancestry (82-545), 15 July 1952; Amendment to Claims Act of 1948 (84-673), 9 July 1956; Credit for Periods of Internment for Certain Federal Employees of Japanese American Ancestry (86-782), 14 September 1960; Social Security Amendments of 1972 (Section 142-92-603), 17 November 1972; and the Japanese American Civil Service Retirement Credit for Periods of Internment, 22 September 1978.

The hopes of former German internees were raised in 1980 when Congress passed Public Law 96-317 creating the Commission on Wartime Relocation and Internment of Civilians (CWRIC). Its purpose was to review America's wartime record on the subject. But it did not seek, hear, or permit any testimony from German or European-American former internees; curiously, the commission sought the testimony only of Japanese-American former internees. Although the group was in existence for over two years, it held only twenty days of hearings. Not surprisingly, the commission's final report, *Personal Justice Denied*, issued in 1982, concluded that the only victims of wartime internment were Japanese-Americans.[32] German-Americans were sure they were finally vindicated when officials such as Edward Ennis, former director of the Alien Control Unit of the Justice Department, and James Rowe, Jr., former assistant attorney general, testified that Japanese-Americans were not treated any differently than German-Americans! There it was: German internees were officially there. And, therefore, they were entitled to identical remuneration. Unfortunately, none of these testimonies made it into the final report. More than that, the commission concluded that there was no need for Roosevelt's original Executive Order 9066, authorizing the exclusion of enemy aliens from restricted zones, and the detention and internment of legal resident aliens and citizens without proof of wrongdoing. The entire program had been unnecessary.

Finally came the landmark Civil Liberties Act of 1988 (100-383), 10 August 1988, which authorized $1.2 billion—or $20,000 per family—to surviving Japanese-American survivors. (No payments were to be made to the families of the 60,000 internees who died before the bill was signed.) On 27 September 1992, Congress passed an amendment to the Civil Liberties Act of 1988 (102-371), increased the amount by an additional $320 million, and included payments to new spouses and family members not of Japanese ancestry. The Civil Liberties Act of 1988 recognized "the fundamental injustice of the . . . internment of United States citizens and permanent resident aliens" and provided an apology on "behalf of the people of the United States" to those of Japanese ancestry who suffered internment. The law specifically excluded German internees.

In 1992 Congress passed an additional law, called the Japanese-American National Historic Landmark Theme Study Act, to locate one-time internment centers and designate them as national historic landmarks. Hearings were convened to consider the importance of various internment facilities, and witnesses were solicited. Jacobs, by now the spokesman for former German internees, prevailed upon Senator Dale Bumpers, chairman of the Subcommittee on Public Lands, to be included. For whatever reason, he was turned down and the Department of the Interior consulted with Japanese-American communities only.

While the German internees do not begrudge their fellow internees the compensation—indeed, quite the contrary—former German internees believe that the government just is unwilling to face the facts. "What it boils down to," says Alfred Plaschke in his retirement home in Katy, Texas, "is that the Japanese have a better lobby in Washington, D.C."

In an unrelated matter, former German internees drew some comfort from the choice of the architect selected to design the wonderfully imaginative memorial to the crew of the U.S.S. *Arizona*, lying at the bottom of Pearl Harbor. Alfred Preis, a famous architect, had been a German internee who spent the war years behind barbed wire in Camp Gloucester, New Jersey.[33] While the scattered community of former German internees are proud of one of their own, they drew greater satisfaction from seeing Preis's Gloucester City war internment mentioned in the national press. It was if they could say: "See? We Germans were interned during World War II as well."

CHAPTER TWELVE

THE ISSUES

In the final analysis, 31,275 enemy aliens were interned during the war. Apart from 16,849 Japanese (not counting the 120,000 relocated Japanese), there were 10,905 Germans, and 3,278 Italians, along with 52 Hungarians, 5 Bulgarians, 25 Romanians, and 161 of other European nationalities, for a total of 14,426 persons of European descent interned. This last figure does not include U.S. citizen family members—spouses and children—who joined internees.

After the passage of the Civil Rights Act of 1988, which concerned only Japanese-Americans and completely excluded German-Americans, several scholars, like John Eric Schmitz and Timothy J. Holian, and a small number of former internees, worked to set the record straight. In particular, free-lance writer Joseph E. Fallon researched the issue extensively and boiled down the following points: (1) Japanese-Americans did not make up the majority of those interned; 56 percent of all internees were European and European-American; (2) 64 percent of those arrested by the FBI from 7 December 1941 to 30 June 1945 were Europeans and European-Americans, including seamen of foreign ships in American ports; (3) the arrest of German legal resident aliens and German-Americans began on 7 December 1941, four days before Germany declared war on the United States; (4) while all Japanese-Americans were released from internment by June 1946, some Europeans and European-Americans were interned until July 1948; (5) the official government report on wartime internment, *Personal Justice Denied*, is misleading since it included no testimony from former European internees and none from high-ranking officials who had mentioned them; and (6) former internment camps that have become historic landmarks according to Public Law 102-248 are identified officially as having only interned Japanese-Americans.[1]

The government position is that the Japanese on the West Coast were rounded up en masse on strictly racial grounds, but the Germans were arrested individually, as security risks, following an accusation and a presumed investigation. Consequently, the Japanese internees (and their heirs and survivors) should be compensated, however belatedly, for their unlawful incarceration. The Germans were in a different position. Not so, says Arthur Jacobs, who took the issue to the U.S. Court of Appeals. First, Jacobs reminded the court that the mass roundup of Japanese by Presidential Executive Order 9066 did not begin until February 1942. Before February, hundreds of Japanese were individually arrested by the FBI. The Civil Liberties Act compensates all the Japanese, however, including the enemy aliens arrested before February. If the government finds it fair to compensate Japanese enemy aliens, they should also compensate their German counterparts.

Moreover, Jacobs told the court of appeals, the Germans were not criminals. They had been accused by anonymous informants, investigated by aggressive FBI agents who were driven to produce results, and tried by hearing boards made up of unsympathetic amateur sleuths and superpatriots. Their rights had been violated at every level of the alien-enemy program. They had not been tried before any judge or jury. Criminals were sent to prison, while the German internees were shipped to civilian detention camps. Hence, the government never considered them to be criminals.

There were other issues as well. Many of those arrested and interned were American citizens, some naturalized and some born in the United States. American-born citizens in particular—most of the children and many wives—should be compensated for the violation of their rights of citizenship. They were seldom permitted an attorney, and the hearing boards varied widely in make-up, standards of accepted alien behavior, and punishments. Many former internees claim to have been bullied and lied to at every turn.

A number saw their businesses close or fall victim to competition; others lost homes and property to unpaid taxes or vandals. Educations suffered, and the health of internees of all ages deteriorated due to poor diets, anxiety, and limited medical and optical care. A number had job opportunities but were denied employment after the war. Some children were orphaned for years while their parents were interned. Jacobs asked for compensation and an apology.

He received neither. In July 1991 the U.S. Court of Appeals disagreed with his arguments and turned down his appeal. The issue hinged on the question of mass exclusion and racial detention. The court of appeals simply stated that no mass exclusion or detention was ordered against American citizens of German or Italian descent.

Undaunted, Jacobs challenged the ruling and, in the fall of 1991, managed to bring the case before the U.S. Supreme Court in *Arthur D. Jacobs v. William Barr et al.* (#91-2061). He argued that the Civil Rights Act of 1988 and the court cases that supported it did not take into account several crucial points: (1) Not one German-American who had been "interned, relocated, paroled and/or interned-at-large" was invited to testify in preparation for the Civil Rights Act; (2) the Commission on Wartime Relocation and Internment of Civilians utilized documents solely related to the case of Japanese-Americans; and (3) in contrast to congressional and legal comments to the contrary, by 9 December 1941, two days before the

United States went to war with Germany, twenty-six German-Americans had been arrested in the state of Washington alone.[2] After many months, the High Court ruled against Jacobs, concluding that under wartime conditions his constitutional rights had not been violated. However crestfallen, Jacobs and a declining number of surviving internees vow to continue the legal struggle.[3]

Nonetheless, it must be remembered that the number of internees was small compared to the multitude of enemy aliens who continued their lives unhampered by the authorities. There were, after all, 314,105 registered German citizens living in America at the time, of whom only 10,905 were interned. More than 300,000 others worked hard, displayed strong feelings of patriotism and loyalty, and kept any pro-German personal beliefs to themselves. Far more of them might have been interned, and under worse conditions, were it not for the availability of the court system, the general levelheadedness of officials like Francis Biddle, Earl Harrison, Amy Stannard, Joseph O'Rourke, and Philip Forman, and the general good sense of the American public, which kept such excesses to a minimum. Still, the relatively small number of victims lessens neither their humiliation nor their lost years.

The internment program and the mass evacuation left a dangerous legacy for America's future. A secret government detention list and the arrest of thousands of noncitizens on mere suspicion of potential danger caused a crack in the Constitution that allowed McCarthyism and the communist witch hunts of the late 1940s and early 1950s. The World War was barely past when national paranoia turned toward a new enemy (and old ally), Soviet Russia. Once again, a small percentage of foreigners and Americans lived in fear of unsubstantiated accusations, blacklists, FBI harassment, and political hysteria. Thousands of people were accused of potential disloyalty by anonymous informants, vigilante groups, and crude FBI probes. Government hearings forced suspects to name others, and the terrain of the period is strewn with lost careers and reputations, shattered friendships, suicides, and, for some, jail time. Fifteen years later, during America's agony over the Vietnam War, the FBI and informants moved through college campuses with impunity, collecting names of antiwar protesters and potentially disloyal groups and individuals. This governmental intolerance for legal dissent led to numerous losses of employment and education, occasional jail sentences, and worse.[4] It is reasonable to say that neither the McCarthy years nor the later FBI crackdown on the antiwar and civil rights movement could have occurred as easily without the previous public toleration of the wartime internment and mass relocation programs.

The irony of their experience was never lost on the internees. America was fighting for democracy and the Four Freedoms, while denying them to a portion of its own population. Magazines and newspapers struggled to define the nation's wartime goals, and Hollywood championed freedom and the right to resist oppression through any of dozens of war films, such as *Bombs over Burma, Flying Tigers, Bataan, Destination Unknown, The Story of Dr. Wassel, The Story of G.I. Joe.*, and *Know Your Emmy.* The nation committed its sons and wealth to allies around the world in defense of their liberty. The contradiction was painful and frustrating: the war to defend freedom abroad led to the curtailment of liberties at home. While German enemy aliens were not the only group under government scrutiny, next to the Japanese, the Germans constituted the largest number interned. Unexplainably, their experiences have been passed over by history.

When he was fourteen years old, young Claude Turner skipped school one April day in 1942, in Gloucester, New Jersey. He went to stand along South King Street to watch the arrival of another group of German enemy aliens at the INS detention center. Two young to enlist in the army, Claude wanted to see these "enemies," as his family called them, in the flesh. He was startled by the scene: a dozen men and women, disheveled from several nights spent in police stations or immigration centers, wrestling suitcases and bags of belongings under the watchful eyes of local police. They were well dressed, the women in print dresses and the men with neckties and hats. Some smiled gamely, a few glowered in defiance, but most averted their eyes in humiliation.

Claude was frankly disappointed. He had hoped to see fierce, dangerous Nazis shouting slogans or marching to German songs—not embarrassed, average-looking people dragging their belongings to a detention center. When he met his friends after school, and they asked him what he thought of the internees, he remembers telling them, "They wuz just ordinary folks, just like you and me. Somehow, it just don't seem right. . . ."[5]

List of Internment/Detention Camps during World War II*

Camp	State	Jurisdiction
San Juan	Puerto Rico	Military
Pine Island	Cuba	Justice
Angel Island	California	Military
Sharp Park	California	INS
Tuna	California	INS
Tujunga	California	INS
Fort Logan	Colorado	Military
Fort Barrancas	Florida	Military
Miami	Florida	INS
Fort Ogelthorpe	Georgia	Military
Fort Screven	Georgia	Military
Fort McPherson	Georgia	Military
Sand Island	Territory of Hawaii	Military
4800 Ellis Avenue	Illinois	INS
Home of Good Shepherd, Chicago	Illinois	INS
Jung Hotel, New Orleans	Louisiana	INS
East Boston	Massachusetts	INS
Fort Howard	Maryland	Military
Fort Meade	Maryland	Military
Detroit	Michigan	INS
Kansas City	Missouri	INS
Fort Missoula	Montana	Military
Grove Park Inn, Ashville	North Carolina	INS
Fort Lincoln, Bismarck	North Dakota	Military
Good Shepherd Convent, Omaha	Nebraska	INS
Gloucester City	New Jersey	INS
Fort Stanton	New Mexico	Military
Lordsburg	New Mexico	INS
Camp Upton	New York	Military
Home of Good Shepherd, Buffalo	New York	INS

Camp	State	Jurisdiction
Ellis Island	New York	INS
Niagra Falls	New York	INS
Home of Good Shepherd, Cleveland	Ohio	INS
Hotel Gibson, Cincinnati	Ohio	INS
McAlester	Oklahoma	Military
Fort Sill	Oklahoma	Military
Stringtown	Oklahoma	Military
Portland	Oregon	INS
Home of Good Shepherd, Philadelphia	Pennsylvania	INS
Camp Forrest	Tennessee	Military
Fort Sam Houston	Texas	Military
Fort Bliss	Texas	Military
Seagoville	Texas	INS
Kenedy	Texas	INS
Crystal City	Texas	INS
Laredo	Texas	INS
Salt Lake City	Utah	INS
Sullivan Lake, Metaline Falls	Washington	Military
Seattle	Washington	INS
Spokane County Jail	Washington	INS
Camp McCoy	Wisconsin	Military
Home of Good Shepherd, Milwaukee INS	Wisconsin	
Milwaukee Barracks (County Jail)	Wisconsin	INS
Greenbrier Hotel, White Sulphur Spring	West Virginia	INS

* Doc. 4, Jacobs and Fallon, *Documents*, 1518–1519.

NOTES

Chapter One

The Lists

1. See Richard Gid Powers, *Secrecy and Power: The Life of J. Edgar Hoover* (New York: Free Press, 1987), 65; and Athan G. Theoharis and John Stuart Cox, *The Boss: J. Edgar Hoover and the Great American Inquisition* (Philadelphia: Temple University Press, 1988), 37–38.

2. Walter Goodman, *The Committee: The Extraordinary Career of the House Committee on Un-American Activities* (New York: Farrar, Straus, and Giroux, 1968), 3–23. An excellent summary of the House Special Committee's activities may be found in George P. Perros, *Preliminary Inventory of the Special House Committee on Un-American Activities Authorized to Investigate Nazi Propaganda and Certain Other Propaganda Activities Under the Authority of H. Res. 198, 73rd Congress* (unpublished), RG 233, Stack Area, 8E-3, 73A-F30.1, Row 14, National Archives, Washington, D.C. (hereafter cited as NA).

3. U.S. Senate, "Supplementary Detailed Staff Reports on Intelligence Activities and the Rights of Americans," book 3, *Final Report of the Select Committee to Study Government Operations with Respect to Intelligence Activities,* 94th Cong., 2d sess. 1976. S. Rept. 94-755, 396, 562. Hereafter cited as *Final Report.*

4. Attorney General Cullen Murphy to President Roosevelt, 17 June 1939, cited in "Supplementary Detailed Staff Reports," Book 3, *Final Report,* 34.

5. U.S. Congress. House. Committee on Appropriations, *Emergency Supplemental Appropriations Bill: Hearings on H.R. 76-7805,* 76th Cong., 1st sess. 30 Nov. 1939, 303–307.

6. *Congressional Record,* 76th Cong., 1st sess., 1939, vol. 84, pt. 5: 5161–5193. In 1941 Congressman Sam Hobbs introduced House Rule 2266, which legalized wiretapping, banned since 1934.

7. Theoharis and Cox, *The Boss,* 156–157n. See also Athan Theoharis, *Spying on Americans: Political Surveillance from Hoover to the Houston Plan* (Philadelphia: Temple University Press, 1978), 40.

8. Louis DeJong, *The German Fifth Column in the Second World War* (New York: Howard Fertig, 1973).

9. Ernst W. Puttkammer, *Alien Friends and Alien Enemies in the United States,* Public Policy Pamphlet no. 39 (Chicago: The University of Chicago, 1943), 15.

10. Hugo Grothe, *Die Deutschen in Übersee, eine Skizze ihres werdens, ihrer Verbreitung und kultur Arbeit,* (Berlin: Zentraverlag, 1982), map 1.

11. Ambassador Dieckhoff to the Auswärtiges Amt, 7 January 1938, in *Documents on German Foreign Policy 1918–1945,* series D, vol. 1 (Washington, D.C., 1949), 667.

12. Puttkammer, *Alien Friends,* 15.

13. *Documents on German Foreign Policy 1918–1945,* 670.

14. U.S. Congress. House. *Investigation of Un-America Activities and Propaganda in the United States,* 76th Cong., 1st sess., 1940, H. Rept. 1476, appen., vol. 4: *German-American Bund,* 1446. Hereafter cited as the *Dies Report, 1940.*

15. LaVern J. Rippley, *The German Americans* (Boston: Twayne Publishers, 1976), 205.

16. Susan Canedy, *America's Nazis: A Democratic Dilemma* (Menlo Park, Calif.: Markgraf Publications, 1990), 86.

17. See, for example, "Bund Rally to Get Huge Police Guard," *The New York Times*, 18 Feb. 1939; "Peewee Hitlers Found in America," ibid., 1 Sept. 1939; "Link German Bund to Army Officers," ibid., 8 Sept. 1939; and "Bundsmen Linked to Defense Plants," ibid., 3 Oct. 1940. Also Klaus Kipphan, *Deutsche Propaganda in den Vereinigten Staaten, 1933–1941*, Beiheft zum Jahrbuch für Amerikastudien (Heidelberg: Universitätsverlag, 1971), 56–57.

18. See "Anti-Nazi Outbreak Feared," *The New York Times*, 20 Feb. 1939; and "22,000 Nazis Hold Rally in Garden: Police Check Foes," ibid., 21 Feb. 1939.

19. "Bund 'Party' Egged on Coast," *The New York Times*, 26 Feb. 1939.

20. "Young Bund Members Drill in Brooklyn; Police Guard Almost Outnumbers Children," *The New York Times*, 13 Mar. 1939.

21. "Index to Publications: German-American, Italian-American, American, Russian, and Miscellaneous," doc. 32, in Arthur D. Jacobs and Joseph E. Fallon, eds., *The World War Two Experience*, sect. 1, pt. 1, vol. 4, 1641–1660, in Don Heinrich Tolzmann, ed., *German-Americans in the World War* (Munich: K. G. Saur, 1995). Hereafter cited as Jacobs and Fallon, *Documents*.

22. Timothy J. Holian, "The German-American Community During the World War II Era, with a Focus on Cincinnati, Ohio" (Ph.D. diss.: University of Cincinnati, 1995), 98.

23. Canedy, *America's Nazis*, xiv–xv.

24. H. M. Glancy, *Confessions of a Nazi Spy*, vol. 1 of *International Dictionary of Films and Filmmakers* (Chicago: St. James, 1990), 205.

25. Eric J. Sandeen, "Confessions of a Nazi Spy and the German American Bund," *American Studies* 20 (fall 1979): 73.

26. U.S. Congress. House. "Propaganda in Motion Pictures," *Hearings Before a Subcommittee of the Committee on Interstate Commerce: United States Senate, Resolution 152*, 77th Cong., 1st sess., 9–26 September 1941, 339.

27. Larry Langman and Ed Borg, *Encyclopedia of American War Films* (New York, 1989), 547. Also Holian, "German-American Community," 155–157.

28. "The Screen," *The New York Times*, 13 June 1942, 11.

29. Jay Robert Nash and Stanley Ralph Ross, *The Motion Picture Guide: C-D, 1927–1983* (Chicago: Cinebooks, 1990), 50.

30. James Combs, *American Political Movies; An Annotated Filmography of Feature Films* (New York: Garland, 1990), 37.

31. *Congressional Record*, 76th Cong., 1st sess., 1939, vol. 84, pt. 5: 5161–5193.

32. Theoharis, *Spying on Americans*, 40.

33. Theoharis and Cox, *The Boss*, 156–157n.

34. President Roosevelt, Statement, 6 Sept. 1939, cited in *Final Report*, 404.

35. Memo, J. Edgar Hoover to Edward A. Tamm, 2 Dec. 1939, cited in *Final Report*, 414.

36. Memo, J. Edgar Hoover to Matthew F. McGuire, 21 Aug. 1940, cited in Frank M. Sorrentino, *Ideological Warfare: The FBI's Path Toward Power* (Port Washington, New York: Associated Faculty Press, 1985), 147, n. 18.

37. Stephen R. Fox, *The Unknown Internment: An Oral History of the Relocation of Italian Americans During World War II* (Boston: Twayne Publishers, 1990), 152.

38. *Final Report*, 404–405.

39. "Declare United States Ready to Run Down Spies," *The New York Times*, 1 Oct. 1939.

40. See, for example, Frank C. Hanigen, "Foreign Political Movements in the United States," *Foreign Affairs* (Oct. 1937): 1–15. For more sensational views, see John Roy Carlson, *Under Cover* (New York: E. P. Dutton, 1943); Michael Sayers and Albert E. Kahn, *Sabotage! The Secret War Against America* (New York: Harper & Brothers, 1942); or William Breuer, *Hitler's Undercover War: The Nazi Espionage Invasion of the U.S.A.* (New York: St. Martin's, 1989).

Chapter Two

Precedents

1. Woodrow Wilson, "War Message to Congress," 2 Apr. 1917, in Arthur Link et al., eds., *The Papers of Woodrow Wilson* (Princeton: Princeton University Press, 1966) 41: 526.

2. Jörg Nagler, "Victims of the Home Front: Enemy Aliens in the United States During the First World War," in Panikos Panayi, ed., *Minorities in Wartime: National and Racial Groupings in Europe, North America and Australia during the Two World Wars* (Providence, R.I.: Berg, 1993), 196.

3. Robert H. Keyserlingt, "Allies or Subversives? The Canadian Government's Ambivalent Attitude towards German-Canadians in the Second World War," in Panayi, *Minorities in Wartime*, 239–260.

4. Jonathan F. Wagner, *Brothers Beyond the Seas: National Socialism in Canada* (Waterloo, Ontario, Canada: Wilfrid Laurier University Press, 1981), 68.

5. Letter from the *Generalstab des Heeres* to the *Luftwaffe-Führungsstab*, 25 Aug. 1938, PS-375, *International Military Tribunal, Nuremberg* vol. 25: 387–388.

6. Stanley Firmin, *They Came to Spy* (London: Hutchinson, 1946), 16.

7. *Führer Conferences on Naval Affairs* (London: Admiralty, 1947) 1940: 72.

8. Ronald Stent, *A Bespattered Page? The Internment of 'His Majesty's Most Loyal Enemy Aliens,'* (London: Andre Deutsch, 1980), 60–61.

9. Ibid., 64.

10. Ibid., 102–106.

11. Puttkammer, *Alien Friends*, 1.

12. There are several excellent articles worth noting: Colin Holmes, " 'British Justice at Work': Internment in the Second World War," in Panayi, *Minorities in Wartime*, 150–165; and Robert M. W. Kempner, "The Enemy Alien Problem in the Present War," *The American Journal of International Law* 34 (July 1940): 443–458. For a more specific examination of the various camps, see John Harwick's reports for the War Prisoners Aid of the World Committee of YMCAs, "Report on Alien Internment Camps in the United Kingdom, April 1941" and "Married Aliens' Internment Camp," June 1941, RG 407 (Records of the Adjutant General's Office, 1917–), Box 146, Army AG, Classified Decimal File, 1940–1942, NA.

Three outstanding histories of the internment of enemy aliens in Britain are Ronald Stent, *A Bespattered Page?*; P. and L. Gillman, *"Collar the Lot!" How Britan Interned and Expelled its Wartime Refugees* (1980). For particular interest in the many Jewish refugee artists, writers, and scientists, even Nobel Prize laureates, who were classed as enemy aliens, see M.

Berghahn, *Continental Britons: German-Jewish Refugees from Nazi Germany* (Leamington Spa, 1988).

Chapter Three

The Net Tightens

1. Theoharis and Cox, *The Boss*, 195.
2. Holian, "German American Community," 166.
3. Prince Franz Hohenlohe, *Steph: The Fabulous Princess* (London: New English Library, 1976), 139.
4. Ibid., 139.

Far from being a brainless twit attracted to the excesses of high society, the princess, according to author Charles Higham in his fascinating and maddening book *Trading with the Enemy*,

> was entirely devoted to Hitler . . . She formed a close relationship with Otto Abetz, the smooth Nazi representative in Paris . . . In 1938 the princess arranged a meeting between Fritz Wiedemann, a devoted Nazi, and Lord Halifax, the British Foreign Minister, to determine Halifax's and Chamberlain's attitude to[ward] Hitler. Wiedemann and the princess were credited by Hitler with helping to pave the way to his annexation of European territories . . . Stefanie [*sic*] also spent much time in Switzerland, where she linked up with German intelligence nets.

She was well rewarded for her efforts. Hitler made a gift to her of Leopoldskron Castle near Salzburg, the former property of the great Jewish theatrical producer Max Reinhardt. *Der Führer* also gave her a swastika-shaped diamond clip, and there seemed to be an unending flow of money. On one occasion, the princess was rewarded with a parcel of shares in the German chemical conglomerate, IG Farben. Far from being innocent, Princess Stephanie Hohenlohe was the very type of enemy alien that the internment program was designed to incarcerate. Charles Higham, *Trading with the Enemy: An Exposé of the Nazi-American Money Plot, 1933–1949* (New York: Delacorte Press, 1983), 190–192.

5. *Time Magazine*, 19 May 18–19; "Protests Arrests of German Seamen," *The New York Times*, 12 May 1941, 64.
6. An earlier group of 410 German seamen, having scuttled their ship to avoid Allied seizure, were the first to be interned at the Fort Stanton, New Mexico, holding facility. See "160 Nazi Seamen Arrested in Raids; Publicists Seized," *The New York Times*, 8 May 1941; "Check-up of Aliens to Go On; 200 Held," *Newsweek*, 19 May 1941, 22; and Ernest Hamburger, "A Peculiar Pattern of the Fifth Column: The Organization of the German Seamen," *Social Research* 9 (1942): 495–509.
7. The story of the enemy seamen has been admirably recorded by author John Christgau in *"Enemies": World War II Alien Internment* (Ames: Iowa State University Press, 1985), 19.
8. The most complete examination of Fort Stanton is William E. Anderson Jr., "Guests for the Duration: World War II and the Crew of the S.S. *Columbus.* An Historical Archaeological Investigation of the Fort Stanton Enemy Alien Internment Camp (1941–1945)" (master's thesis, Eastern New Mexico University, 1993).

9. "Few Elated Over Internment Camp," *Bismarck Tribune*, 12 Apr. 1941.

10. Holian, "German American Community," 168.

11. Francis Biddle, *In Brief Authority* (Garden City, N.Y.: Doubleday, 1962), 117.

12. Beulah Amidon, "Aliens in America," *Survey Graphic*, February 1941: 58.

13. Biddle, *Brief Authority*, 107.

14. Earl G. Harrison, "How State and Local Officials Can Assist in the Alien Registration Program," *State Government*, Oct. 1940, 204–205. The alien community may also have become mindful of its growing vulnerability, for the year 1940 witnessed a record 235,260 people becoming naturalized American citizens. See *Newsweek*, 26 May 1941, 22.

15. "2 Seized in Phila. as 'Spy Ring' Cogs," *Camden* (New Jersey) *Courier Post*, 12 Feb. 1941.

16. Testimony of James Rowe Jr., *Hearings before the Commission on Wartime Relocation and Internment of Civilians (CWRIC)*, Washington, D.C., 14 July 1981, 45–77, RG 220 (Records of the Commission on Wartime Relocation and Internment of Civilians), NA.

17. Memo, Assistant Chief of Staff to Chief of Staff, War Department, 19 July 1940, Sub: "Internment of Alien Enemies," 2. AG 014.311 (7-13-40) RG 407 (Records of the Adjutant General's Office), NA.

18. Memo, Lt. Col. R. B. Patterson, AG, to AG Washington, Sub: "Disposition of Crews of Foreign Merchant Vessels and Other Alien Enemies in the Event of War," 3 Apr. 1941, AG 014.311 (1-13-41) (Sect. G), RG 407, NA.

19. Memo, "Completion of Camp Upton Enclosure," AG 014.311 (1-13-41)(Sect. 3), NA.

20. Memo, Col. C. A. Easterbrook, AG, to PMGO, Washington, 23 Mar. 1942. Sub: "Use of Electrically Charged Wire around Prisoner of War Enclosure." SP AG. 014.311 (3-28-42), NA.

21. Memo, Major N. J. Safourek, Asst AG, to Commanding General, Services of Supply, Washington, 10 Mar. 1942. Sub: "Evacuation and Housing of Alien Enemies." 014.311 (3-10-42), NA.

22. Joint Agreement of the Secretary of War and the Attorney General respecting Internment of Alien Enemies, 18 July 1941, 2. AG 014.311 (1-13-41)(Sect. 5), NA.

23. J. Edgar Hoover, "Alien Enemy Control," *Iowa Law Review* vol. 29 (Mar. 1944): 396.

24. Francis Biddle, "American-Aliens and the Registration Act of 1940," *State Government*, Aug. 1940, 145.

25. Earl G. Harrison, "Axis Aliens in an Emergency," *Survey Graphic*, Sept. 1941, 465, 467–468.

26. "Roundup and Rally," *Newsweek*, 26 May 1941, 22.

27. "Wisconsin Federation of German-American Fight Against Pro-Nazi Groups in Milwaukee," *The New York Times*, 23 April 1939, sect. 4, 7; Ingeborg Kayko, "On Being a German-American," *Atlantic Monthly*, May 1943, 97–98.

28. Wolfgang zu Putlitz, "Your German-American Neighbor and the Fifth Column," *Harper's Magazine*, Feb. 1942, 324.

29. Memo from Joseph Savoretti for Lemuel B. Schofield, Special Assistant to the District Attorney, to District Director of Immigration and Naturalization, Ellis Island, N.Y. harbor, 10 Oct. 1941, "Special Delivery and Confidential," 2 pp., File 56125/3, Box 2399, Accession Nr, 85-58A734. INS Records, Washington, D.C.

Until very recently, the INS records concerning the detention of alien enemies were available to the public only through the Freedom of Information Act. However, they were transferred from the INS to the National Archives in September 1996 and are finally available to all. The only research guide is Marian L. Smith's "INS Records Related to the Detention and Internment of Enemy Aliens during World War II," Historical Reference Library and Reading Room Section, INS Information Services Branch, 1 July 1991, 57 pp.

Chapter Four

The Arrests

1. Ken Ringle, "The Untold Story of One Man's Fight for the Nisei," *The Los Angeles Times*, 6 Dec. 1981, pt. 5.

2. Memo, J .Edgar Hoover to Major Lemuel B. Schofield, "Immigration and Naturalization Service, On Various Individuals Being Considered for Custodial Detention," 8 Dec. 1941, doc. 14, Jacobs and Fallon, *Documents*, 1556.

3. Biddle, *Brief Authority*, 207. Also see U.S. Congress. House, Select Committee Investigating National Defense Migration. *Recommendations on the Mobilization of Manpower for the All-Out War Effort. Fifth Interim Report* pursuant to H. Res. 113. H. Rept. 2396, 77th Cong., 2d sess, 10 Aug. 1942, 294–315. Hereafter "National Defense Migration."

4. "28 Axis Nationals Arrested by FBI in Gulf Arms Area," *Houston Post*, 10 Dec. 1941, 1, 15; "FBI Continues Roundup of Aliens in Houston Area," ibid., 11 Dec. 1941, 1, 10.

5. Biddle, *Brief Authority*, 206.

6. Earl G. Harrison, "Civilian Internment—American Way," *Survey Graphic*, May 1944, 229–233, 270.

7. Testimony of James Rowe Jr., hearings before the CWRIC, RG 220, Washington, D.C., 14 July 1980, 52.

8. Memo, J. Edgar Hoover to Mr. Tolson, Tamm, and Ladd, 9 Dec. 1941, doc. 18, Jacobs and Fallon, *Documents*, 1560.

9. Memo, Lemuel B. Schofield, Immigration and Naturalization Service, to Edward J. Ennis, director of the Alien Enemy Control Unit, Department of Justice, "On Number of Germans Arrested by December 9, 1941," 10 Dec. 1941, doc. 19, Jacobs and Fallon, *Documents*, 1561.

10. Department of Justice, *Announcing the Number of Dangerous Alien Enemies Arrested*, press release, 13 Dec. 1941, doc. 23, Jacobs and Fallon, *Documents*, 1570.

11. Samuel Eliot Morison, *The Battle of the Atlantic* (Boston: Little, Brown & Co., 1960), 128.

12. Alan Hynd, *Passport to Treason: The Inside Story of Spies in America* (New York: R. M. McBride & Co., 1943), 113–114.

13. J. Edgar Hoover, encoded telegram, 17 Dec. 1941, *Papers of the U.S. Commission on Wartime Relocations and Internment of Civilians*, pt. 1, Numerical File Archive, University Publications of America.

14. *United States Reports*, vol. 339, *Cases Adjudicated in the U.S. Supreme Court of October Term, 1949* (Washington, D.C.: U.S. Government Printing Office), 763–798.

15. Arnold Krammer, "In Splendid Isolation: Enemy Diplomats in World War II," *Prologue*, spring 1985, 25–43. The government records of the internment of enemy diplomats

are located in Record Group 85 (Immigration and Naturalization Service), entries 297 to 300, location 5/62/00/04, containers LTA-S 1-4, NA.

The Axis diplomats complained continually about the disposition of their mountains of luggage, and official correspondence between Germany and Switzerland fills a substantial folder in the Auswärtiges Amt archives in Bonn, Germany. Gesandtschaft Bern, Folder 5039 ["Nachforschungen nach Gepäck von aus den USA nach Deutschland zurückgekehrten Reichsdeutschen, 1942–1945"] the Political Archives of Germany's Auswärtiges Amt (AA), Bonn. Hereafter cited as "Folder"/"Document," AA, Bonn.

16. Charles B. Burdick, *An American Island in Hitler's Reich: The Bad Nauheim Internment* (Menlo Park, Calif.: Markgraf Publications Group, 1987).

17. Lists compiled by Arthur D. Jacobs from official rosters from Ellis Island, Fort Lincoln, and Crystal City, 29 Feb. 1944.

18. Frank J. Donner, *The Age of Surveillance* (New York: Vintage Books, 1980), 163.

19. Arthur L. Smith Jr., *The Deutschtum of Nazi Germany and the United States* (The Hague: M. Nijhoff, 1965), 161. See also Sander A. Diamond, *The Nazi Movement in the United States, 1924–1941* (Ithaca: Cornell University Press, 1974), 345–346; and Leland V. Bell, "The Failure of Nazism in America: The German-American Bund, 1936–1941," *Political Science Quarterly*, vol. 85, no. 4 Dec. 1970: 585–599.

20. *Freeport (Texas) Facts*, 8 Jan. 1942. Alfred Plaschke, interview with author, Houston, Texas, 14 Apr. 1990.

21. Gerd Erich Schneider, interview with author, Evergreen, Colorado, 31 May 1997.

22. R. J. Abbaticchio, Special Agent in Charge, to J. Edgar Hoover, director, 26 Dec. 1941, FBI Records, Custodial Detention, File No. 100-2-21. *Alien Roundup*, 15 min., available in NA: NNSM(m)-111-BW-403; and Time, Inc., *The F.B.I. Front*, 20 min., NNSM(m)-200-MT-9.1.

23. Hoover to Abbaticchio, 2 Jan. 1942; Abbaticchio to Hoover, 6 Jan. 1942, FBI Records, ibid.

24. Hohenlohe, *Steph*, 148.

25. "Princess Stephanie Is Interned in Jersey; Nazi Agent Was Believed to be in Mexico," *The New York Times*, 11 Dec. 1941, 24.

26. Hohenlohe, *Steph*, 149.

27. Lacy McCrary, "Forgotten Internees End Silence," *The Philadelphia Inquirer*, 16 Dec. 1989, 1-A, 4-A; "World War II German-American Internees Seek Reparations," *Riverside (California) Press Enterprise*, 24 Dec. 1989.

28. Paul Grayber, letter to author, St. Martin, French West Indies, 25 Dec. 1993.

29. Cited in John Eric Schmitz's excellent thesis, "Democracy Under Stress: The Internment of German-Americans in World War II" (master's thesis, North Carolina State University, Raleigh, 1993), 66–67.

30. Memo, W. F. Kelly, Supervisor of the Border Patrol, to E. Ennis, Director, Alien Enemy Control Unit, July 1942; W. C. Bruppacher, Swiss Legation, to W. F. Kelly, 20 Apr. 1944., ibid.

Chapter Five

The Process

1. Edward J. Ennis, "Government Control of Alien Enemies," *State Government*, May 1942, 100.

2. Circular No. 3389, "To All United States Attorneys, Re: Alien Enemy Hearing Boards," 2 Feb. 1942, doc. 27, Jacobs and Fallon, *Documents*, 1578.

3. Record of the Hearing of Officers and Civilians Convened Pursuant to Paragraph 33, Special Orders No. 130, HQ, Hawaiian Department, Fort Shafter, T.H., 15 May 1942: The Case of Edmund Adolph Dropman. RG 153, Office of the Judge Advocate General (Army), Litigation Division, Record of Exclusion Cases, 1942–1947, Box 3, NA.

4. Biddle, *Brief Authority*, 208.

5. *Personal Justice Denied: Report of the Commission on Wartime Relocation and Internment of Civilians* (Washington, D.C., 1982), 285.

6. Eugene V. Rostow, "Our Worst Wartime Mistake," *Harper's Magazine*, September 1945, 194.

7. Papers of Martin George Dudel in possession of Deborah Ann (Dudel) Lincoln, Vashon, Washington, loaned to author, 1996.

8. Instruction No. 58, Lemuel Schofield, Special Assistant to the Attorney General, to the Immigration and Naturalization Service, 28 Apr. 1942, doc. 28, Jacobs and Fallon, *Documents*, 1580–1589.

9. Ibid.

10. James Rowe Jr., "The Alien Enemy Program—So Far," *Common Ground*, summer 1942, 21–22.

11. Memo for the Director, 1 Sept. 1943, Re: "Alien Enemy Control." 3 pp. Custodial Detention, File No. 100-2, Main File, Section 188, Serial #3955, FBI Records, Washington, D.C.

12. "National Defense Migration," 249.

13. Robert E. Cushman, "The Impact of the War on the Constitution," in *The Impact of the War on America: Six Lectures by Members of the Faculty of Cornell University* (Ithaca: Cornell University Press, 1942), 18.

14. "Property Collected by Police from Aliens Here," *The New York Times*, 7 Jan. 1942, 21.

15. Geoffrey Perrett, *Days of Sadness, Years of Triumph: The American People 1939–1945* (New York: Coward, McCann & Geoghegan Inc., 1973), 222.

16. Personal Justice Denied (CWRIC), 65.

17. "Travel for Aliens Made Easier Here; Applicants for Permits Need Only One Personal Appearance, Renewals to be Mailed," *The New York Times*, 7 Jan. 1942, 21.

18. *San Francisco Chronicle*, 9 Feb. 1942, 10.

19. See Alexander Stephan, *Im Visier des FBI. Deutsche Exilschriftsteller in den Akten amerikanischer Geheimdienste* (Stuttgart: Verlag J. B. Metzler, 1995).

20. Perrett, *Days of Sadness*, 361.

21. *Time Magazine*, 14 Feb. 1944.

22. Perrett, *Days of Sadness*, 363.

23. Francis Biddle, "Axis Aliens in America—Statement of Policy Issued December 19, 1941," *Survey Graphic*, January 1942, 13, 47.

24. "The Foreign-Language Press," *Fortune*, November 1940, 90–93, 102–104.

25. "Hungarian Papers Split on War," *The New York Times*, 7 Dec. 1941. See Joseph S. Roucek, "Foreign-Language Press in World War II," *Sociology and Social Research* 27, no. 6 (July–Aug. 1943): 462–471.

26. Loula D. Lasker, "Friends or Enemies?" *Survey Graphic*, June 1942, 278. Most surviving former internees believe that they were lured into complacency and think it laughable that Harrison later became president of the American Civil Liberties Union.

27. "Willkie Issues Plea for Alien Group Here," *The New York Times*, 29 Jan. 1942, 23.

28. "Alien Camps Made Enclosed Prisons," *The New York Times*, 12 Jan. 1942, 6.

29. "Foreign Born Held Loyal to America," *The New York Times*, 28 June 1942, 26.

30. U.S. Department of Justice, *Questions and Answers on Regulations Concerning Aliens of Enemy Nationalities* (Washington, D.C., 1942), 26, 36, 43. Also see *The New York Times*, 3 July 1942.

31. Ruth E. McKee, *Wartime Exile: The Exclusion of the Japanese Americans From the West Coast*, vol. 10 of *War Relocation Authority Monograph* (Washington, D.C.: U.S. Government Printing Office, 1946), 114.

32. Stetson Conn, Rose C. Engelman, Byron Fairchild, "Japanese Evacuation from the West Coast," chap. 5 in *The Western Hemisphere: Guarding the United States and Its Outposts*, a vol. of *The United States Army in World War II* (Washington, D.C.: Office of the Chief of Military History, 1964), 126.

33. Quoted in Rostow, "Worst Mistake," 195–196.

34. See Emory S. Bogardus, "Relocation Centers as Planned Communities," *Sociology and Social Research* 28, no. 3 (Jan.–Feb. 1944): 218–234.

35. North of the Pacific States, the Canadian government and army carried out a similar program for the forced evacuation of British Columbia's 21,000 Japanese residents, three-fourths of them Canadian-born. See Forrest Emmanuel La Violette, *The Canadian Japanese and World War II: A Sociological and Psychological Account* (Toronto: University of Toronto Press, 1948, reprinted in 1987), 44; Roy Mickey, *Justice in Our Time: The Japanese-Canadian Redress Settlement* (Vancouver, British Columbia: Talonbooks, 1991); and William Minoru Hohri, *Repairing America: An Account of the Movement for Japanese-American Redress* (Pullman: Washington State University Press, 1988).

36. *Time Magazine*, 6 Apr. 1942.

37. Carey McWilliams, "Moving the West Coast Japanese," *Harper's Magazine*, September 1942.

38. Ringle, "Untold Story," 6.

39. Perrett, *Days of Sadness*, 217, 219, 223.

40. "FBI Tightens Curb on 256,000 Aliens," *The New York Times*, 1 Apr. 1942, 23.

41. "Tent Town Built for Aliens at Fort Devens," *The New York Times*, 2 Apr. 1942, 23.

40. RG 226 (OSS—Foreign Nationalities Branch), Entry 100: "Press" (Report No. INT-13GE-41, -65, -95, -1356); "Emigration" (INT-13GE-68, -105); "Bund" (INT-13GE-7, -110, -114, -138, -192, -193); "New York City" (INT-13GE-77, -80); "San Francisco" (INT-13GE-110), "Illinois" (INT-13GE-187); "Pittsburgh" (INT-13GE-196); "Detroit" (INT-13GE-1342); "Wisconsin" (INT-13GE-1356); "War Aid" (INT-13GE-57); and "Indirection" (INT-13GE-141).

43. "Alien Restriction Tightens On Coast," *The New York Times*, 14 June 1942, E9.

44. Memo, Lt. Col. William A. Boekel to Col. Karl R. Bendetsen, 4 May 1942, cited in Stetson Conn, Rose Engelman, Byron Fairchild, "Japanese Evacuation From the West Coast," chap. 5, *United States Army in World War II: The Western Hemisphere—Guarding the United States and its Outposts* (Washington, D.C.: OCMH, 1964), 144.

45. "National Defense Migration," 24–25; Walter Lipmann, *New York Herald Tribune*, 5, 12, and 14 Feb. 1942. Also see Peter S. Sheridan, "The Internment of German and Italian Aliens Compared with the Internment of Japanese Aliens in the United States during World War II: A Brief History and Analysis," Hearings before the CWRIC, Washington, D.C., 24 Nov. 1980, 816–817. Mimeographed copy on file in the Library of Congress, Congres-

sional Research Service, Main File, D-521 USA, and JV-6201 USA-Japanese, Washington, D.C.

46. "National Defense Migration," 27–30.

47. Stephen C. Fox, "General John De Witt and the Proposed Internment of German and Italian Aliens during World War II," *Pacific Historical Review* 55, no. 4 (1988): 407–437.

48. LaVern J. Rippley, *The German-Americans* (Boston: Twayne Publishers, 1976), 204.

49. John J. McCoy to Francis Biddle, 4 Aug 1943, ASW 014.311 E.D.C., as well as a large collection of Exclusion Orders and related correspondence. RG 107 (Records of the Office of the Secretary of War), Box 7, NA.

The exclusion orders were divided by areas as follows: Eastern Defense Command = 69; Southern Defense Command = 16; and Western Defense Command = 173. "Statistical Report Showing Case, Name and Number, and Present Status of All Exclusion Cases of This Command as of 13 January 1944," 2 pp. RG 107. ASW 014.311, EDC Exclusion Order, Box 7, NA.

50. "Philadelphia Woman Defies Army Order That She Must Leave the Eastern Area," *The New York Times*, 8 May 1943, 17; and "Forbids Exclusion From a Coast Area," ibid., 21 Aug. 1943, 13.

51. Civil Action File No. 1811, *Henry L. Beach v. Lt. General John L. De Witt, Lt. Colonel Randall Larson, Colonel John Doe, Colonel Richard Doe, Major John Doe, and John Doe.* 13 Feb. 1943. RG 153, Litigation Division, Box 3, NA.

52. John J. McCloy to Charles Fahy, Solicitor General, 26 Mar. 1943, ibid.

53. RG 153, Box 2, NA.

54. General Thomas Green to Colonel Archibald King, 24 Sept. 1942, ibid.

55. Archibald King, "The Legality of Martial Law in Hawaii," *California Law Review*, Sept. 1942.

56. "Hawaii Doctor Seized by Army Seeks $575,000," *Chicago Daily Tribune*, 29 May 1946, 18.

57. Frank E. Thompson Jr. to Thomas Clark, Subject: Member Enemy Alien Hearing Board, Honolulu, Hawaii, 4 June 1946. RG 153, Litigation Division, Box 3, NA.

58. Ibid.

59. H. A. Drum to John J. McCoy, assistant secretary of war, 28 May 1943, RG 153, Litigation Division, ibid.

60. Memo, Francis Biddle to the president, 17 Apr. 1943, 2. RG 107, ASW 014.311 EDC, Exclusion Order, Box 7, NA.

57. "Statistical Report Showing Case, Name and Number, and Present Status of All Exclusion Cases of This Command as of 13 January 1944," 2 pp. RG 107. ASW 014.311, EDC Exclusion Order, Box 7, NA.

62. Hoover, "Alien Enemy Control," 407.

63. Memo to D. M. Ladd, Sub: "Apprehension and/or Denaturalization of Rueckwanderer Mark Purchases," 4 Oct. 1943, 2. Custodial Detention, File No. 100.2, Main File, Section 189, Serial #3964, FBI Records.

64. "Report of the Director of the Federal Bureau of Investigation, John Edgar Hoover, For the Fiscal Year 1945" (Washington, D.C.: U.S. Government Printing Office), 2.

65. *San Francisco Chronicle*, 13 Oct. 1942.

66. The story of the Italian experience is best told by Stephen Fox in *The Other Internment: An Oral History of the Relocation of Italian Americans during World War II* (Boston: Twayne Publishers, 1990).

67. *San Francisco Chronicle*, 16 and 19 Oct. 1942.

68. According to Mangione, a Justice Department inspector of the internment camps, "By about 1944 about half of the interned Italian civilians were either paroled or released unconditionally. (One man was released a few hours after it was learned that his American soldier son had been killed in action during the invasion of Sicily.) The rest of the civilians, about one hundred hard-core admirers of the fascist regime, remained in internment until the end of the war. Nearly all of them, willingly or not, were then deported to Italy." Jerre Mangione, *An Ethnic at Large: A Memoir of America in the Thirties and Forties* (New York: Putnam, 1978), 345.

69. Lasker, "Friends or Enemies?" 301.

70. "No More Aliens in Army," *Army and Navy Register* 58 (28 Aug. 1937): 5.

71. John M. Curran, "The Companies of the Damned," *Army*, February 1982, 62.

72. Ibid., 54.

73. "Two Ex-U.S. Soldiers Seized as Alien Foes," *The New York Times*, 7 Jan. 1943.

74. "Rueckwanderer Mark Purchases," FBI Records.

75. "Alien Interned by FBI, Had Officers' Club Job," *The New York Times*, 9 Jan. 1942, 10.

76. "Alien Released, Recently Again Held in Dallas," *The Dallas Journal*, 25 Feb. 1942.

77. "Nazi Family of 5 Seized in Brooklyn," *The New York Times*, 27 June 1943, 28.

78. "Alien Found Dead in East River," *The New York Times*, 25 June 1942, 11.

79. "Army Court to Try 8 Nazi Saboteurs," "Nazi Aide in Detroit Convicted," "One of Few U.S. Treason Cases," *The New York Times*, 3 July 1942, 1.

80. W. A. Swanberg, "The Spies Who Came in From the Sea," *American Heritage*, April 1970, 91. See also Shirley J. Burton and Kellee Green, "Oaths of Allegiance, Acts of Treason: The Disloyalty Prosecutions of Max Stephan and Hans Haupt," *Prologue*, fall 1991, 236–247; and Eugene Rachlis, *They Came to Kill* (New York: Random House, 1961).

81. "Bundist Gets Six Months," *The New York Times*, 20 June 1942, 28.

82. "German is Accused of Seeking War Job," *The New York Times*, 26 June 1942, 22.

83. " 'Dangerous' Bundist Arrested," *The New York Times*, 23 June 1942, 4.

84. "Chicago Inquiry to Call Bundists," *The New York Times*, 30 June 1942, 6.

85. Higham, *Trading with the Enemy*, 41.

86. "Bail Fixed at $100,000, Man of German Flag is Accused of Insulting Flag," *The New York Times*, 19 June 1942, 15.

87. "Bars Alien Students," *The New York Times*, 16 June 1942, 25.

88. The Swiss authorities received copies of all dealings regarding the German enemy aliens, which, in turn, were turned over to the German Foreign Office in Bonn, Germany. See Gesandtschafts Bern, Folder 5040 ["Verordnungen des Departementes of Justice über feindliches Ausland, Internierung, Freilassung auf Parole etc., Band 1, 1941–1942/Documents DA-496, DA-1383, and DA-1412], AA, Bonn.

89. Eberhard Fuhr, letter to author, 26 Jan. 1991.

90. Arthur Jacobs interview with author.

91. Papers of Martin George Dudel.

92. FBI Reports, 1941–48, Decimal File, 291.2 Germans—291.2 Italians, RG 319 (Army Intelligence), Box 384, Folder 3.1.43–12.31.43, NA.

93. Department of Justice news release, 5 Apr. 1942, Folder 5040/Document DA-496, AA, Bonn.

94. Memo, Daniel B. Priest, chairman of Civilian Hearing Board, to Hon. C. E. Rhetts,

acting assistant attorney general, 13 Nov. 1944, Re: Alien Enemy, Lambert Dietrich Jacobs, 146-13-2-52-1690. In possession of Arthur Jacobs, Tempe, Arizona.

95. Arthur Jacobs interview with author.

96. Holian, "German American Community," 274.

97. *Spotlight*, 20 May 1991, 12–13.

98. Eberhard Fuhr, letter to author, 1991; see also Kitry Krause, "Dangerous Enemy Alien," *Chicago Weekly Reader*, 3 Sept. 1993, 1, 11–17, 20–21. See also "Brothers Want to Help Hitler," *Cincinnati Enquirer*, 24 Mar. 1943; "Brothers Face Alien Hearing," *Cincinnati Times Star*, 25 Mar. 1943.

99. Eberhard Fuhr interview with author.

100. Charlotte Krause correspondence with author, 20 Sept. 1996.

101. Memo, J. Edgar Hoover to Edward J. Ennis, director, Alien Enemy Control Unit, 19 Mar. 1942; Memo, J. Edgar Hoover to J. C. Strickland, 7 Mar. 1942. Custodial Detention, File 100, Sub. 2-60, Sect. 7, FBI Records.

102. Memo, J. Edgar Hoover to D. M. Ladd, 24 Feb. 1942. Custodial Detention, File 100, Sub 2-60, Sect. 4, FBI Records.

103. Postal telegraph, Biddle to Hon. William Fleet Palmer, 26 Feb. 1942, ibid.

104. Roosevelt to Hoover, 3 Apr. 1942, Papers of Franklin D. Roosevelt, President's Secretary's Files (PSF)—Hoover, Justice, Box 77, Franklin D. Roosevelt Library, Hyde Park, New York.

105. "Panel of 22 Set Up For Alien Hearings," *The New York Times*, 22 Aug. 1943, 36.

106. "Only 3,771 Enemy Aliens Interned in U.S. Camps," *The New York Times*, 11 Nov. 1943, 16.

Chapter Six

The Camps

1. Government records of Camp Kenedy, Texas, are in RG 85, entries 301–305, location 5/62/05/07, containers LGA-S 1, 1-80, 1-2, 81, 82-84, NA. See also INS records, File 56125/57, Box 2423, Accession Nr. 85-58A734, Washington, D.C.

2. Government records of Camp Seagoville, Texas, are in RG 85, entries 310–316, location 5/62/13/07, containers LTA-S 1, IND-A 1-2, PHO-G 1, NA; INS records: File 56125/60, Box 2424, Accession Nr. 85-58A734, Washington, D.C.

3. Government records of Camp Stanton, New Mexico, are in RG 85, entries 294–296, location 5/62/05/07, containers LTA-S 1-25, NA.

4. Government records of Camp Crystal City, Texas, are in RG 85, entries 275–280, location 5/61/53/7, containers LTA-S 1-280, NA; INS records: File 56125/88, Box 2431, Accession Nr. 85-58A734, Washington, D.C.

5. Government records of Fort Missoula, Montana, are in RG 85, entries 289–293, location 5/60/00/03, NA.

6. Government records of Fort Lincoln, North Dakota, are in RG 85, entries 281–288, location 5/63/58/2, container LTA-S 1, NA.

7. Swiss inspection records of Camp Gloucester City, New Jersey, are in Folder 5087 ["Gloucester City, New Jersey, 1942–1945"], AA, Bonn.

8. Swiss inspection records of Stringtown, Oklahoma, are in Folder 5095 [mislabeled "Springtown" [sic], "1942–1945"], AA, Bonn.

9. Internee letters to Mr. Phillip Forman, Folder 5085 ["Zivilinterniertenlager Ellis Island"]/Document D-3676, AA, Bonn.

10. Swiss Inspection Report, Ellis Island, New York Harbor, 27 July 1944, ibid; INS records: File 56125/3, Box 2400, and File 56125/60, Box 2425, Accession Nr. 58-85734, Washington, D.C.

11. Fragebogen, Bericht Nr. 4, Camp Forrest, Tennessee, 13–14 Apr. 1943, Folder 5086 ["Lager Forrest, Tennessee"]/Document DA-598, AA, Bonn.

12. Swiss Inspection Reports, Gloucester City, New Jersey, 31 Aug. 1943, 7 Apr. 1944, and 9 Oct. 1944, Folder 5087 ["Zivilinterniertenlager Gloucester City, New Jersey, USA"], AA, Bonn.

13. Eberhard Fuhr interview; Kitry Krause, "Dangerous Enemy Alien."

14. Alfred Plaschke interview.

15. O.S.S., Latin American Section, "Preliminary Report on the Elements of Instability in Brazil," 13 Oct. 1941. O.S.S. Records, Latin America, 1941–1961, Part 14, Reel 6, Frame 0143; "The Relation of Brazil to the Defense of the Northeast," ibid., 6, Frame 0164; "Nazi Activity and Labor Unrest in Columbia," ibid., 1 Dec. 1941, Part 14, Reel 8; "Survey of the Elements of Instability in the Latin American Sector," ibid., 30 Jan. 1942, Part 14, Reel 1, Frame 0015, 7; ibid., 24, Frame 0032; ibid., 26; "Special Report: The Spanish Falange in Latin America," ibid., 2 Feb. 1942, 1–15, Frames 1048–1063, NA. Allan Chase, Falange: The Axis Secret Army in the Americas (New York: G.P. Putnam's Sons, 1943); and Reiner Pommerin, Das Dritte Reich und Latinamerika: Die deutsche Politik gegenüber Süd- und Mittelamerika (Dusseldorf: Froste, 1977).

16. "Mexico Deporting Jews," The New York Times, 4 Dec. 1937, 2; "Jews in Mexico Hit," ibid., 20 Dec. 1937, 15; "Mexico Lays Plans to Oust Many Jews," ibid., 24 Dec. 1937, 7.

17. "Nazi Spy Activity in Mexico Charged," ibid., 28 June 1938, 1.

18. J. Edgar Hoover to Col. E. R. Warner McCabe, assistant chief of staff, G-2, 29 Sept. 1939, RG 165 (Military Intelligence Division), #2801-304-8, NA.

19. Ladislas Farago, The Game of the Foxes: The Untold Story of German Espionage in the United States and Great Britain During World War II (New York: D. McKay Company, 1971), 311. See also H. Montgomery Hyde, Room 3603: The Story of the British Intelligence Center in New York during W.W. II, forward by Ian Fleming (New York: Farrar, Straus and Company, 1962), 52–53, 56–58, 69, 100, 149, 227.

20. "Race Row Divides Wives of Nazis in Nicaragua," The New York Times, 27 June 1942, 4.

21. Ibid.

22. Memo, Cordell Hull to President Roosevelt, 27 Aug. 1942, 740.00115 EW 1939/ 5835, 5649, and 4476; and Memo, Department of State, 3 Nov. and 30 Dec. 30, 1942. RG 59 (Records of the Department of State), NA.

23. Memo, "Regarding the Activities of the United States Government in Removing from the Other American Republics Dangerous Subversive Aliens," 3 Nov. 1942, 3. RG 59, Subject Files, Box 180, Records of the Special War Problems Division, NA.

24. See Leslie B. Rout Jr. and John F. Bratzel, The Shadow War: German Espionage and United States Counterespionage in Latin America During World War II (Lanham, Md.: University Press of America, 1986).

25. "Third Meeting of Ministers of Foreign Affairs of the American Republics," U.S. Department of State, *Bulletin* 6, no. 137 (7 Feb. 1942): 128–131.

26. Regina Wagner, *Los Alemanes en Guatemala, 1828–1944* (Asociacion de Educacion y Cultura 'Alejandro von Humboldt' Comite de Investigaciones Historicas, Editorial IDEA: La Universidad en su Casa, Universidad Francisco Marroquin, Guatemala, 1991), 373–374. A list of the Germans and German-Guatemalans and their families sent to the U.S. may be found on 430–442.

27. C. Harvey Gardiner, *Pawns in a Triangle of Hate* (Seattle: University of Washington Press, 1981), 107–108.

28. "Guatemala Sends Aliens to U.S.," *The New York Times*, 13 Jan. 1942, 9.

29. Memo, Francis M. Sullivan, American Legion, to Secretary Hull, 20 Oct. 1942. RG 59, 740.00115 EW 1939/7518, NA.

30. *The Fargo(North Dakota)Forum*, 22 Feb. 1946.

31. Mangione, *Ethnic at Large*, 321–322.

32. Memo, General Allen Gullion, PMG, to chief of staff, sub. "Letter of Inquiry as to 'Santa Lucia' Internees," 16 Feb. 1942. AG 014.311 (1-13-41) (2-16-42) Sec. 3, RG 407, NA. See INS records "Arrival of Women and Children on the S.S. *Santa Lucia* in New York," File 56125/45x, Box 2415, Accession Nr. 58-85734, Washington, D.C.

33. Family interview, examination of documents, and ten-page written recollection by Walter Klein's grandson, John Cramer, Jan.–Apr. 1994, Tübingen, Germany.

34. Clara Kruse and son Reinhard, interview with author, 30 Mar. 1996, 16 Dec. 1996, 12 Jan. 1997, 25 Feb. 1997, Philadelphia.

35. "Axis Espionage and Propaganda in Latin America," 16 May 1946, 95. RG 165, Military Intelligence Division, War Department, NA; also see Gardiner, *Pawns in a Triangle of Hate*, 134.

36. Edward N. Barnhart, "Japanese Internees from Peru," *Pacific Historical Review* 31 (1962): 169–178. See INS records, "Arrival of Alien Enemy Detainees from Central and South America," File 56125/64, Box 2426, Accession Nr. 85-58A734, Washington, D.C. See also Thomas Connell III, "The Internment of Latin American Japanese in the United States During World War II: The Peruvian Japanese Experience" (Ph.D. diss., Florida State University, 1995).

The first official revelation of the Latin American program came in the FBI's 1947 "Summary of Accomplishments." During the seven-year period when the FBI was responsible for intelligence in the entire Western Hemisphere, 1 July 1940 to 28 Apr. 1947, a "total of 7,064 enemy aliens were moved from strategic areas in Latin America; 2,172 were interned locally; and 5,893 were deported or expelled"—many to the United States. "In addition, hundreds of Axis espionage and propaganda agents were identified, as well as smugglers of strategic materials. Lastly, thirty clandestine radio transmitters and eighteen clandestine radio receiving sets were confiscated." *Report of the Director of the Federal Bureau of Investigation, John Edgar Hoover, For the Fiscal Year 1947*, 11–12. Research Office, Public and Congressional Affairs, J. Edgar Hoover Building, Washington, D.C.

37. Cited in the National Broadcasting Company's television program "Round-Up," on *Dateline*, Nov. 1994.

38. Harvey Strum, "Jewish Internees in the American South, 1942–1945," *American Jewish Archives* 42, no. 2(fall/winter 1990): 27–48.

See the official lists of German citizens en route from Latin America to Seagoville, particularly Folder 5040, "C-Jüdische Gruppe aus Nikaragua," "F-Jüdische Gruppe aus Honduras" and "Folgende Juden . . . ." [Documents DA-1354, DA 1451], AA, Bonn.

39. NBC program, "Round-Up."

40. Alex-Edmund S. DaHinten, interviews with author, 19 Mar. 1997 and 3 May 1997.

41. *Federal Correctional Institution: Seagoville, Texas. 1940–1990: 50th Anniversary* (UNICOR, FCI Seagoville, 1990), 10.

Chapter Seven

Life in the Camps

1. "Comments to Dr. Stannard from Spokesman's meeting on Food Service," 6 July 1943, doc. 48 xi, Jacobs and Fallon, *Documents*, 1903–1906.

2. Swiss Inspection of Camp Seagoville, 22–23 Aug. 1944, 9, Folder 5092 ["Seagoville, Texas"]/Document D-3927, AA, Bonn; also "Changes, Inside and Out," *Dallas Morning News*, 10 Oct. 1990.

3. "Treasury Notification to Civilian Internees that their Assets are Being Frozen and Providing Instructions to Them for Preparing a Financial Report Form," 18 July 1944, doc. 48 xxxviii, Jacobs and Fallon, *Documents*, 1966–1972.

4. Bouquets and Brickbats File of Dr. Stannard, ibid., 2025–2038.

5. Memo, Dr. Stannard to officer in charge, steward, liaison officer, social services consultant, and chief medical officer, Re: Ration Revision, 24 Apr. 1945, doc. 48 xii, ibid., 2021.

6. The diplomatic letters between Berlin and Washington on matters concerning the mutual safety and repatriation of official and nonofficial citizens, as exchanged through the Swiss government, are located in Folder 5040/Documents 77 (23 Jan. 1942), 160 (1 Mar. 1942), 314 (13 Apr. 1942), 358 (28 Apr. 1942); Folder 5045 ["Dritte Fahrt mit dem Dampfer Drottningholm"]/Document 675 (2 July 1942), 680 (3 July 1942); and Folder 5054 ["Deutsch-Amerikanischer Austausch, Band 1"]/Document 1764 (10 Dec. 1943), AA, Bonn.

7. K. A. Susuki to the Spanish Consulate, New Orleans, 30 Apr. 1942. RG 389 (Records of the Office of the Provost Marshal General), Administrative Division, Mail and Records Branch, Unclassified Decimal File, Project—Technical Services—1941–1945, Box 423, Folder 383.7 "Fort Houston." NA.

8. Responses by Germans in New York to the random telegrams notifying them of passage space aboard the *Drottningholm* on 15 July 1942 are located in Folder 5045, AA, Bonn.

9. Swiss inspection reports of Camp Tuna Canyon can be found in Folder 5080 ["Durchgangslager für Männer in Tuna Canyon, USA, und Frauenlager in Los Angeles"], AA, Bonn.

10. Swiss inspection reports of Camp Algiers, Louisiana, can be found in Folder 5076 ["Übergangs—und Durchgangslager für Zivilinternierte Algiers, Louisiana in USA"], AA, Bonn.

Chapter Eight

Camp Crystal City, Texas

1. United States Immigration and Naturalization Service film, Alien Enemy Detention Facility (1947), available from the Audio-Visual Division of the National Archives.

2. See, for example, "Germans Now in Detention Camp," *Zavala County Sentinel*, 18 Dec. 1942, A1; "Population at Camp Increasing Fast," ibid., 26 Mar. 1943, A1; "Two Japanese Girls Drowned at Camp," ibid., 18 Aug. 1944, A1; and "Post Office Has Big Business Increase, ibid., 29 Dec. 1944, A1.

3. "Historical Narrative of the Crystal City Internment Camp." RG 85, 101/161 Camp Progress Narrative and Reports, 32, NA.

4. Jacobs and Fallon, *Documents*, 2038.

5. The first comprehensive investigation of the Crystal City Federal School is Karen Lea Riley's, "Schools Behind Barbed Wire: A History of Schooling in the United States Department of Justice Internment Camp at Crystal City, Texas, During World War II, 1942–1946" (Ph.D. diss., The University of Texas at Austin, 1996).

6. Gerd Erich Schneider.

7. Mangione, *Ethnic at Large*, 333–334, 347. See the eighteen-minute INS film, "Alien Enemy Detention Facility" (Crystal City, Texas, 1947).

8. McCrary, "Forgotten Internees of WW II Share Bitter Memories," *The Philadelphia Inquirer*, 16 Dec. 1989, 1, 4–5.

Chapter Nine

Nazis and Troublemakers in the Internee Camps

1. A collection of camp newspapers, *Das Lager*, *The Latrine*, and the *Bismarck Echo*, are reprinted in Jacobs and Fallon, *Documents*, 2653–2904.

2. RG 85 (Immigration and Naturalization Service), Investigations and Disciplinary Actions, Entry 214/033, Box 28, NA.

3. Albert Benz, Kurt Biederbeck, Fritz Eckstein, Johann Schranner, and Louise Wilkins to N. D. Collaer, 21 Apr. 1943. RG 85, ibid., WW II Internment Camps, Crystal City, General Files, 100/071 Part I. For additional letters of complaint, see also Entries 101/011, also 214/032, Box 27, NA.

4. N. D. Collaer to INS Commission, 28 Apr. 1943. RG 85, ibid.

5. Tessy Hohenreiner to Willard Kelly, Chief Supervisor of Border Patrol, 28 Dec. 1943. RG 85, ibid., File No. 103/22, Box 3, 103/031, and 103/63, Box 4, NA.

6. Ibid., Complaints and Disciplinary Action, File 201/022, Box 17, NA.

7. Jerre Mangione to Joseph O'Rourke, 27 Oct. 1943, and N. D. Collaer to Joseph O'Rourke, 19 Jan. 1945. RG 85, ibid., 56125/88-E, NA.

8. "Internees at Ft. Lincoln Deny Nazi Sympathies," *Bismarck (North Dakota) Tribune*, 8 Jan. 1946, 1, 7.

9. *The Fargo Forum*, 22 Feb. 1946.

10. "Interned German Seaman Tunnels His Way Out," *Bismarck Tribune*, 13 June 1941, and "Authorities Capture German Seaman," ibid., 16 June 1941.

11. Martin George Dudel Papers.

12. Swiss Inspection Report, Fort Lincoln Internment Camp, 18–20 Oct. 1944. Folder 5089 ["Fort Lincoln bei Bismarck, North Dakota"]/Document D-1100, AA, Bonn.

13. Martin George Dudel Papers.

14. Mangione, *Ethnic at Large*, 351–352.

15. Folder 5094 ["Zivilinterniertenlager Fort Stanton, New Mexico, 1942–1945"]/ Documents DA-538, 739, AA, Bonn.

16. Anderson, "Guests for the Duration," 60.

17. *Kenedy (Texas) Advance*, 30 Apr.1942, 21 May 1942, 2 July 1942, and 20 Aug. 1942. See also Gardiner, *Pawns in a Triangle of Hate*; and Memo, Bernard Gufler, Department of State, 22 May 1942, 740.00115 EW 1939/4715; and *Supplemental Report on Alien Enemy Camp at Kenedy, Texas, August 7, 1942*, 740.00115 PW/968, RG 59, NA.

18. Swiss Inspection Report, 29–30 Oct. 1942, 12, Folder 5088 ["Kenedy, Texas"]/ Document DA-1408, AA, Bonn.

19. "Vorschau auf die Olympiade," and "Ergaenzungen zum Frageboden," Alien Detention Center, Kenedy, Texas, 30 June–1 July 1943. Folder 5088/Document 1102, AA, Bonn.

20. Mangione, *Ethnic at Large*, 347.

21. Ibid., 327.

22. "Kuhn To Be Deported as Dangerous Alien," *The New York Times*, 7 Sept. 1945, 25; "Kuhn Departed Today, On Way to Germany," ibid., 15 Sept. 1945, 20.

23. Folder 5067 ["Zivilinterniertenlager, Allgemeines, Band 1"]/Document DA 815, AA, Bonn.

24. "By Order of Colonel Frankenberger, Headquarters, Stringtown Internment Camp, Stringtown, Oklahoma, September 1, 1942," Folder 5095 [Zivilinterniertenlager Stringtown in USA]/Document 1303, AA, Bonn.

25. "415 Jap Aliens Arrive at Fort," *Bismarck Tribune*, 9 Feb. 1942.

26. "Reporter Goes Inside the Gates to Learn How Enemy Aliens Lived during the War," *The Morton County (Mandan, North Dakota) News*, 21 Feb. 1946.

Chapter Ten

The Exchanges

1. Docs. 6, 57, 58, 59, 60, Jacobs and Fallon, *Documents*, 2309–2316.

2. RG 389, Administrative Division, "Administrative Division, Ft. Houston," 4 Apr. 1942, NA.

3. Repatriation Hearing: Karl Eppeler, Crystal City, 26 Aug. 1946. RG 85, File 210/ 51, Box 25, NA.

4. FBI Report by Agent James F. Gardner, San Antonio, Texas, District, 19 Feb. 1944, No. 100-270. RG 319, Decimal File, 1941–48, 291.2 Germans, Box 384, NA.

5. "List of Articles Which May or May Not Be Taken Out of the United States by German Repatriates," December 1944, doc. 106, Jacobs and Fallon, *Documents*, 2444–2445.

6. Docs. 76, 77, 78, ibid., 2354–2363.

7. T. F. Fitch, chief special agent, to Mr. Fletcher, "Special Instructions for Mr. Fletcher for Receiving the German Nationals From Mexico," n.d. RG 59 (Department of State), Special War Problems Division, NA.

8. Folder 5086 ["Deutsch-Amerikanischer Austausch von Zivilpersonen, 1944-1945, Band 1"]/Documents DA-4744, 4830, 815, AA, Bonn.

9. *Federal Register* 10, no. 144 (1945): 8947.

10. *United States Statutes at Large* 59, pt. 2, 880–881. 10 *Federal Register,* 11635, Modified by Presidential Proclamation 2685, 11 Apr. 1946 (11 *Federal Register,* 4075) authorizing the alien thirty days to prepare for repatriation/departure. U.S. Department of State, *Bulletin* 13, no. 332 (1945): 737–738. *Foreign Relations of the United States, 1945* 9: 283.

Chapter Eleven

The War Is Over

1. U.S. Department of State, *Bulletin* 13, no. 332 (4 Nov. 1945): 737–738.

2. Arthur Jacobs, Alfred Plaschke interviews.

3. Letter to the editor, Roger N. Baldwin, "Deporting Enemy Aliens," *Washington Post,* 5 Oct. 1945, 16.

4. Department of Justice, War Division, "Notice of Determination of Repatriation of Alien Enemy," "Acknowlegment of Notice and Request for Alien Enemy Repatriation Hearing," RG 85, entry 268, location 5/62/17/2, container LTA-C 1, NA.

5. Ibid.

6. Memo, Ugo Carusi, commissioner, INS, to all district directors and the officer in charge, Crystal City, 4 June 1946, doc. 131, Jacobs and Fallon, *Documents,* 2511–2514.

7. Ibid.

8. Anderson, "Guests for the Duration," 74–77.

9. Krause, "Dangerous Enemy Alien," 20–21.

10. Ibid.

11. *Daily Counts, German Spokesman, March 14, 1947,* RG 85, 206/023, General Files, Crystal City, Box 19, NA.

12. Hohenlohe, *Steph,* 154.

13. Charlotte Krause interview and correspondence.

14. *Congressional Record,* 80th Cong., 1st sess., vol. 93, pt. 8, 9466, 9898.

15. Krause, "Dangerous Enemy Alien."

16. McCrary, "Forgotten Internees," 4.

17. Gerd Erich Schneider interview.

18. Jo Anne Terwege interview and correspondence.

19. *The Bismarck Tribune,* 5 June 1969, 3.

20. See, for example, Joy Nozakiegee, ed., *Crystal City Internment Camp, 50th Anniversary Reunion, October 8–10, 1993, Monterey, California,* Crystal City Association, Sacramento, California; as well as *The Crystal City Chatter,* edited by Sumi Shimatsu-Utsushigawa, Los Angeles; and the Japanese American National Museum, Los Angeles.

21. Alan Garthright, "Memories of Injustice," *San Jose (California) Mercury News,* 2 Jan. 1991, 1.

22. Rostow, "Worst Mistake," 198–201.

23. "Intelligence Activities and the Rights of Americans," book 2, 24.

24. Ibid., 35.

25. Arnold Krammer, "Feinde Ohne Uniform: Deutsche Zivilinternierte in den USA, 1941–1945," *Vierteljahrshefte für Zeitgeschichte* (Munich), no. 4, Oct. 1996, 581–603. Also, Theoharis and Cox, *The Boss,* 173–174.

26. U.S. Congress. House. Subcommittee on Appropriations, Testimony of the Director

on 17 Jan. 1946, 163; also Justice Department, Appropriations Bill, 1946, 259. These numbers do not take into consideration the percentage of each ethnic population that these arrests represent. For example, of some 600,000 registered Italian aliens, 3,503 arrests represent only 1 percent of the Italian alien community; of over 300,000 German aliens, 7,164 arrests represent 2 percent of registered German aliens; but of about 90,000 registered Japanese aliens in the United States, 6,026 arrests represent a full 7 percent of all Japanese aliens.

27. Letter to the editor, Arthur D. Jacobs, "Germans, Italians also were interned," *The Arizona Republic*, 19 Aug. 1988, A16. By the same author, see "Fifty Years of Silence," *Society for German-American Studies Newsletter* (University of Cincinnati, Ohio), June 1991, 10ff; and "History Quiet on the Arrest and Internment of German-Americans in the United States During World War II," ibid., Sept. 1991, 18, 19, 23. Also Dianna Hatfield, "Internment of Germans and German-Americans During World War II: The Untold Story," ibid., June 1993, 12–14.

28. Guillermo X. Garcia, "Prisoners of War: Texas Camps Held Hostages of WW II Hysteria," *Austin American-Statesman*, 18. Sept. 1989, 1, 5.

29. August C. Boliano, *The Ellis Island Source Book* (Washington, D.C.: Kensington Historical Press, 1985).

30. Cited in Roger Daniels, *Coming to America: A History of Immigration and Ethnicity in American Life* (New York: Harper Collins, 1990), 303.

31. John Leo, "An Apology to Japanese-Americans," *Time Magazine*, 2 May 1988; "America's Debt to Japanese-Americans," *The New York Times*, 4 Oct. 1987, sec. 4, 22.

32. *Personal Justice Denied* (U.S. Commission: 1992), 293, 295–301.

33. *USA Today*, 6 Dec. 1991, 9A; Michael Slackman, *Remembering Pearl Harbor: The Story of the USS Arizona Memorial* (Honolulu: Arizona Memorial Museum Association, University of Hawaii Press, 1984), 74.

Chapter Twelve

The Issues

1. Joseph E. Fallon, "The Facts About Internment," cited in Holian, "German-American Community," 314–315.

2. Arthur D. Jacobs, Circuit of Appeals (District of Columbia Circuit), decision dated 28 Mar. 1992, in the case of Arthur D. Jacobs, 30 Mar. 1992, 1–4.

3. Clay Thompson, "At War with U.S.," *The Phoenix Gazette*, 6 Oct. 1992, 1, 10.

4. See, for example, Richard E. Morgan, *Domestic Intelligence: Monitoring Dissent in America* (Austin: University of Texas Press, 1980).

5. Interview with Claude Turner, 15 Aug. 1993, Gloucester, New Jersey.

BIBLIOGRAPHY

Books

Biddle, Francis, *In Brief Authority* (Garden City, New York: Doubleday, 1962).

Boliano, August C., *The Ellis Island Source Book* (Washington, DC: Kensington Historical Press, 1985).

Breuer, William, *Hitler's Undercover War: The Nazi Espionage Invasion of the U.S.A.* (New York: St. Martin's Press, 1989).

Burdick, Charles B., *An American Island in Hitler's Reich: The Bad Nauheim Internment* (Menlo Park, Calif.: Markgraf Publications Group, 1987).

Canedy, Susan, *America's Nazis: A Democratic Dilemma* (Menlo Park, Calif.: Markgraf Publications, 1990).

Carlson, John Roy, *Under Cover* (New York: E. P. Dutton & Co., Inc., 1943).

Chase, Allan, *Falange: The Axis Secret Army in the Americas* (New York: G. P. Putnam's Sons, 1943).

Christgau, John, *'Enemies': World War II Alien Internment* (Ames: Iowa State University Press, 1985).

Combs, James, *American Political Movies; An Annotated Filmography of Feature Films* (New York: Garland, 1990).

Cushman, Robert E., "The Impact of the War on the Constitution." In *The Impact of the War on America: Six Lectures by Members of the Faculty of Cornell University* (Ithaca: Cornell University Press, 1942).

Daniels, Roger, *Coming to America: A History of Immigration and Ethnicity in American Life* (New York: Harper Collins, 1990).

DeJong, Louis, *The German Fifth Column in the Second World War* (New York: Howard Fertig, 1973).

Diamond, Sander A., *The Nazi Movement in the United States, 1924–1941* (Ithaca: Cornell University Press, 1974).

Documents of German Foreign Policy, 1918–1945. Vol. 1 (Washington, D.C. 1949).

Donner, Frank J., *The Age of Surveillance* (New York: Vintage Books, 1980).

Fallon, Joseph E., "The Facts About Internment," unpublished manuscript.

Farago, Ladislas, *The Game of the Foxes: The Untold Story of German Espionage in the United States and Great Britain During World War II* (New York: D. McKay Company, 1971).

Federal Correctional Institution: Seagoville, Texas, 1940–1990: 50th Anniversary. (UNICOR, FCI Seagoville, 1990).

Firmin, Stanley, *They Came to Spy* (London: Hutchinson, 1946).

Fox, Stephen R., *The Other Internment: An Oral History of the Relocation of Italian Americans during World War II* (Boston: Twayne Publishers, 1990).

Fox, Stephen R., *The Unknown Internment: An Oral History of the Relocation of Italian Americans During World War II* (Boston: Twayne Publishers, 1990).

Führer Conferences on Naval Affairs. Vol. 1940 (London: Admiralty, 1947).

Gardiner, C. Harvey, *Pawns in a Triangle of Hate* (Seattle: The University of Washington Press, 1981).

Glancy, H. M., *Confessions of a Nazi Spy, Vol. 1 of International Dictionary of Films and Film-makers* (Chicago: St. James, 1990).

Goodman, Walter , *The Committee: The Extraordinary Career of the House Committee on Un-American Activities* (New York: Farrar, Straus, and Giroux, 1968).

Higham, Charles, *Trading With the Enemy: The Exposé of the Nazi-American Money Plot, 1933–1949* (New York: Delacarte Press, 1983).

Hohenlohe, Prince Franz, *Steph: The Fabulous Princess* (London: New English Library, 1976).

Hohri, William Minoru, *Repairing America: An Account of the Movement for Japanese-American Redress* (Pullman: Washington State University Press, 1988).

Hyde, H. Montgomery, *Room 3603: The Story of the British Intelligence Center in New York during W.W. II, Forward by Ian Fleming* (New York: Farrar, Straus and Company, 1962).

Hynd, Alan, *Passport to Treason: The Inside Story of Spies in America* (New York: R. M. McBride & Company, 1943).

Langman, Larry and Ed Borg, *Encyclopedia of American War Films* (New York, 1989).

La Violette, Forrest Emmanuel, *The Canadian Japanese and World War II: A Sociological and Psychological Account* (Toronto: University of Toronto Press, 1948, 1987).

Mangione, Jerre, *An Ethnic at Large: A Memoir of America in the Thirties and Forties* (New York: Putnam, 1978).

Mickey, Roy , *Justice in Our Time: The Japanese-Canadian Redress Settlement,* (Vancouver, British Columbia: Talonbooks, 1991).

Richard E. Morgan, *Domestic Intelligence: Monitoring Dissent in America* (Austin: University of Texas, 1980).

Morison, Samuel Eliot, *The Battle of the Atlantic* (Boston: Little, Brown & Company, 1960).

Nash, Jay Robert and Stanley Ralph Ross, *The Motion Picture Guide: C-D, 1927–1983* (Chicago Cinebooks, 1990).

Panayi, Panikos (ed.), *Minorities in Wartime: National and Racial Groupings in Europe, North America and Australia during the Two World Wars* (Providence, R.I.: Berg, 1993).

Perrett, Geoffrey, *Days of Sadness, Years of Triumph: The American People 1939–1945* (New York: Coward, McCann & Geoghegan Inc., 1973).

Personal Justice Denied: Report of the Commission on Wartime Relocation and Internment of Civilians (Washington, D.C., December 12, 1982).

Pommerin, Reiner, *Das Dritte Reich und Latinamerika: Die deutsche Politik gegenüber Süd-und Mittelamerika* (Düsseldorf: Froste, 1977).

Powers, Richard Gid, *Secrecy and Power: The Life of J. Edgar Hoover* (New York: Free Press, 1987).

Puttkammer, Ernst W., *Alien Friends and Alien Enemies in the United States*, Public Policy Pamphlet No. 39 (Chicago: The University of Chicago, 1943).

Rachlis, Eugene, *They Came to Kill* (New York: Random House, 1961).

Rippley, LaVern J., *The German Americans* (Boston: Twayne Publishers, 1976).

Rout, Jr., Leslie B., and John F. Bratzel, *The Shadow War: German Espionage and United States Counterespionage in Latin America During World War II* (Maryland, University Publications of America, Inc., 1986).

Sayers, Michael and Albert E. Kahn, *Sabotage! The Secret War Against America* (New York: Harper & Brothers, 1942).

Slackman, Michael, *Remembering Pearl Harbor: The Story of the USS Arizona Memorial* (Honolulu: Arizona Memorial Museum Association, University of Hawaii Press, 1984).

Smith, Jr., Arthur L., *The Deutschtum of Nazi Germany and the United States* (The Hague: M. Nijhoff, 1965).

Sorrentino, Frank M. *Ideological Warfare: The FBI's Path Toward Power* (Port Washington, N.Y.: Associated Faculty Press, 1985).

Stent, Ronald, *A Bespattered Page? The Internment of 'His Majesty's Most Loyal Enemy Aliens,'* (London: Andre Deutsch, Ltd., 1980).

Stephan, Alexander, *Im Visier des FBI. Deutsche Exilschriftsteller in den Akten americanischer Geheimdienste* (Stuttgart: Verlag J. B. Metzler, 1995).

Theoharis, Athan G. and John Stuart Cox, *The Boss: J. Edgar Hoover and the Great American Inquisition* (Philadelphia: Temple University Press, 1988).

Theoharis, Athan, *Spying on Americans: Political Surveillance from Hoover to the Houston Plan* (Philadelphia: Temple University Press, 1978).

Tolzmann Don Heinrich, ed., *German-Americans in the World War*. Vol. 4, Arthur D. Jacobs and Joseph E. Fallon, eds., *The World War Two Experience,* Section 1, Part I (Munich: K. G. Saur, 1995).

United States Army in World War II: The Western Hemisphere—Guarding the United States and its Outposts (Washington, D.C. OCMH, 1964).

Wagner, Jonathan F., *Brothers Beyond the Seas: National Socialism in Canada* (Waterloo, Ontario, Canada: Wilfrid Laurier University Press, 1981).

Wagner, Regina, *Los Alemanes en Guatemala, 1828–1944* (Asociacion de Educacion y Cultura 'Alejandro von Humboldt' Comite de Investigaciones Historicas) Editorial IDEA, Universidad Francisco Marroquin Guatemala, 1991.

Wilson, Woodrow, War Message to Congress, April 2, 1917, in Arthur Link, et al., eds., *The Papers of Woodrow Wilson* (Princeton: Princeton University Press, 1966).

Government Documents

Congressional Record, House, 76th Cong., 1st session

Congressional Record, House, 77th Cong., 2nd session

Congressional Record, House, 80th Cong., 1st session

Congressional Record, House, 95th Congt., 2nd session

Department of State Bulletin

Federal Bureau of Investigation, Report of the Director, Fiscal Years 1941, 1942, 1943, 1944, 1945, 1946, 1947.

Immigration and Naturalization Service Records, Washington, D.C.

National Archives, Washington, D.C.

    Record Group 59 (General Records of the Department of State)

    Record Group 85 (Records of the Immigration and Naturalization Service)

    Record Group 107 (Records of the Office of the Secretary of War-Old Army/Modern Army)

    Record Group 153 (Records of the Office of the Judge Advocate General-Army)

    Record Group 165 (Records of the War Department General and Special Staffs)

    Record Group 220 (Records of Temporary Committees, Commissions, and Boards)

    Record Group 319 (Records of the Army Staff-Modern Army)

    Record Group 389 (Records of the Provost Marshal General's Office 1941)

The diplomatic letters between Berlin and Washington on matters concerning the mutual safety and repatriation of official and nonofficial citizens, as exchanged through the Swiss Government, are located in the archives of the Auswärtiges Amt, Bonn.

Journals And Newspapers

" 'Dangerous' Bundist Arrested," *The New York Times*, June 23, 1942.

"160 Nazi Seamen Arrested in Raids; Publicists Seized," *The New York Times*, May 8, 1941.

"2 Seized in Phila. as 'Spy Ring' Cogs," *Camden (New Jersey) Courier Post*, February 12, 1941.

"22,000 Nazis Hold Rally in Garden: Police Check Foes," *The New York Times*, February 21, 1939.

"28 Axis Nationals Arrested by FBI in Gulf Arms Area," *Houston Post*, December 10, 1941.

"415 Jap Aliens Arrive at Fort," *Bismarck Tribune*, February 9, 1942.

"Alien Camps Made Enclosed Prisons," *The New York Times*, January 12, 1942.

"Alien Found Dead in East River," *The New York Times*, June 25, 1942.

"Alien Interned by FBI, Had Officers' Club Job," *The New York Times*, January 9, 1942.

"Alien Restriction Tightens On Coast," *The New York Times*, June 14, 1942.

"America's Debt to Japanese-Americans," *The New York Times*, October 4, 1987.

"Anti-Nazi Outbreak Feared," February 20, 1939, *The New York Times*, February 21, 1939.

"Army Court to Try 8 Nazi Saboteurs," *The New York Times*, July 3, 1942.

"Authorities Capture German Seaman," *Bismarck Tribune* , June 16, 1941.

"Bail Fixed at $100,000, Man of German Flag is Accused of Insulting Flag," *The New York Times*, June 19, 1942.

"Bars Alien Students," *The New York Times*, June 16, 1942.

"Brothers Face Alien Hearing," *Cincinnati Times Star*, March 25, 1943.

"Brothers Want to Help Hitler," *Cincinnati Enquirer*, March 24, 1943.

"Bund 'Party' Egged on Coast," *The New York Times*, February 26, 1939.

"Bund Rally to Get Huge Police Guard," *The New York Times*, February 19, 1939.

"Bundist Gets Six Months," *The New York Times*, June 20, 1942.

"Bundsmen Linked to Defense Plants," *The New York Times*, October 3, 1940.

"Changes, Inside and Out," *Dallas Morning News*, October 10, 1990.

"Check-up of Aliens to Go On; 200 Held," *Newsweek*, May 19, 1941.

"Chicago Inquiry to Call Bundists," *The New York Times*, June 30, 1942.

"Declare United States Ready to Run Down Spies," *The New York Times*, October 1, 1939.

"Dr. Zimmerman, Former Storm Center Here, Sues 37 Hospitals," *Honolulu Advertiser*, June 19, 1945.

"FBI Continues Roundup of Aliens in Houston Area," *Houston Post*, December 11, 1941.

"FBI Tightens Curb on 256,000 Aliens," *The New York Times*, April 1, 1942.

"Few Elated Over Internment Camp," *Bismarck Tribune*, April 12, 1941.

"Forgotten Internees End Silence, *Philadelphia Inquirer*. December 16, 1989.

"Forbids Exclusion From a Coast Area," *Bismarck Tribune*, August 21, 1943.

"Foreign Born Held Loyal to America," *The New York Times*, June 28, 1942.

"German is Accused of Seeking War Job," *The New York Times*, June 26, 1942.

"Germans Now in Detention Camp," *Zavala County Sentinel*, December 18, 1942.

"Guatemala Sends Aliens to U.S.," *The New York Times*, January 13, 1942.

"Hawaii Doctor Seizes by Army Seeks $575,000," *Chicago Daily Tribune*, May 29, 1946.

"Hungarian Papers Split on War," *The New York Times*, December 7, 1941.
"Interned German Seaman Tunnels His Way Out," *Bismarck Tribune*, June 13, 1941.
"Internees at Ft. Lincoln Deny Nazi Sympathies," *Bismarck (North Dakota) Tribune*, January 8, 1946.
"Jews in Mexico Hit," *The New York Times*, December 20, 1937.
"Kuhn Departed Today, On Way to Germany," *The New York Times*, September 15, 1945.
"Kuhn To Be Deported as Dangerous Alien," *The New York Times*, September 7, 1945.
"Link German Bund to Army Officers," *The New York Times*, September 8, 1939.
"Mexico Deporting Jews," *The New York Times*, December 4, 1937.
"Mexico Lays Plans to Oust Many Jews," *The New York Times*, December 24, 1937.
"Nazi Aide in Detroit Convicted," *The New York Times*, July 3, 1942.
"Nazi Family of 5 Seized in Brooklyn," *The New York Times*, June 27, 1943.
"Nazi Spy Activity in Mexico Charged," *The New York Times*, June 28, 1938.
"No More Aliens in Army," *Army and Navy Register 58* (August 28, 1937).
"One of Few U.S. Treason Cases," *The New York Times*, July 3, 1942.
"Only 3,771 Enemy Aliens Interned in U.S. Camps," *The New York Times*, November 11, 1943.
"Panel of 22 Set Up For Alien Hearings," *The New York Times*, August 22, 1943.
"Peewee Hitlers Found in America," *The New York Times*, September 1, 1939.
"Philadelphia Woman Defies Army Order That She Must Leave the Eastern Area," *The New York Times*, May 8, 1943.
"Princess Stephanie Is Interned in Jersey; Nazi Agent Was Believed to be in Mexico," *The New York Times*, December 11, 1941.
"Property Collected by Police from Aliens Here," *The New York Times*, January 7, 1942.
"Protests Arrests of German Seamen," *The New York Times*, May 12, 1941.
"Race Row Divides Wives of Nazis in Nicaragua," *The New York Times*, June 27, 1942.
"Reporter Goes Inside the Gates to Learn How Enemy Aliens Lived during the War," *The Morton County News*, February 21, 1946.
"Roundup and Rally," *Newsweek*, May 26, 1941.
"Tent Town Built for Aliens at Fort Devens," *The New York Times*, April 2, 1942.
"The Foreign-Language Press," *Fortune*, November, 1940.
"The Screen," *The New York Times*, June 13, 1942
"Travel for Aliens Made Easier Here; Applicants for Permits Need Only One Personal Appearance, Renewals to be Mailed," *The New York Times*, January 7, 1942.
"Two Ex-U.S. Soldiers Seized as Alien Foes," *The New York Times*, January 7, 1943.
"Willkie Issues Plea for Alien Group Here," *The New York Times*, January 29, 1942.
"Young Bund Members Drill in Brooklyn; Police Guard Almost Outnumbers Children," *The New York Times*, March 13, 1939.

Amidon, Beulah, "Aliens in America." *Survey Graphic*, February 1941.
Baldwin, Roger N., "Deporting Enemy Aliens." *Washington Post*, October 5, 1945.
Barnhart, Edward N., "Japanese Internees from Peru." Vol. 31, *Pacific Historical Review* (1962).
Bell, Leland V., "The Failure of Nazistm in America: The German-American Bund, 1936–1941." *Political Science Quarterly*, December 1970.
Biddle, Francis, "American-Aliens and the Registration Act of 1940." *State Government*, August 1940.

Biddle, Francis, "Axis Aliens in America—Statement of Policy Issued December 19, 1941." *Survey Graphic*, January 1942.

Bogardus, Emory S., "Relocation Centers as Planned Communities." *Sociology and Social Research* (January–February 1944).

Burton, Shirley J. and Kellee Green, "Oaths of Allegiance, Acts of Treason: The Disloyalty Prosecutions of Max Stephan and Hans Haupt." *Prologue* (Fall 1991).

Curran, John M,. "The Companies of the Damned." *Army* (February 1982).

Ennis, Edward J., "Government control of Alien Enemies." *State Government* (May 1942).

Ennis, Edward J., "Federal Control Measures for Enemy Aliens." *Police Yearbook* 1943.

Fox, Stephen C., "General John DeWitt and the Proposed Internment of German and Italian Aliens during World War II." *Pacific Historical Review*, 57, no.4, (1988).

Garcia, Guillermo X., "Prisoners of War: Texas Camps Held Hostages of WW II Hysteria," *Austin American-Statesman*, September 18, 1989.

Garthright, Alan, "Memories of Injustice," San Jose (*California*) *Mercury News*, January 2, 1991.

Hamburger, Ernest, "A Peculiar Pattern of the Fifth Column: The Organization of the German Seamen." *Social Research* 9 (1942).

Hanigen, Frank C., "Foreign Political Movements in the United States." *Foreign Affairs*, (October 1937).

Harrison, Earl G., "Axis Aliens in an Emergency." *Survey Graphic* (September 1941).

Harrison, Earl G., "Civilian Internment—American Way." *Survey Graphic* (May, 1944).

Harrison, Earl G., "How State and Local Officials Can Assist in the Alien Registration Program." *State Government* (October 1940).

Hatfield, Dianna, "Internment of Germans and German-Americans During World War II: The Untold Story." *Society for German-American Studies Newsletter* (June 1993).

Hoover, J. Edgar, "Alien Enemy Control." *Iowa Law Review* (March 1944).

Interview with Alfred Plaschke, Houston, Texas, April 14, 1990. *Freeport (Texas) Facts*, January 8, 1942.

Jacobs, Arthur D., "Fifty Years of Silence." Society for German-American Studies Newsletter (University of Cincinnati, Ohio), June 1991.

Jacobs , Arthur D., "History Quiet on the Arrest and Internment of German-Americans in the United States During World War II." *Society for German-American Studies Newsletter* (September 1991).

Jacobs, Arthur D., "Germans, Italians also were interned," *The Arizona Republic*, August 19, 1988.

Kempner, Robert M. W., "The Enemy Alien Problem in the Present War." *The American Journal of International Law* 34, no. 3 (July 1940).

Kenedy (Texas) Advance, April 30, May 21, July 2, 1942, and August 20, 1942.

Krammer, Arnold, "In Splendid Isolation: Enemy Diplomats in World War II." *Prologue* (spring 1985).

Krammer, Arnold, "Feinde Ohne Uniform: Deutsche Zivilinternierte in den USA, 1941–1945." *Vierteljahrshefte für Zeitgeschichte* (Munich), no. 4 (October 1996).

Krause, Kitry, "Dangerous Enemy Alien." *Chicago Weekly Reader,* 22, no. 48, September 3, 1993.

Lasker, Loula D., "Friends or Enemies?" *Survey Graphic* (June 1942).

Leo, John, "An Apology to Japanese-Americans," *Time Magazine*, May 2, 1988.

Lippmann, Walter, *New York Herald Tribune*. February 5, 12, and 14, 1942.

McCrary, Lacy, "World War II German-American Internees Seek Reparations." *Riverside (California) Press Enterprise*, December 24, 1989

McWilliams, Carey, "Moving the West Coast Japanese." *Harper's Magazine*, September 1942.

Nozakiegee, Joy, ed., *Crystal City Internment Camp, 50th Anniversary Reunion*. October 8–10, 1993, Monterey, California, Crystal City Association, Sacramento, California.

Putlitz, Wolfgang zu, "Your German-American Neighbor and the Fifth Column." *Harper's Magazine*, February 1942.

Ringle, Ken, "The Untold Story of One Man's Fight for the Nisei." *The Los Angeles Times*, December 6, 1981.

Rostow, Eugene V., "Our Worst Wartime Mistake." *Harper's Magazine*, September 1945.

Roucek, Joseph S., "Foreign-Language Press in World War II." *Sociology and Social Research* (July–August 1943).

Rowe, James Jr., "The Alien Enemy Program—So Far." *Common Ground* (summer, 1942).

San Francisco Chronicle, February 9, 1942, p. 10.

Sandeen, Eric J., "Confessions of a Nazi Spy and the German American Bund." *American Studies*, 20 no. 2 (fall 1979).

Smith, Deborah McCarty, "Years of Silence," *University of Dayton Quarterly* 6 (summer 1997)

Spotlight, May 20, 1991.

Swanberg, W. A., "The Spies Who Came in From the Sea." *American Heritage*, April 1970.

The Crystal City Chatter, edited by Sumi Shimatsu-Utsushigawa, Los Angeles; and the Japanese American National Museum, Los Angeles.

The Fargo (North Dakota) Forum, February 22, 1946.

Thompson, Clay, "At War with U.S." *The Phoenix Gazette*, October 6, 1992.

USA Today, December 6, 1991.

Map

Hugo Grothe, *Die Deutschen in Übersee eine Skizze ihres werdens, ihrer Verbreitung und Kultur Arbeit* (Berlin: Zentraverlag, 1982) map 1.

Interviews

Reinhard Kruse
Arthur D. Jacobs
Paul Graber
Charlotte Maier
Alex-Edmund DaHinten
Alfred Plaschke
John Cramer
Juergen Koetter
Gunter Koetter
Joseph E. Fallon

Claude Turner
Eberhard Fuhr
Julius Fuhr
Deborah Ann Dudel Lincoln
John Heitmann
JoAnne Wartemann Terwege
Jerre Mangione

Theses/Dissertations

Anderson, Jr., William E., "Guests for the Duration: World War II and the Crew of the S.S. Columbus. An Historical Archaeological Investigation of the Fort Stanton Enemy Alien Internment Camp (1941–945)" (Master's thesis, Eastern New Mexico University, 1993).

Connell III, Thomas, "The Internment of Latin American Japanese in the United States During World War Two: The Peruvian Japanese Experience" (Ph.D. diss., Florida State University, 1995).

Holian, Timothy J., "The German-American Community During the World War II Era, With a Focus on Cincinnati, Ohio" (Ph.D. diss.: University of Cincinnati, Ohio, 1995).

Riley, Karen Lea, "Schools Behind Barbed Wire: A History of Schooling in the United States Department of Justice Internment Camp at Crystal City, Texas, During World War II, 1942–1946" (Ph.D. diss., The University of Texas at Austin, 1996).

Schmitz, John Eric, "Democracy Under Stress: The Internment of German-Americans in World War II" (Master's thesis, North Carolina State University at Raleigh, 1993).

Film/Television

National Broadcasting Company's television program "Round-Up," on *Dateline*, November 1994.

United States Immigration and Naturalization Service film, Alien Enemy Detention Facility (1947), available from the Audio-Visual Division of the National Archives.

Index

Abbaticchio, R. J., 39
Ackerman, Max, 63, 65
Adkins, Gov. Homer, 59
Agne, Herman, 72
Alexander, Kenneth, 63
alien enemies in the armed forces, 70
Alien Enemy Control Unit, 43, 45–46, 76–77, 80, 112, 153, 164
Alien Registration Act, 4, 25, 77
America First, 52
American Civil Liberties Union, 64, 99
American Committee for Protection of the Foreign Born, 55
American Jewish Joint Distribution Committee, 99
American Legion, 51, 74–75, 95
Angel Island, 25, 84
anti-Semitism, 6–8, 52–53, 99, 113
Arandora Star, 21
Arthur D. Jacobs v. *William Barr et al.,* 172–173
Attorney General, 1, 12, 23–33, 53, 55, 60, 66–68, 72, 81, 152–153, 165–166, 168. *See* Francis Biddle, Tom Clark, Justice Department
Australia, 21

Balboa Detention Center, 98
Bauer, Alfred, 133
Beach, Henry L., 62–63
Belz, Emil, 133
Benesch, Horst Werner, 130
Berle, Adolph, 92
Betz, Emil, 135
Biddle, Francis, 26–27, 32–33, 45, 53, 55, 60, 66–68, 72, 80–81, 165–166, 173. *See also* Attorney General, Justice Department
Biddle's Columbus Day speech, 69
Bill 1749, 159
Bismarck Echo, 117, 126

Bismarck Tribune, 125, 138
Boeck, Willy, 119, 123
Bremen, Lloyd, 133
Bremer, Otto, 86
Brincker, Walter, 130
Britain, 18–21
Bunker, Raymond, 108
Bushfield, Gov. Harlan, 59

Camp Algiers (LA), 108
Camp Bismarck (ND), 97
Camp Blanding (FL), 93, 98
Camp Forrest (TN), 117
Camp Fort Sam Houston (TX), 84
Camp Kenedy (TX), 131–136, 143
Camp McCoy (WI), 27, 64
Camp Meade (MD), 73
Camp Seagoville (TX), 73, 83, 100–104, 108–110
Camp Sharp Park (CA), 84
Camp Stringtown (OK), 84, 93, 137–138
Camp Tuna Canyon (CA), 107
Camp Upton (NY), 27
Canada, 15–18
Canion, Darrel, 120
Carusi, Ugo, 153
Civil Liberties Act of 1988, 169
Civilian Alien Enemy Hearing Boards, 45
Civilian Conservation Corp (CCC), 25, 27, 36, 70, 83, 107, 131
Clark, Charles, 59
Clark, Attorney General Tom, 66, 153. *See also* Attorney General, Justice Department
Clay, Gen. Lucius, 151
Collaer, N. D., 120–122
Commission on Wartime Relocation and Internment of Civilians (CWRIC), 60, 168, 172
Confessions of a Nazi Spy, 7
confidential informants, 64

Cordes, Hermann, 127
Crantz, Christel, 130
Crystal City Federal High School, 114
Custodial Detention Index (CDI), 10–11, 28, 33, 37, 39–40, 61, 164–166

Daehne, Capt. Wilhelm, 129–130
DaHinten, Dr. Alex-Edmund, 99
Das Lager, 113–114, 117, 146
Dathe, Bruno, 130
De Jong, Louis, 90
De Martin, Joseph, 85
De Witt, Lt. Gen. John L., 50–51, 55, 58, 62–65, 69
denaturalization (decertification), 68
detainees, 49
Dodd Field Internment Camp (TX), 106–107
Dropman, Edmund Adolph, 46–47
Drum, Lt. Gen. Hugh A., 66–67
Dudel, Martin G., 47–48, 67–68

Eastern Defense Command, 61, 66–67 (*See also* Lt. Gen. Hugh A. Drum)
Ebell, Dr. Wolfgang, 34
Effinger, Max, 133
Ehrhard, Walter, 37
Elwood, Larry, 119
Emergency Detention Program, 10
Endo v. *United States,* 167
enemy aliens (*See also* alien enemies); anti-fascists among, 52 (*See also* Chapter 9, "Nazis and Troublemakers"); confidential information, 64; denaturalization (decertification), 68; effects of movies on American fears, 7–9; in armed forces, 70; number in America, 4–5, 26–27, 31–32; registration of, 25–30
Enemy Alien Detention Centers (*See* Camps); *Bismarck Echo,* 117; camp commanders (*See* Chapter 6, "The Camps" and individual camps); camp spokesman (*See* Chapter 6, "The Camps," and individual camps); *Das Lager,* 113–114, 117, 146; food and entertainment (*See* Chapter 7, "Life in the Camps"); escapes (*See* Chapter 9, "Nazis and Troublemakers");

German Council, 120–122; *The Latrine,* 117; Nazism in camps (*See* Chapter 9, "Nazis and Troublemakers"); schools and education (*See* Chapter 7, "Life in the Camps"); Swiss inspectors, 85–87, 122, 130, 136
England, 18–21
Ennis, Edward J., 45–46, 153, 168
Executive Order 9066, 55, 58, 61, 168–169, 171
Executive Order 9106, 59

Fallon, Joseph E., 171
Federal Bureau of Investigation (FBI), 1–2, 10–12, 45, 50–57, 67–68, 71–81, 90, 102, 118, 144, 151, 164–166, 171–173 (*See also* Chapter 4: "The Arrests" and Chapter 5: "The Process")
Fengler, Alfred K. H., 133
Flechsel, Anna, 113
Foreign Nationalities Branch (FNB), 57–58
Fox, Stephen C., 59–60
Frankenberger, Lt. Col. Bertram, 137
Franz, Martin, 38
Friedman, Max Paul, 92, 98
Fuhr, Carl, 77–78
Fuhr, Eberhard, 77–79, 88, 107, 156, 159, 163–164
Fuhr, Julius, 77–78, 88, 164

Garay, Jose Maria, 132
Gast, Max, 133
Gebhard, Mr., 122
Geneva Convention (1929), 49, 105, 132
German-American Bund, 4–7, 23, 34, 45, 77 (*See also* Fritz Kuhn)
German-American Societies, 29, 118
German Council, 120–122
German newspapers, 53
German seamen, 23–25, 75, 124, 129, 134
Gibbe, Gunther, 86
Gloucester City (NJ), 41, 86, 144, 169
Gotthelf, Ina, 87
Graber, Heinrich, 41–42
Green, Brig. Gen. Thomas, 65
Gregeratzki, Albert, 127
Gregg, Wayne, 46

Harrison, Earl G., 28, 33, 45, 54, 112, 173.
    See also Immigration and Naturalization
    Service
Hasenburger, Heinrich Johann, 113, 117,
    119, 122
Hearing Boards, 45–47, 62–66. *See also* Im-
    migration and Naturalization Service,
    Justice Department, and Federal Bureau
    of Investigation
Heitmann, Alfred Heinrich R., 73, 102,
    155, 158
Hohenlohe, Prince Franz, 24, 41
Hohenlohe-Waldenburg-Schillingfurst,
    Princess Stephanie, 23–24, 41, 102, 157
Holian, Timothy J., 171
Hoover, J. Edgar. *See also* Federal Bureau of
    Investigation; arrests of, evidence, and
    search warrants against enemy aliens (see
    Chapter 4); concern about foreigners,
    1–2; development of CDI lists/index,
    10–11; evaluation of FBI role. *See*
    Chapter 12, "The Issues"; presidential
    authorization, 2, 14; renaming of CDI,
    Hoover's manipulations, 165–166
Hudson, Aubrey S., 132–133
Hull, Cordell, 92, 95

Iden, Christian, 39
Immigration and Naturalization Service
    (INS), 28–31, 45–46, 80–81, 83–85,
    88, 102, 108–109, 113, 117, 124–125,
    146, 152–154
Individual Exclusion Program, 61–68; ex-
    cludees, 67–68

Jackson, Robert, 23
Jacobs, Arthur, 75, 161–162, 171–173
Arthur D. Jacobs v. William Barr et al., 161–
    162, 171–173
Jacobs, Lambert Dietrich, 158–159
Japanese-American National Historic Land-
    mark Theme Study Act (1992), 169
Jensen, Lloyd H., 138
Johnson, Sen. Hiram, 50
Johnson v. *Eisentrager,* 35
Justice Department, 1, 10–11, 27–28, 33–
    34, 45–46, 55, 63–64, 67–70, 72–76,

83, 99, 151–154. *See also* Francis Biddle,
    Tom Clark, Federal Bureau of Investiga-
    tion

Karch, Louis, 123
Keller, John, 120
Kelly, Willard F., 43
Kenedy Advance, 131
Kiessling, Otto, 74
Klein, Walter, 93, 95–96, 132–133, 135,
    143, 148, 162
Kleinmond, Frank, 88
Koehlein, Anna, 80
Koeller, Heinz, 135
Koetter, Gunter, 163
Koetter, Hermann, 30–40, 47, 103, 115,
    142, 163
Koetter, Juergen, 163
Kolb, Karl, 120, 137, 142
Kriechbaum, Herr, 114
Kruse, Heinrich, 93, 96–98
Kuhn, Fritz, 5, 8, 122, 136, 149. *See also*
    German-American Bund
Kunze, Gerhard Wilhelm, 34

Langer, Sen. William, 158–159
The Latrine, 117
Laughlin, James J., 153
Lechner, Karl, 123

Maier, Charlotte, 157–158
Mains, George Calvin, 72
Mangione, Jerre, 95, 115, 129, 136, 138
Marggraff, Joachim, 126
Marquenie, Johann, 128
Max Ackerman v. *General DeWitt,* 65
McAlexander, E. D., 119
McCloy, John J., 63, 65
McCoy, Ike P., 95, 126–127, 129
McDermott, Thomas D., 87
Mertig, Kurt, 153
Meyer, Frank, 108
Michel, Willy, 130
Military Intelligence Division, 2, 11, 98
Military Tribunal, 67
Molzahn, Rev. Kurt E. B., 34
Munson, Curtis B., 56

National Censorship Office, 42
National Japanese American Student Relocation Council, 112
National Refugee Service, 99
Neuoff, Hermann, 131
Neutrality Laws Unit, 23
Nicolini, Teodor, 134

Office of Coordinator of Information, 57
Office of Naval Intelligence (ONI), 2, 11, 31, 33–35, 57, 147
Office of Strategic Services (OSS), 57–58, 89, 112
Osborn, Gov. Sidney, 59

Pitts, Ruth, 120
Plaschke, Alfred, 37–38, 103, 107, 109, 111, 115, 128, 139, 142, 147, 159–162, 169
Plaschke, Rudy, 37
Poielski, Reinhold, 130
Preis, Alfred, 169
Presidential Proclamation 2525, 32
Priest, Daniel, 76
Proclamation 2662, 149
provost marshal general's office, 83

Rankin, John, 53
Rayburn, Sam, 29
Reckefuss, Herbert, 135
Renken, Heinrich, 131
Reseneder, Othilia, 41, 159
Rhetts, C. E., 76, 153
Ringle, Lt. Cdr. Kenneth, 31
Rio Conference, 92
Roberts Report, 51
Rostow, Eugene V., 47, 165
Rowe, James Jr., 26–27, 33, 49–51, 168
Runne, Hermann, 130

Schiavo, Adolph, 87
Schickert, Dr. A. G., 86
Schmitz, John Eric, 171
Schneider, Erich Alfred, 38
Schneider, Gerd Erich, 38, 115
Schofield, Maj. Lemuel B., 24, 31, 157
Schubert, Heinz, 134

Schueller, Olga, 61
Schuler, William A., 34
Schurwerk, Joseph, 123
Scott, M. N., 108
Seattle Immigration Station (WA), 48
Secretary of State, 92, 95, 151
Security Index, 166
Seifert, Werner Ernest, 38–39, 163
Selective Training and Service Act of 1940, 70
Senate Judiciary Subcommittee on Immigration, 159
Smith Act, 26
Sohnius, Alfred, 87
Special War Policies Unit, 23
Sprenger, Dr. Gerhard, 126
Stannard, Dr. Amy N., 101–104, 158, 167, 173
Steimle, Karl, 120
Stephenson, William, 90
Stubbe, George Karl Gerhard, 39
Supreme Court, 35, 56, 65, 67, 167
Swiss inspectors, 85–87, 122, 130, 136

Tachibana, Itaru, 34
Taniguchi, Alan, 167
Tenney, Ammon, 129
Theberath, Peter, 42
Tolan Committee, 58–59
Trautmann, Capt. Otto, 126
Truman, Harry S., 149
Turner, Claude, 174

Uhse, Bodo, 52

Vandervort, Carl, 97
Veis, Harry Oscar, 39
Vogl, Anna, 122
von Falkenstein, Baron Georg, 119, 122–123
von Opel, Fritz, 108, 158

Wagner, Johann, 133
Walter, Peter Josef, 108
War Relocation Authority, 83
Wartemann, Wilhelm, 74, 142–143, 162
Wartime Civil Control Administration, 62

Weinberg, Gerhard, 52
Western Defense Command, 5–6, 50, 62–
   63, 67
Westphal, Edwin, 72
Wiedemann, Captain Fritz, 24
Willumeit, Dr. Wilhelm, 34
Wirz, Franz, 101, 141

Woeltje, Heinz, 39

Zeitsch, Otto, 131
Zillmer-Zoser, Mrs. Theolinda, 137
Zimmerman, Dr. Hans, 65
Zimmerman v. Walker, 65

ABOUT THE AUTHOR

Arnold Krammer is professor of history at Texas A&M University. He was educated at the University of Wisconsin, Madison, and at the University of Vienna, Austria. Author of such books as *The Forgotten Friendship*, *Nazi Prisoners of War in America*, *Hitler's Last Soldier* (with Georg Gaertner), and more than fifty articles, Krammer has also taught on the faculty of Rice University and the University of Tübingen.